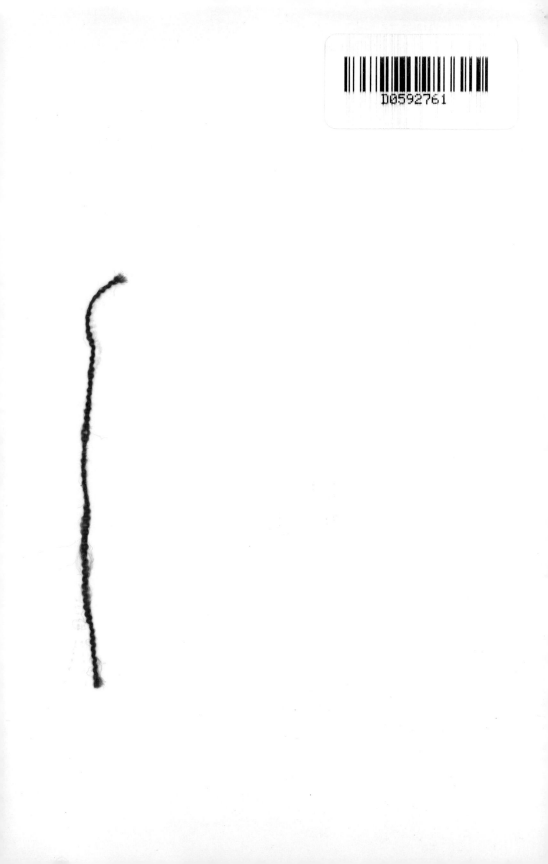

THE GREAT
AMERICAN
DECEPTION

THE GREAT AMERICAN DECEPTION

WHAT POLITICIANS WON'T TELL YOU ABOUT OUR ECONOMY AND YOUR FUTURE

Ravi Batra

JOHN WILEY & SONS, INC.

New York • Chichester • Brisbane • Toronto • Singapore

Library of Congress Cataloging-in-Publication Data:

Batra, Raveendra N.
     The Great American Deception: what politicians won't
tell you about our economy and your future / by Ravi Batra.
          p.   cm.
     Includes bibliographical references.
     ISBN 0-471-16556-5 (cloth)
     1. Tariff—United States.   2. Free trade—United States.
3. Budget deficits—United States.   4. Balance of trade—United
States.   5. Income tax—United States.   I. Title.
HF1753.B38   1996
330.973—dc20   96-24021

Printed in the United States of America

10 9 8 7 6 5 4 3 2 1

To My Toddler Rishi

Acknowledgments

S ome ventures are more cooperative in spirit than others. This book is one of them. With most manuscripts, the author's spouse is often last on the list of those receiving thanks. This work, however, is an exception. My wife Sunita is first on my list. She has been enthusiastically involved at every stage of the publishing process.

Others indispensable to this work were Jim Childs, Mike Hamilton, Bjarni Ingason, Tahir Islahi, Bhagwanti Khushlani, Amitabh Singh, Geoffrey Smith, and Thor Thorgeirsson. Without their help and encouragement, my ideas might not have materialized.

RAVI BATRA

Dallas, Texas
June 15, 1996

Contents

CHAPTER 1

Introduction:
America, What Is Wrong?

The ideas of economists and political philosophers, both when
they are right and when they are wrong, are more powerful
than is commonly understood. Indeed the world is ruled by
little else.

John Maynard Keynes, 1936[1]

Americans have a nagging feeling today that something
is wrong with their economy and society. They have
been groping for answers since the beginning of the
1990s, but, in the absence of rational explanations, they are
very confused. They have repeatedly thrown incumbents out
of office to express their anger and frustration, but the pall
of gloom continues to thicken. The new leaders have no better answers than the old.

In 1992, voters dethroned President George Bush, the hero
of the Persian Gulf War, in which the reputation of the U.S.
military, sullied in the debacle of Vietnam, was restored. In
1994, they vented their anger over Congressional Democrats,
who had been controlling the House for the past forty years.
Voters hoped the Republicans would offer fresh ideas to
counter the nonideas of the new President, Bill Clinton. Instead, the GOP has offered stale old wine in a new bottle—the
trickle-down version of economics, wherein prosperity seeps
through little by little, drop by drop, from the rich to the poor.

Strange events seem to be multiplying today. Whenever a
company lays off workers by the thousands, its directors shower

the management with raises, bonuses, and perks. Whenever the economy sinks, the stock market soars. Whenever jobs abound, share prices nosedive.

This is not how our system is supposed to function. This is not how our economy has operated in the past. Share prices were then a leading indicator of prosperity. A thriving stock market meant that a boom was around the corner. Today, the opposite is true. Soaring share prices nowadays herald a feeble economy.

A strong economy generates a variety of investment opportunities—gold, real estate, antiques, and stocks—in which people can park their savings, maintain a diversified portfolio, and earn respectable returns. In a feeble economy, however, interest rates are low and few desirable avenues other than shares are available to investors. The stock market is then the only game in town.

Share prices vary inversely with interest rates, which tend to rise when business is robust. News of a healthy economy today tends to depress the stock market, whereas the market zooms at every whisper of a slowdown. Booming stock exchanges in America since January 1991 are actually a manifestation of paltry growth and the continuing crisis of the 1990s.

Meanwhile, thousands of skilled and talented people are being fired by robust corporations. Yet, the rate of unemployment, at 5.4 percent in April 1996, was the lowest since 1974. Under such circumstances in the past, businesses would hoard labor and hold on to their experts. Today, nobody seems to care—neither the companies nor the political leaders.

Our economy is very sick today. Its sickness is new; nothing of this kind has been seen in the past. It needs a fresh diagnosis and prescription. Old cures are not working and will not work, no matter how often they are renamed and reintroduced.

The purpose of this book is to examine America's economic ills and offer new but effective medicine. We need to overhaul the system, not just tinker with it and indulge in wishful thinking that the economy will heal itself.

The economic illness of the 1990s is not a surprise to me. I have been predicting it since 1978 in a number of books and articles. Unfortunately, as I was always on the opposite side of official policy, my alarms went unheeded.

As recently as 1993, when I participated in many debates on the North American Free Trade Agreement (NAFTA), my statements were frequently ignored on both sides of the aisle. I opposed NAFTA on the grounds that it would cripple Mexico and hurt the United States. Even the opponents of NAFTA had few doubts about Mexico benefiting from the treaty. But I argued that NAFTA would destroy our southern neighbor and damage U.S. real earnings, which are wages adjusted for inflation. I discuss the subject in detail in Chapter 9, but here is a snippet from my book, *The Myth of Free Trade*, published in the Spring of 1993:[2]

> NAFTA will simply compound the ills created by the administration's policy. . . . Mexico would face great disruption as a result of opening its borders. . . . U.S. productivity would, of course, rise as the emigrating firms reduce their costs, but real earnings would tumble. . . .
>
> Mexico's industrial structure is also monopolistic, and initially a large number of domestic plants would shut down, thereby further worsening the current depression. *Things could get really ugly before they get better.*

This is exactly what has happened; things have gotten ugly in Mexico. NAFTA went into effect in January 1994; and in less than two years the Mexican economy collapsed. Unemployment and inflation soared while real wages and economic growth plummeted. In his recent book, *Bordering on Chaos*, Andres Oppenheimer, a Pulitzer Prize winner and the chief Latin American correspondent at the *Miami Herald*, aptly describes the state of Mexico today. The country is undergoing "a gradual meltdown."[3]

Similarly, in *The Great Depression of 1990*, first published in 1985, I forewarned the American public that, because of growing wealth disparity, a great depression would start as a recession in 1990 and would linger over the whole decade.[4] Depression is not too strong a word. In the past, any downturn in income or employment that festered for six or more years has been termed by historians a great depression.

Experts are now divided on this point. Some think we are currently in a depression; others say we are not. But few venture that life has been normal in the 1990s. My own view, presented in detail in Chapter 10, is that we have been in a quiet depression ever since 1990. It has not been as concentrated and dramatic as the Great Depression of the 1930s. But it has afflicted a far greater portion of the population. It has been spread out among almost 100 million people; they have suffered quietly, waiting patiently for it to end. Now they are becoming vocal about it because they see no light at the end of the tunnel.

True, unemployment has been low in the 1990s, but the rate of growth in America and Europe has been the worst since the 1930s. Annual growth averaged 0.8 percent in the 1930s; it has been around 1.2 percent in Europe and no greater than 1.7 percent in America between 1990 through 1995. (See Figure 1.1.)

The quiet crisis in the 1990s has been, in some ways, worse than the calamity of the 1930s. At the end of the 1930s, real wages had actually risen—by 17 percent. So far in the 1990s, real family income has tumbled by 6 percent. In five out of the six years, 1990 through 1995, real family income has dropped— for the first time since the Great Depression. (See Figure 1.2.)

The quiet crisis of the 1990s is clearly the worst in sixty years. No wonder Americans today are furious and confused. Democratic pollster Celinda Lake concedes that a lot of people are incensed with President Clinton. Her voter surveys reveal that "1996 makes 1992 look like voters were happy. The anger out there and the frustration are palpable."[5] In the May 6, 1996 issue of *Time,* Jill Smolowe offers a true portrait of the public agony today: "for millions of Americans, each week becomes a stressful triage between work and home that leaves them feeling guilty, exhausted and angry."[6]

In terms of unemployment, Europe and the United States have switched places. In 1933, America suffered from a debilitating 24 percent jobless rate, but Europe fared much better.[7]

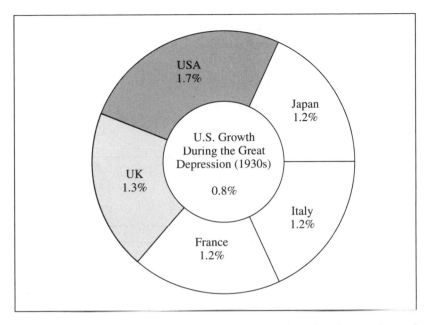

**FIGURE 1.1   U.S. annual GDP growth during the depression of
the 1930s relative to growth in some G-7 countries in the 1990s.** Average annual economic growth in the G-7 countries of America,
Japan, Italy, U.K., and France in the 1990s has not been much
above that of the 1930s, when the world was trapped in the worst
ever depression. There is thus a quiet crisis around the world
masked by booming stock markets in North America. In fact, U.S.
GDP growth in the 1990s is less than half of the normal long term
rate of growth. (*Source:* Appendix Tables A.10 through A.29.)

In France, for instance, the jobless rate did not exceed 4.2 percent in the 1930s; yet output fell for a few years—an indication
that depressions can coexist with low joblessness, as in America today. Now, when Western Europe has a much higher rate
of unemployment, America is afflicted only by underemploy-
ment or millions of part-time jobs. Figure 1.3 displays the jobless rates in Germany, France, Italy, and Spain between 1990
and 1996. In all four countries, the rate of unemployment was
very high, at double-digit rates, by April 1996. Spain suffered
a 24 percent rate in 1994, the same rate as in America in 1933.

What has masked the gravity of the situation in the United
States and Europe are the booming stock markets in North

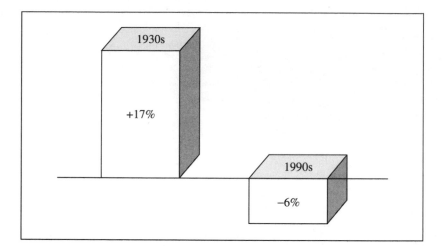

FIGURE 1.2   Real family income or wages in America, 1930s vs. 1990s. In some respects the quiet American crisis of the 1990s has been worse than that of the Great Depression in the 1930s. At the end of that decade, real wages had jumped 17 percent. In the 1990s (1990–1995), however, real family income has dropped in five out of six years by a total of 6 percent. (*Source:* Tables 10.2 and 10.3 in Chapter 10.)

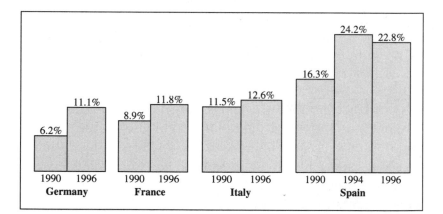

FIGURE 1.3   Unemployment rates in the 1990s in Europe. In terms of unemployment, America and Europe have switched places in the 1990s. In the 1930s, U.S. unemployment rate was as high as 24 percent, but Europe fared much better. In the 1990s, by contrast, America has mostly lower wage employment, but some parts of Europe have had unemployment as high as 24 percent. (*Source:* Appendix Tables A.17 through A.29.)

America. But people are beginning to realize that what is good for shareholders is no longer good for America. The growing affluence of the wealthy may be another reason why the crisis of the 1990s has remained hidden and been ignored by the politicians. Unlike in the 1930s when both the poor and the rich were hurt, in the 1990s the poor have been devastated while the rich have grown richer. The U.S. economy is clearly suffering from a new type of sickness. This book diagnoses it and then offers proper prescriptions.

Let us explore the burning questions in today's headlines. Why are thousands of skilled workers being fired by thriving corporations? Why are wages and family incomes constantly lagging behind inflation? Why is our economy, the world's largest, addicted to huge budget and trade deficits? Why have we borrowed hundreds of billions of dollars from countries that were practically destroyed in the Second World War? Why does the burden of payroll taxes rise every year? Why do the rich keep getting richer no matter which party is in power on Capitol Hill or in the White House?

The confusion and anger in America over the state of the union are traceable to one social cancer—the botched-up tax policy of incumbent politicians and their precursors. Ever since the turn of the century, for variegated self-interest, most of the presidents, representatives, and senators have been cutting taxes on foreign goods and, then to make up for lost revenue, raising taxes on American goods, and on the incomes of the poor and the middle class. The tax burden was first shifted from tariffs to income-related levies, and then onto the backs of those who can least afford it. All this was a great American deception done in the name of preserving prosperity or the Social Security system, but actually to enrich the rich.[8]

Our tax system has become ultra-regressive; it also imposes a heavy load on local goods and producers while sparing foreign manufacturers altogether.

Such a monumental shift in tax policy may appear innocuous, but it has gradually devastated the U.S. economy and, as I will show, has transformed the country, once the world economic leader, into the world's leading debtor. For over nineteen straight decades after its birth, our nation imposed giant tariffs, and inflation-adjusted wages never fell.

Since the early 1970s these wages have tumbled, in spite of rising productivity. A country that gave rise to the legend of the American Dream now worries about the future nightmare. A middle class that used to enjoy one of the puniest tax burdens in the world now coughs up virtually half its income to the government. A society that once welcomed millions of immigrants into its thriving factories at ever growing incomes now contemplates shutting its borders. All these ills are linked to the monstrous shift in the tax structure. Here, in brief, is a foretaste of what the present book is about.

Chapter 2 examines the extent of the suffering in America today; Chapter 3 explains the popular ideas that have long coexisted with our faltering economy.

Chapters 4 and 5 demonstrate that high taxes on the wealthy lead to high growth, whereas high taxes on the middle class and the poor decimate growth. Chapter 6 takes a detailed look at the mindset that replaced tariffs with the income tax, and at today's monstrous Social Security taxes. The disinflationary effects of tariffs, contradicting the commonly held view, are described in Chapter 7.

Chapter 8 offers an alternative view of economic development, wherein manufacturing is more important than trade; it also shows that domestic competition is superior to foreign competition. Chapter 9 makes a case for how NAFTA has hurt our economy. Chapter 10 deals with the economic effects of extreme inequality. Chapter 11 reveals that the self-destructive U.S. tax policy has spread to other nations, creating serious unemployment in Canada and Europe. Finally, Chapter 12 offers a comprehensive plan to revive the U.S. and the world economy, without destroying the environment.

CHAPTER 2

The Ugly Secret

S enate majority leader Bob Dole was puzzled the night before the 1996 New Hampshire primary election. "I didn't realize," he said, "that jobs and trade and what makes America work would become a big issue in the last few days of this campaign."[1] Considering that the American worker has been suffering for a long time, the Republican presidential candidate was clearly out of touch with reality. As I pointed out in my earlier work, *The Myth of Free Trade,* the agony of the workforce began in 1972, when U.S. real wages began tumbling.[2]

In Table 2.1, real wages are portrayed as *inflation-adjusted figures:* wages are expressed in terms of the prices of some past year (called the base year) in order to measure their purchasing power. In the Table, the base year is 1982. Therefore, in terms of purchasing power, the average hourly wages of nonsupervisory workers were $8.53 in 1972, $7.52 in 1990, and $7.42 in 1995. These earnings had declined by 13 percent in 1982 dollars. Select any other base year and the result remains the same. Weekly wages fell even faster, from $315.44 to $255.90 or by 18 percent. If tax hikes are taken into account, the weekly earnings have fallen by as much as 25 percent. In 1972, the Social Security tax was 4.8 percent; today, it is 7.65 percent. Similarly, the median sales tax rate across all the states was 3 percent. Today, it is 7 percent.

How many nonsupervisory workers are there? Almost all of us fit the description. For every one supervisor or manager, there are about ten nonmanagerial workers. Leaving aside

TABLE 2.1   Average hourly and weekly earnings of nonsupervisory workers in 1982 dollars: 1972–1995 (selected years).

Year	Hourly Earnings	Weekly Earnings
1972	$8.53	$315.44
1975	8.12	293.06
1980	7.78	274.65
1985	7.77	271.16
1990	7.52	259.47
1995	7.42	255.90

Source: Economic Report of the President, 1996, The Council of Economic Advisers, Washington, DC, p. 330.

professionals and the self-employed, 80 percent of the American labor force is in the nonsupervisory category. The U.S. Bureau of Labor Statistics puts the number at a minimum 75 percent of the workforce. Thus, for over three-fourths of the workforce, inflation-adjusted wages have fallen by 25 percent. In other words, for most working Americans, consumer prices have outpaced after-tax salaries by that amount.

My fellow economists have reacted with disbelief to this information. Even though the statistics come from the *Economic Report of the President,* they have challenged their accuracy because the data excluded what they claimed was a huge rise in pension and health benefits.

That argument is equally faulty. As MIT Professor Lester Thurow writes:[3]

What has happened cannot be explained as a diversion of cash income into fringe benefits. From 1979 to 1989 the percentage of the workforce with private pensions declined from 50 to 43 percent, and the percentage of those with health insurance declined from 69 to 61 percent. While the top quintile of wage earners' employer-paid health care fell only marginally, the lowest quintile took very substantial cuts.

Stated another way, if you take shrinking health and pension benefits into account, the real wage decline for 80 percent of the labor force is even greater than 25 percent. In 1995, less than 40 percent of employees enjoyed corporate pension benefits.[4]

Others, including the president of the National Association of Manufacturers, Jerry Jasinowski, suggest that the fall in the real wage is a myth resulting from an overestimate of the rate of inflation. Even if true, this should not make any difference to the analysis of real earnings, because the same inflation formula has been applied to the data before and after 1972. If inflation is overestimated now, it was also overestimated prior to the 1970s; but the real wage trends are remarkably different in the two periods, even though the inflation formula is the same.[5]

Americans have coped with the drastic fall in the real wage and in fringe benefits by working longer hours and by putting more of their family members to work. As a result, as shown in Table 2.2, the *pre-tax* real family income generally rose after 1972 and fell after 1990. However, the *after-tax* income remained more or less constant because Social Security and sales tax rates were almost doubled. The maximum Social Security tax on an individual was $374 in 1970 but soared to

TABLE 2.2   Median family income (in 1994 dollars) and poverty rate: 1972–1994 (selected years).

Year	Family Income	Poverty Rate
1972	$37,959	9.3%
1976	37,319	9.4
1980	37,857	10.3
1985	38,200	11.4
1990	40,087	10.7
1994	38,782	11.6

Source: Economic Report of the President, 1983 and 1996, The Council of Economic Advisers, Washington DC.

$3,924 in 1990 and $5,529 in 1993. Not only did the tax rate climb, the taxable income threshold also jumped.[6]

After 1990, under the relentless onslaught of the shriveling paycheck, even family income began to fall. But taxes continued to rise. The bite of the family income's stagnation was more severe than the figures indicate. With both husband and wife working in most families, expenses grew faster. Two-earner families needed two cars to commute to work. They had to make extra payments for auto loans, insurance, and license fees. They needed baby-sitters to watch their children, cleaning persons to wash their floors and dust their homes, money for restaurant and fast-food meals, and so on.

Not surprisingly, the rate of family poverty—the percentage of families living below the official poverty line—began to climb, from 9.3 percent in 1972 to 11.6 percent by 1994.

The poor and middle class were working harder and longer hours and still could not preserve their living standard even though the economy kept expanding. National productivity and real per-capita gross domestic product (GDP) continued to climb after 1972.

Take a look at Table 2.3. Per-capita GDP is another term for national output per person. It reached an all-time high in 1994 at $20,476. So did output per hour, a measure of labor productivity. Yet, for 22 years, real wages had been dwindling and the poverty rate had risen. The nation was as productive as ever, but 80 percent of the labor force, along with their families and children, were suffering.

The suffering was needless: the country was now more productive than ever. What went wrong in the *management* of the economy? We will examine the causes in the coming chapters. The economic blight that occurred between 1972 and 1994 is represented in Figure 2.1. Note the huge rise in the Social Security tax and its taxable wages base, against a background of falling real earnings and rising poverty.

With real wages falling and family incomes stagnant for 80 percent of the workforce, who benefited from the rise in productivity? The other 20 percent of the workforce. During the 1980s, 64 percent of the wage gains among males went to the

TABLE 2.3   Per-capita GDP (in 1987 dollars) and output per hour: 1972–1994 (selected years).

Year	Per-Capita GDP	Output per Hour
1972	$14,801	75.2
1975	14,917	79.0
1980	16,584	84.1
1985	17,944	91.9
1990	19,593	96.2
1994	20,476	101.0

Source: Economic Report of the President, 1996, The Council of Economic Advisers, Washington, DC, p. 332; *Statistical Abstract of the United States,* 1995, U.S. Department of Commerce, Washington, DC, p. 456.

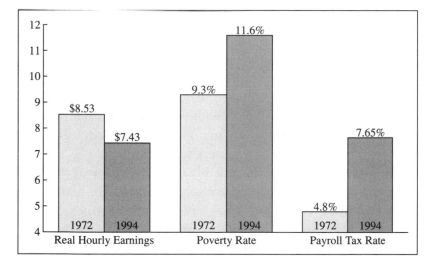

FIGURE 2.1   U.S. economic conditions in 1972 and 1994. In 1972, real wages were higher, and the poverty rate lower than in 1994. Moreover, the payroll tax rate was much greater in 1994 than in 1972. The American living standard had tumbled in two decades. (*Source: Statistical Abstract of the United States,* 1995, U.S. Department of Commerce, Washington, DC, various issues.)

top 1 percent of earners. Their income gains were a spectacular 90 percent if we include earnings from capital.

CEOs did extremely well. The average pay of the chief executives of Fortune 500 companies jumped from 35 times to 157 times the salary of the average nonsupervisory worker. Not surprisingly, the concentration of wealth reached an all-time high, with the top 1 percent of the population owning more than 40 percent of assets, as opposed to owning just 21 percent in 1949.

Until the 1970s, much of the wage debacle struck blue-collar workers; by and large, white-collar workers, especially managers, had escaped the corporate ax. But in the 1980s, white-collar workers increasingly became victims of company mergers and debt, in what is called "downsizing."

Downsizing means pruning the workforce in order to squeeze maximum effort out of the remaining employees. If a company's motive is to trim losses and restore profitability, the action is understandable. But if a profitable firm resorts to layoffs to raise profits and its stock price, and to pad the pockets of its CEO and other executives, it is ultimately self-destructive. Workers are also customers for goods and services, and impoverished consumers are forced to trim product demand. At best, this process hurts GDP growth because of lost sales. At worst, it creates economic downturns.

Downsizings began in the 1980s and reached epic proportions in the 1990s. In the process, millions of productive citizens, who had held good jobs, were laid off.

The first wave of downsizing occurred in the recession of 1981–1982, when three blue-collar jobs were eliminated for every one white-collar job. This was the typical American response to a slump. As the 1980s came to a close, the relative job losses for managers increased.

A second wave of downsizing, more drastic than the first, hit after 1989. Table 2.4 compares announced layoffs and after-tax corporate profits by major corporations. Between 1990 and 1995, profits soared from $229 billion to $390 billion, or 70 percent in just five years. Meanwhile, some 3 million good jobs were eliminated. Yet our Presidents, George

TABLE 2.4   **Announced corporate layoffs and after-tax profits: 1990–1995.**

Year	Layoffs	After-Tax Profits (Billions)
1990	300,000	$229.0
1991	550,000	249.1
1992	400,000	258.4
1993	600,000	300.7
1994	516,000	331.2
1995	600,000	390.0
Total	2,966,000	

Source: Economic Report of the President, 1996, The Council of Economic Advisers, Washington, DC, p. 379; Lester Thurow, *The Future of Capitalism: How Today's Economic Forces Shape Tomorrow's World,* William Morrow, New York, 1996, p. 26.

Bush and Bill Clinton, watched the horror of mass firings as cavalier bystanders.

Contrast this with what President John F. Kennedy did in April 1962, when faced with a 5 percent price hike from the United States Steel Corporation. The country was in a recession at the time, and the Kennedy Administration was worried about rising unemployment. Even though the inflation rate was low at 1.2 percent, the president didn't like the idea of prices galloping in the midst of mounting layoffs.

At the president's request, the steelworkers' union had limited its wage demands, but the U.S. Steel management promptly announced a major increase in steel prices. Kennedy was incensed. Under heavy jawboning that involved a threat of tax audits and antitrust lawsuits, U.S. Steel caved in and revoked the price increase. In the 1980s and the 1990s, the presidents didn't lift a finger even as big business announced a string of needless layoffs, mostly created by business mergers.

Yet, politicians of all persuasions wonder why America is so angry today. As *Newsweek* put it recently: "You can practically smell the fear of white-collar America, because no one in

CEO-land seems to care. Where will I find a new job if I get downsized? Stop whining, unemployment statistics have barely budged despite huge white-collar firings. Will my boss ruin my life to make another cent of profit on her stock options? Cheer up, you are being blown away by . . . . the gale of creative destruction."[7]

The sheer magnitude of America's quiet crisis has been staggering. Two reporters, Louis Uchitelle and N. R. Kleinfeld, write:[8]

> More than 43 million jobs have been erased in the United States since 1979, according to a *New York Times* analysis of Labor Department numbers. Many of the losses came from the normal churning as stores fail and factories move. And far more jobs have been created than lost over that period. But increasingly the jobs that are disappearing are those of higher-paid, white-collar workers, many at large corporations, women as well as men, many at the peak of their careers. Like a clicking odometer on a speeding car, the number twirls higher nearly each day.

The number of lost jobs exceeds the entire populations of Canada and Australia combined. Yet our politicians—from presidents down to local mayors—have done nothing about it.

While wages were tumbling for the vast majority of the workforce, our representatives and senators were awarding themselves one raise after another. Their salaries more than doubled during the 1980s, and their pension benefits tripled. Yet these same leaders did not raise the minimum wage in the entire decade during which prices jumped 40 percent.

When the purchasing power of the minimum wage falls, real wages go down for millions of people. The minimum wage serves as a floor for the wages of most nonsupervisory workers. As the inflation-adjusted minimum wage tumbled in the 1980s, the average real wage fell for millions more.

At the time of this writing, there is no respite in downsizing. The future of skilled workers seems to be as ominous as it has been since the 1970s. According to one estimate, manufacturing employment could dwindle to just 4 percent of the workforce by the year 2000. In view of the huge decline in manufacturing jobs that has already occurred, no estimate appears far-fetched.[9]

The corporate predators of today are reminiscent of those who throve in America at the end of the 19th century—the group of businessmen who gobbled up numerous small businesses in a frenzy that earned them the label "robber barons." According to Gilbert Fite and Jim Reese, these men "built poor railroads, turned out shoddy products, cheated honest investors, sweated labor, and exploited the country's natural resources for their own wealth and satisfaction."[10]

Compared to today's predators, robber barons of the 19th century were benevolent. They sweated labor but did not uproot their workers' lives through mass firings. As Fite and Reese emphasize, "Few can deny that these men made some valuable contributions to American life."[11]

Time wondered aloud, in its January 29, 1996 issue, why politicians and economists alike were puzzled by the state of the economy, especially when inflation, interest rates, and unemployment had all been low or falling since 1993. As *Time* put it: "Bill Clinton is puzzled. He would love to open his reelection campaign by bragging about inflation, low interest rates, and 7.8 million new jobs since he took office. But his advisers warn that in all 50 states many voters feel that prosperity is only for the rich and would resent any White House happy talk."[12]

Recently, Newt Gingrich and Dick Armey authored books in which they offered ways to regenerate American civilization. One would think that they might have had at least one word to say about the wage blight in their respective tomes on national revival. No, not a single word.

The much ballyhooed *Contract with America* was about "individual liberty, economic opportunity, limited government, personal responsibility, security at home and abroad."[13] Beautiful words. But what about shrinking paychecks and downsizing? Why would these concerns not warrant a mention? In his best-selling work, *To Renew America,* Newt Gingrich outlines six challenges facing the country, but none of them is about the shrinking real wage.[14] He worries about poverty and down-sizing, but sees no reason to chastise big business. To him, as to many others, downsizing is just a natural and healthy response of businesses in a global economy.

Stanford University Professor Paul Krugman is an influential economist who is often cited by the *Wall Street Journal* and the *New York Times*. In his 1994 textbook, co-authored with Maurice Obstfeld, he is clueless about the U.S. real wage decline.[15] In an oversized volume (795 pages) that touches, as a textbook should, on every subject in international economics, Krugman and Obstfeld cannot bring themselves to pen a line about the American wage blight.

What about the media luminaries—Rush Limbaugh and George Will, among others? Do they have a kind word for those downsized? In *The Way Things Ought To Be,* Rush Limbaugh writes: "Why is that whenever a corporation fires workers it is never speculated that workers might have deserved it?"[16]

Mr. Limbaugh hates the poor for their poverty. In his own words:[17]

> The poor and the lower classes of this country have gotten a free ride since the Great Depression when it became noble to be poor. Look at how we treat the homeless. We celebrate them, make romantic figures out of them. We make movies about them and teach them to dine in dumpsters.

Mr. Limbaugh berates the destitute, because "they're the ones who get all the benefits in this country. They are the ones that are always pandered to."[18]

> Do the poor pay anything back? Do they pay any taxes? They contribute nothing to this country. They do nothing but take from it. There are people who are putting into this economy. There are people who are working hard every day, playing by the rules and contributing. They are the givers. Who are the takers? The poor.

He sidesteps the government handout of billions of dollars to rich corporations in the form of tax credits, defense contracts, and business subsidies.[19] What Mr. Limbaugh has not cared to explore is that millions of *working* Americans are extremely poor. In 1994, retail trade, with 20.9 million employees, was the largest single employer in America.[20] Retailing workers also had the lowest earnings—barely $216 per week. Assuming that a retail worker labored for 50 weeks a year, he earned $10,800. Out of this, he paid a Social Security tax of $826, a sales tax of $864, and about $600 in income tax. His after-tax income was just $8,500. He paid a total tax of $2,290, or some 21 percent, of his wages. This is a far greater percentage than the zero tax paid by some giant corporations in the 1980s.

Mr. Limbaugh is not the only media guru who is out of touch with reality. George Will is a regular commentator for the American Broadcasting Corporation (ABC-TV) and moonlights as a syndicated columnist for the *Washington Post.* In a column headlined by the *Dallas Morning News* as "Why are we unhappy when we've never had it so good?" he lamented: "We are richer, freer, healthier and work at less exhausting jobs than ever before. So why during this epoch of unprecedented achievement has America become preoccupied with perceived failure?"[21]

For his standard of comparison, Mr. Will selects the 1930s and 1940s, when the United States was trapped in either the depression or the war. And, in terms of life expectancy, average earnings, hours worked, and possession of cars and appliances, most Americans today *are* better off than in the pre-war period, although most retail-trade workers today live from hand to mouth. But this shows how bad things must be in America today, if one has to compare them with the 1930s.

Most Americans have no memory of the 1930s, but they do remember the 1950s and the 1960s, when one parent alone could earn enough to afford a car, a house, healthcare insurance, and college tuition, and still save about 8 percent of income for the future. Now, two earning parents are unable to provide, without going into debt, what one was able to afford just forty years ago.

When we have to compare the 1990s with the 1930s and the 1940s to make today's America look good, we shouldn't wonder why people are so unhappy. Remember the early 1970s, when the real wage reached its peak? Americans have not suddenly become lazier or illiterate. The nation as a whole is more productive than ever. Why then did we have the largest population of poor Americans, 39 million, in 1993?

Not since the Great Depression has there been such a wide chasm between the attitudes of politicians, elites and economists on the one side and the feelings among America's populace on the other. As *New York Times* columnist Bob Herbert, citing a poll by the Marist Institute of Public Opinion, writes: "The poll shows that more than 100 million Americans are worried that their total family income is not enough to meet expenses. At the same time the cost of health insurance is going up and payroll benefits are going down."[22]

The fact that more than 100 million people are hurting should not be a surprise. After all, the nonsupervisory workers, whose real earnings on the average have sunk by 25 percent since 1973, constitute as much as 80 percent of the workforce.

The current anxiety of a vast number of Americans is not difficult to explain. If the real family income stagnates and taxes and family expenses escalate, there is little left for saving, retirement, and entertainment. On top of it all, if you worry that you could be the next prey of downsizing, you are bound to have sleepless nights.

The irony is that those who have been completely out of touch with the plight of millions of Americans insist that they alone have the solutions. These people want the country to trust policies that have coexisted with the real wage debacle for more than two decades. Isn't it wonderful that foxes seek to guard the henhouse?

CHAPTER 3

The Twelve Commandments of Modern Economics

I n 1980, George Bush, then a candidate for the Republican presidential nomination, used the term "voodoo economics" to describe the ideas of another Republican presidential candidate, Ronald Reagan, who claimed that he would cut taxes, raise defense spending, and balance the federal budget—all at the same time.

Anyone with a semblance of common sense knew that it was impossible to do what Reagan had promised. But voters are sometimes swayed by a candidate's charm and eloquence; the idea that they could eat their cake and have it too held terrific appeal for the electorate in November 1980. Reagan was swept into office in a landslide. Ironically, his running mate was George Bush, who had a last-minute change of heart toward Reaganomics. He recanted his past characterization of Reagan's program and offered his whole-hearted support to get it enacted through an understandably reluctant Congress, if elected vice president.

The rest is history: President Reagan got his tax cuts and a sizable jump in defense spending. But he could not get the laws of mathematics to bend to his oratory. The federal deficit, instead of evaporating into thin air, soared first to an unheard-of $100 billion, then $150 billion, and finally $221 billion. It would have climbed to as much as $300 billion, had Reagan not engineered what he called a "revenue enhancement" in 1982, and then a massive and extended rise in the Social Security tax in 1983.[1]

In spite of the giant tax increases, the U.S. budget deficit broke record after record. The government borrowed billions not only from affluent Americans but also from affluent Japanese, Arabs, Canadians, Germans, Mexicans, and even citizens of the Third World. So huge was the annual deficit that, in Reagan's first term alone, the federal debt exceeded the combined debt accumulated by all thirty-nine presidents who preceded him.

In 1980, the federal debt was less than $1 trillion. By the end of Reagan's second term in 1988, it stood at $2.6 trillion. By the start of 1996, it approximated $5 trillion.[2]

In hindsight, the Reagan budget program deserved the sobriquet of "voodoo economics." George Bush's words, offered in a rare moment of candor, aptly described not only Reaganomics but much of modern economics as well.

Harvard Professor J. K. Galbraith offers an eloquent judgment on the Reagan achievement:[3]

> There have been few periods in American or world history . . . that have been more scrupulously examined from an economic and social viewpoint than the 1980s. Much of the resulting judgment, though to be sure not all, has been unfavorable. Tax reduction oriented to the affluent, unduly enhanced defense expenditures and a large deficit in the federal budget were the prize manifestations of error. Related was the large and persistent deficit in the American balance-of-payments account, causing the United States to shift from being the world's largest creditor to being, by a wide margin, its largest debtor. . . . Eventually came the political reckoning: Mr. Reagan's party and his successor in office were thrown out of power.

The ideas favored by today's politicians are just as outrageous as Reagan's promise of a free lunch. Some of the current theories are so self-serving that they don't even warrant serious discussion. Others have hoodwinked the public for a long time and have been the basis for public policy. Some economists have even won Nobel prizes espousing them. Today's popular economic ideas need to be put to public scrutiny, because they will determine the economic future of each and every one of us.

MODERN VOODOO ECONOMICS

Any theory that affects our living standard and is so preposterous that it insults our intelligence qualifies as voodoo economics. In his best-selling book, *The Death of Common Sense,* Philip Howard cites myriad American laws that defy comprehension.[4] Philip Howard should read modern economics! He would be just as appalled by some of the theories that have earned their authors world-wide acclaim from their peers. Queer ideas have been always present in economics, but today, with its enormous emphasis on mathematical models, the so-called "dismal science" has queer ideas in abundance. Economics, now totally divorced from common sense, is causing untold suffering that will continue until its obnoxious theories are exposed to the public and put to shame.

From the many currently popular ideas, I have selected twelve. The first nine are theories that some luminaries have popularized in this century. On the final three, the profession is quiet and lends support by its silence.

1. *Depressions are unlikely, if not impossible, in a capitalist economy.* This viewpoint was demolished by the 1930s but is now sneaking back under the pseudonym "rational expectations."[5]

2. *All unemployment is voluntary and therefore painless.* Robert Lucas, a professor at the University of Chicago, won a Nobel prize in 1995 for pioneering the idea of rational expectations, which espoused this notion.[6]

3. *Unemployment can be permanently reduced through deficit financing.* Some Nobel laureates, among many other economists, supported this hypothesis for a long time.[7]

4. *Unilateral free trade benefits every nation.* Regardless of whether other countries reciprocate with their own tariff cuts, a prudent nation should eliminate all tariffs and thereby raise its living standard. This theory is the brainchild of another Nobel laureate, Paul Samuelson of the Massachusetts Institute of Technology.[8]

5. *Free trade, by itself, may equate the wages between developed and underdeveloped nations.* Thus, if India, with its teeming population of 900 million, has free trade with the United States, then its wages may rise to the U.S. level, so argues Samuelson.[9]

6. *Currency depreciation eliminates trade deficits.* Furthermore, in a global economy, a trade deficit does not matter, just as it makes no difference whether some states within America have a deficit in their domestic trade with other states.[10]

7. *Income taxes and Social Security taxes are better than tariffs as means of financing government spending, because protectionism creates depressions.*[11]

8. *High income taxes levied on the rich hurt savings, investment, and growth.*[12]

9. *Low corporate taxes are needed to raise economic growth and the general living standard, because high profits lubricate business investment.*[13]

10. *High Social Security taxes are immaterial to growth and the living standard.* (Economists rail against income taxes, but seldom denounce the payroll tax.[14])

11. *Inequality and the concentration of wealth make no difference to prosperity; moral issues are beyond the scope of economics.*[15]

12. *Speculation in financial assets is benign to economic well-being.*[16]

Most economists revere these ideas as their gospel. These are virtually the twelve commandments of modern voodoo economics. They are scattered in a wide spectrum of magazines, books, and journals, but most of them can be found in any introductory textbook, notably the one authored by Paul Samuelson. Not that the distinguished professor agrees with all these theories, but they have to be included in any broad text on economic principles.

These pronouncements of modern economic thought have been inspired by a multitude of economic events spread over the past 100 years.[17] They have been culled from a large basket of ideas that have been important to people's well-being. In one way or another, they have shaped economic policy and daily life since the turn of our century.

At times, these commandments have created poverty in the wake of widespread unemployment; at other times, roaring inflation resulted, and then stagflation—the coexistence of high unemployment and inflation—developed. Seldom have they generated long periods of prosperity without creating a serious problem as an aftermath. They became popular as cures for the crisis of the day, but were then abandoned when unexpected troubles appeared.

History is a great guide in the choice of economic policy. When various strategies were tested in the past, some worked and some did not. To cure our current ills, we should select those that succeeded and discard the ones that failed.

Even a cursory look at the twelve economic commandments reveals that they are divorced from observed economic reality. The first three are examined in this chapter. Others will be explored in the topical discussions in subsequent chapters.

THE ORIGIN OF VOODOO ECONOMICS

The idea that depressions are unlikely in a market economy dates back to the 18th century. It was pioneered by Adam Smith, David Ricardo, and J. B. Say. Today, they are lumped together and called classicists or classical economists.[18]

The classicists were mostly concerned with what the Reagan program in the 1980s called supply-side economics. They focused on the supply side of the macro economy while neglecting the demand side. Their main worry was inflation, not unemployment.

Classical economics begins with Say's law of markets, which holds that supply creates its own demand. The profit from everything produced in the economy is mostly distributed among households in the form of wages, rents, interest income, and dividends. The rest goes to the government as a sales tax or remains with corporations as the depreciation expense of capital goods such as machines and office buildings.

Buyers in turn spend money out of their incomes, and that spending generates product demand. Since the market value of a country's aggregate production, called the gross domestic product (GDP), always equals the distributed incomes, supply automatically creates demand.

To understand this concept, picture yourself as a small businessperson who owns a retail store—say, a china shop. Your net sales are a miniature version of the GDP. What remains after paying for inventory is net revenue. Out of that amount, you pay your own wages and those of your employees, rent and insurance for the store, interest for any money borrowed, sales tax to the state government, and depreciation for wear and tear on equipment. What remains is your profit. Your costs are incomes for others. The GDP accounting system works in the same way. Total production or revenue in the economy automatically equals the total of various forms of income.

However, incomes need not be spent fully. Some households save a part of their earnings, even in today's climate of living from paycheck to paycheck. Supply will then exceed spending or demand at least by the amount of household savings. Classical economists solved this problem by arguing that savings find their way into the hands of investors through the medium of commercial banks. As long as businesses spend that money for investment, supply again equals demand. Business investment or capital spending is thus the key to the validity of Say's law. It is also the key to prosperity. Furthermore, it is the origin of what some today call "trickle-down economics." I call it "tricklism."[19]

Say's law (supply creates its own demand) has profound implications for us all. It implies that the economy can never suffer from overproduction. At most, the excess supply of goods is temporary, and it automatically vanishes within a few months. And it is in the self-interest of banks to pass household savings onto companies for investment. This is how the banks make money.

In the labor market, there is no possibility of excess supply or unemployment in the long run. Excess supply occurs if labor demand is less than labor supply, or when businesses lay off workers. However, no one likes to remain without work. Joblessness leads to a fall in wages, and other employers find it profitable to increase their hiring. Thus, falling wages eliminate unemployment.

In this way, free markets solve all their problems without any government intervention. No regulations are necessary for a smooth operation of the economy. In fact, according to the classicists, government interference in the name of minimum wage legislation or occupational safety generates more trouble than it solves.

On its face, the classical logic is simple and appealing. Why would anyone champion state interference with markets? Unfortunately, the reality is very different from the classical rhetoric.

The classical insistence on the absence of overproduction and joblessness in the long run implied the absence of depressions. But depressions occurred frequently during the 19th century. Even ignoring two-year-long recessions, there were many disastrous slumps when unemployment remained stubbornly high for several years.

The downturn of the early 1780s lasted five years; the one beginning in March 1839 lasted at least 47 months and lingered for a total of seven years. Another seven-year depression occurred in the 1870s; a three-year depression that occurred in the 1880s was followed by a four-year disaster in the 1890s.[20] To be sure, years of calamity gave way to longer expansions, and the economy grew at an extraordinary pace in the 19th century.

But that is not the issue. Classical economists focused on prosperous decades and ignored those of poverty and starvation.

THE RATIONALE FOR BUDGET DEFICITS

When an illogical idea reigns for a long time, the end result is a catastrophe. That's what happened in 1929, when a lofty stock market crashed and ushered in the Great Depression. The slump was the granddaddy of all slumps, and its impact could not be ignored even by economists.

Moved by mass suffering, a brilliant economist named John Maynard Keynes offered an alternative to the classical paradigm. Keynes turned Say's law around and argued that demand creates its own supply. This made far more sense than the thesis that supply creates its own demand. If there is adequate spending or demand, companies automatically come forward to match that demand through supply. It is in their self-interest to do so.

However, if demand is insufficient, businesses are stuck with unsold goods. There is overproduction, and workers are fired. Under these circumstances, according to classical economists, wages fall and employers expand their investment until excess supply disappears in both the product and the labor market.

Keynes, however, saw the outcome differently. If the producers have already overinvested, they are in no position to expand capital spending; they may also be reluctant to do so in the wake of inadequate product demand. In this case, overproduction will remain a problem for a long time to come.

In the labor market, wages may not fall: the unions may have long-term contracts with employers. To maintain the morale of their employees and to keep productivity high, employers may be unwilling to cut wages.

Even if wages decline, they may do so at a slow rate, and joblessness may plague the country for a long time. What is worse, falling wages initially precipitate another round of shrinking demand; in the process, they create panic among companies.

Therefore, because of insufficient demand, the economy will be trapped in a downward spiral of unemployment, poverty, and mass starvation.

Here then is a rationale for government intervention in the economy. When the system cannot free itself and move out of the trap, someone from outside has to give it a nudge.

Keynes' medicine was linked to his diagnosis of the illness. The government must artificially expand aggregate demand by increasing its spending or by cutting taxes. When people have more money, they increase their spending.

Another way that government could help was by inducing the banks to lend more money to businesses to stimulate investment. But with business confidence so low during the Depression, Keynes preferred budgetary expansion to monetary case.

Keynesian logic made a lot of sense at the time. But only as a last resort will men and women of letters discard their outdated dogmas. Throughout history, intellectuals as a class have been the last to adopt new ideas. One proof of this hypothesis is that, in spite of the Great Depression, the classical theory that depressions are unlikely in a market economy was not discarded until the late 1940s.[21]

Ernest pleas by Keynes to President Franklin Delano Roosevelt (FDR) to follow his prescription proved abortive. Classical experts had always championed balanced budgets to avoid market intervention and inflation. Keynes' advocacy of budget deficits to stimulate demand was ideologically anathema to them.

President Herbert Hoover had already ignored Keynes; Hoover more than doubled the income tax in 1932. FDR added another insult by further raising the tax in 1934 and then again in 1935 and 1937. The results were predictably disastrous. The Great Depression lasted all through the decade, and the rate of unemployment was as high as 15 percent in 1939. This is what happens when irrationality shapes economic policy. People suffer because the leaders trust the self-serving theories of established economists, most of whom are engaged in pleasing their affluent patrons.

Only during the Second World War, when the Western world was forced to adopt deficit budgets, did Keynesian economics replace the classical school. Europe and the United States had no choice except to spend massive amounts on armaments and defense production. Soon, unemployment disappeared and even gave way to spot shortages of workers. Keynes was right after all. Demand was creating its own supply.

Unfortunately, every rational idea falls into the hands of extremists who abuse it with abandon and ultimately bring discredit to its author. Keynes had advocated massive budget deficits to fight depressions, not to combat low levels of unemployment. But his followers, known as Neo-Keynesians and Post-Keynesians—of whom some won Nobel Prizes—argued for monetary and fiscal ease whenever joblessness rose in the economy.

THE DOGMA OF DEFICIT FINANCING

Regardless of the initial cause, governments, under the sway of Keynesians, adopted budget deficits and monetary expansion to cure unemployment. A new problem now arose. While employment remained high, prices began to rise, never to fall back to their old levels again. Keynesians argued that high inflation was the evil that we had to endure to escape the greater evil of layoffs. Persistent inflation, in other words, was a small price that the developed economies had to pay to avoid the recessions that had afflicted workers in the past. And all that was needed was high levels of money growth to finance budget shortfalls. Thus was born the dogma that deficit financing can keep the rate of unemployment at a low level.

On the surface, this was a myopic thesis. If it is so simple to eradicate unemployment and hence poverty, all a country has to do is to print money to finance its budget deficits. One doesn't have to be a genius to see the flaws in this dogma of deficit financing. Yet the economists persisted with it and eventually hurled the world into another major crisis—this time, stagflation.

John F. Kennedy was the first president to adopt budget deficits for the sole purpose of economic growth. He followed the advice of Keynesians by urging that taxes be lowered for individuals and for corporations. But those tax cuts were enacted in 1964, the year following his assassination. Then came a long period of expansion during which unemployment fell from 6 percent to about 3.5 percent. However, the rate of inflation, which climbed from 1.3 percent in 1964 to 5.4 percent in 1969, became a major headache. The Vietnam War, which boosted defense spending, was partly to blame.

After 1969, both unemployment and inflation began to rise, and the world was exposed to a new menace. Those who seemed to have discovered a permanent cure for unemployment were now on the defensive. They had viewed inflation as a small price for high employment. But now, joblessness and inflation rose together, for the first time since 1920. No longer was there a trade-off between soaring prices and layoffs.

The worst was yet to come. In 1973 and again in 1979, the price of oil soared. The Organization of Petroleum Exporting Countries (OPEC), a powerful cartel, raised the oil price from $2.59 per barrel to $10 in 1973, to $12 in 1976, and then all the way to $35 by 1980. The world economy suffered a traumatic shock.

The Great Depression had resulted from plummeting demand. The stagflation of the 1970s arose from tumbling supply. Soaring oil and energy prices sent production costs into an upward spiral, forcing employers to trim their output of goods and services. When supply falls relative to demand, Keynesian strategy becomes self-destructive. Keynes tackled the problem of deficient demand, not deficient supply.

Deficit financing had already generated higher inflation; the supply shock pushed prices into the stratosphere. As production fell, employers needed fewer employees, forcing further layoffs in the process. Stagflation was now at its peak.[22]

The government policy, still in the hands of Keynesians, offered the same old remedy of deficit financing even though circumstances were dramatically changed. The result was persistent unemployment with rising inflation, which reached a 13.5 percent peak in 1980.

Persistent stagflation made a reaction to Keynesian economics inevitable in the 1970s. The response came from two schools of thought: monetarism and rational expectations. Professor Milton Friedman, the pioneer of the monetarist school, argued that money supply is the main determinant of economic activity. In his view, recessions and depressions were caused by sharp declines in money growth. Monetary expansion, on the other hand, only created inflation, without any long-term impact on unemployment. Friedman denounced the ever-present budget deficits as an addictive drug that produces a tense hangover after withdrawal. He offered a policy of steady money growth no higher than the long-run annual growth rate of GDP, which comes to about 4 percent.

This remedy was in sharp contrast to the Keynesian prescription, which had favored money growth rates as high as 14 percent during the 1970s. In Friedman's view, inflation is ultimately a monetary phenomenon, with too many dollars chasing too few goods. Hence, price stability and high employment require that money printing does not outpace the growth of goods.

Friedman believes that low and steady money growth is just as critical to low joblessness as it is to low or zero inflation. This is because high inflation eventually creates high interest rates that choke inflation and economic growth. Friedman was very emphatic on this point, and the stranglehold of stagflation in the late 1970s proved his point. He suggested that the government adopt balanced budgets along with monetary restraint compatible with steady GDP growth.[23]

THE MODERN RATIONALE FOR VOLUNTARY UNEMPLOYMENT

Robert Lucas was another economist who offered prescriptions similar to Friedman's. But his counter to Keynesian economics was far more ambitious than monetarism. He sought to rejuvenate the entire classical thesis, but, in the process, offered views bordering on the ridiculous. Friedman would at least permit a meager dose of government intervention in the case of emergencies such as the Great Depression. Lucas would not.

Lucas' new classical economics believes that individuals are rational and they like to maximize their happiness within the limits of their income and wealth. The sources of happiness, Lucas argued, are consumption and leisure. Work effort creates unhappiness. In the matter of labor supply, therefore, each individual makes a choice between leisure and labor. The cost of leisure is the real wage, which is the purchasing power of a person's salary. If the real wage rises, leisure becomes expensive and the person chooses to work more. Conversely, if the real wage falls, work effort declines and leisure time increases. If the real wage falls sufficiently, a person may choose to move out of the workforce entirely and just relax, at least for a while.

In this rendition of labor supply, unemployment becomes completely voluntary, because a person then chooses leisure over work.[24] As it is a personal choice, there is no pain either, because the unemployed person has all the time in the world to enjoy leisure. In other words, there is no such thing as forced leisure through layoffs. Unemployment simply means that people have quit working because of their disgust with the lower real wage.

A new version of the voluntary unemployment syndrome appeared in the 1980s in the so-called theory of the real business cycle. As Harvard University Professor Gregory Mankiw points out, "Real business cycle theorists assume that fluctuations in employment are *fully voluntary*"[25] (italics added). In this version, if the real wage falls, some employees prefer leisure now and will choose work at a propitious time in the future. Unemployment, in the current period, again becomes a choice of the unemployed.

Workers, being rational, also try to anticipate the movement of prices. Having been burned in the past by high inflation induced by deficit financing, they demand higher wages the moment the government raises its budget deficit or money growth. Rising wages in turn create cost pressures on employers, who are then unable to increase output and hence employment. Thus, with rational expectations about prices, the government intervention to cure unemployment cannot be successful. It will only raise the rate of inflation. Hence, the state should keep its hands off the economy and let the unemployed workers enjoy their leisure without any interference. Now, we are back in the classical world, with a sinister twist.

At least the classical economists never asserted that those out of work, even though voluntarily unemployed, were satisfied with their circumstances. They were not heartless enough to suggest that joblessness is a substitute for leisure. But today's classicists believe that the government need not interfere with the personal choice of the unemployed to relax and enjoy leisure.

Professor Samuel Morley explains the logic of new classical economists in this way: "After all, they argue, if the labor force would accept a reduction in the money wages . . . , there need be no involuntary unemployment."[26] In other words, a manager who is laid off from AT&T can always go to work at Burger King for $5 an hour. He or she need not be unemployed. Managers who don't accept the Burger King job are voluntarily unemployed and seek to enjoy leisure.

However, fired workers who have been managers all their worklife will hardly rush to Burger King for jobs that pay far less. They will search and search in their own areas and be ready to take modest pay cuts. The idea of working for the fast-food chain will come only as a last resort, when all their savings and credit card limits have been exhausted. Meanwhile, they could be without work for years. Are they relaxing all this time and happy about their situation? Hardly. This is the practical reality that economics frequently ignores.

Lucas is not alone in his belief that because leisure and employment are substitutes, unemployment is voluntary.[27] He is just the most celebrated exponent of this view. In October 1995, the Royal Swedish Academy of Sciences awarded him the Nobel prize for "having developed and applied the hypothesis of rational expectations, and thereby having transformed macroeconomic analysis and deepened our understanding of economic policy."[28]

Here is a person who believes that unemployment is voluntary and that the unemployed enjoy leisure. He has not only "had the greatest influence on macroeconomic research since 1970,"[29] but has also received a Nobel prize. In the voluntary unemployment view, joblessness persists because the workers refuse to accept wage cuts. But is this really so? The *New York Times* has raised just such questions with victims of downsizing and with other employees who are afraid they might be next in the layoff queue: "Worried that their grip on their jobs is loosening, most workers say they are willing to make concessions to employers if it would help save their jobs. They are especially willing to get more training and work longer hours; a cut in pay or benefits would go down harder."[30]

The classical school, the new and the old alike, believes that unemployment exists only because workers refuse to take wage cuts. Table 3.1 summarizes the responses to questions posed by the *New York Times* poll. The responses came from two groups: people who had been laid off recently and people who were still working. Among those fired, 59 percent said they would have accepted a wage cut to keep their job. But they were laid off anyway and given no chance to do anything about it. As many as 95 percent would have gone for more training, and a slightly lower percentage would have worked longer hours and accepted smaller benefits.

In other words, more than half would have done anything dignified to retain their positions with their companies. But they were summarily dismissed. Were these people voluntarily unemployed, and did they enjoy the "leisure" of frantically engaging in a job search?

The Lucas tirade against unemployment has, of course, been challenged by economists. In an angry retort, Princeton University Professor Albert Rees denounced the Lucas outlook: "Though scientific discussion is supposed to be dispassionate, it is hard for one old enough to remember the Great Depression not to regard as monstrous the implication that

TABLE 3.1 Workers' willingness to make concessions to their employers, 1996.

Questions Asked	"Yes" Replies among Respondents Who Are Working	"Yes" Replies among Respondents Hard-hit by a Layoff
Will you:		
1. Get more training?	93%	95%
2. Work longer hours?	82	87
3. Accept smaller benefits?	53	69
4. Challenge the boss less often?	49	66
5. Accept a smaller wage?	44	59

Source: *New York Times,* March 4, 1996, p. A9.

the unemployment of that period could have been eliminated if only all the unemployed had been more willing to sell apples or to shine shoes."[31]

It is not just at the practical level that classical economics breaks down. There are also logical flaws in the argument. Most people would take a wage cut and work harder to retain their job rather than face the harshness, uncertainty, and stigma of unemployment. This means that work is valued far more than leisure. Modern economics believes that people are indifferent between work and leisure and that they choose a combination of the two that maximizes their happiness without exceeding the limit of their resources. The logical flaw here is that, up to a certain level of income, work is far more important than relaxation because, without a job, survival may be at stake.

Note too that the classical model assigns the same bargaining power to workers and their employers. In reality, however, the employers are in a much stronger position than the employees, especially in today's global economy where factories can move abroad to low-wage countries.

In the world of rational expectations, a policy of inflation does not lower unemployment even in the short run, because well-informed workers immediately demand higher wages to maintain their purchasing power. However, facing the threat of a factory moving to Mexico or China, where wages are about a dollar per hour or less, the employees are not likely to press for a raise to match inflation. In that case, inflation, expected or unexpected, will raise employment at least in the short run. Thus, the theory of rational expectations is illogical on both practical and logical grounds.

Not surprisingly, the modern classical economists have no idea about the real wage blight that has afflicted America since 1972. In a news conference in Chicago on October 10, 1995, Professor Lucas parroted the Clintonian view: "The U.S. economy is in excellent shape. The government is not trying to do things with economic policy that it isn't capable of doing."[32]

I find it difficult to believe that anyone could think like this, but then perhaps I don't have rational expectations. According to the acolytes of the classical dogma, the unemployed during the Great Depression chose leisure over work, and then laughed about it. Similarly, the millions of fired workers who are recent victims of downsizing have no gripe against their employers because they all chose to be unemployed. The fact that almost all of them went back to work at lower salaries is *not* evidence that unemployment is actually forced leisure. They all just happened to make a wrong choice to quit work at the time of downsizing and regretted it later.

One wonders about the sanity of a profession that rewards such views with acclaim, research grants, Nobel prizes, and distinguished professorships? How would a tenured professor mulling these ideas feel if he or she were offered leisure of the type that the victims of downsizing are now "enjoying"? Would he or she rejoice?

The new classical economics has not been espoused by politicians. When Ronald Reagan took office in 1981, stagflation was roaring. He and Paul Volcker, then Chairman of the Federal

Reserve Bank (the Fed); first applied brakes to runaway inflation by restraining money growth. This was the high point of monetarism. But then came a serious recession, arguably the worst since 1950, and monetarism fell into disrepute.

The Fed followed a tight money policy in 1981 to choke off inflation, which began a slow but steady decline. After 1982, as the Reagan tax cuts took effect, the budget deficit began to soar. This pumped so much spending into the economy that economic growth picked up, but inflation continued to fall. Reagan's popularity recovered with the reversal of fortunes and he was re-elected in 1984 in a landslide.

What Reagan had done was the old-fashioned deficit financing advocated by Keynesians. The tax cuts of 1981 were similar to the Kennedy cuts proposed in 1963. But Reagan gave them a different label and, as stated earlier, called his program supply-side economics. Even though growth picked up after 1982, the rate of unemployment was slow to decline. In spite of high unemployment and a continuing rise in the rate of poverty, Reagan, with all his charm and eloquence, remained popular with the public.

Troubles mounted after Reagan left office in early 1989. The recession that began in 1990 was the worst yet. Galbraith calls it the recession cum depression. As a consequence, George Bush was dethroned in 1992 and Bill Clinton was sworn in as president in early 1993. Since then, real family income has continued its tumble, in spite of rising productivity and profits.

Today, the economic profession is greatly bewildered. The economy has grown slowly since 1992; both inflation and interest rates have declined to lows not seen since the early 1960s. Some economists scoff: "What are people complaining about? They are spoiled by success—after all, the fundamentals are so sound." Such is the refrain of economists today.

The fundamentals are far from sound. Real wages have been tumbling for 80 percent of the workforce since 1972. Social Security and sales tax rates have more than doubled. Income inequality and the concentration of wealth are at their all-time highs. Federal and consumer debt set new records daily. The fundamentals are indeed cause to sound an alarm.

Economists have been caught napping in their ivory towers. None of the schools of thought that gained prominence in the 1970s and the 1980s has even been aware of plummeting wages. Most of our basic textbooks reveal no inkling of the tumbling living standard. Yet their authors will insist that they've got the right answers.

CHAPTER 4

Do Low Taxes on the Rich Stimulate Savings and Investment?

T he eighth commandment of modern economics is that low income taxes and low capital gains taxes on the rich stimulate savings, investment, and economic growth. This has been the gospel of Republicans and conservative economists throughout this century. Self-serving as this may sound, given the personal wealth of many Republican leaders, it was taken seriously and actually implemented in the 1980s. Former HUD (Housing and Urban Development) Secretary Jack Kemp is a vocal supporter of this policy. In his view, "All proposals to expand the economy by lowering taxes on work, saving and entrepreneurship—including the flat tax plans of Steve Forbes and representative Dick Armey—deserve to be discussed and debated, without being dismissed as a boon to the rich."[1]

Kemp, Forbes, Armey, and Gingrich have tried to revive the ghost of Reaganomics, aka supply-side economics. They have done this by offering the so-called flat-tax principle, the imposition of one single tax rate on all taxable income. Steve Forbes and Dick Armey favor a flat tax of 17 percent; Jack Kemp would put it at 19 percent; Milton Friedman is for any rate below 20 percent.[2] The top-income-bracket tax rate at present is 39.6 percent. Every flat-tax proposal will cut the top rate by more than half. Hence the nagging suspicion that the flat-tax principle will be a handout to the rich and may prove even costlier than the Reagan tax cuts enacted in 1981 and again in 1986.

The argument for cuts in the income tax is usually cloaked in a masquerade of Public Benefit. The income tax should be trimmed not for the welfare of the well-to-do, but for social welfare. Such has been the persistent refrain of Republican politicians and their think tanks.

Jack Kemp argues that low taxes stimulate economic growth by promoting work effort, savings, and investment. But the evidence doesn't support this view. For example, look what happened in 1981, when the average income tax rates were reduced by 25 percent but were not fully effective until 1984.

Table 4.1 compares the top-bracket income tax rates from 1980 to 1995 with what is often called the *personal rate of saving*—the amount of income people save out of their disposable or after-tax income.

The saving rate was 8.2 percent in 1980 with a top-bracket income tax rate of 70 percent. Notice that as the tax rate fell to 50 percent, the saving rate did not rise. It fell instead to 6.9

TABLE 4.1   Top-bracket income tax rate and personal rate of saving: 1980–1995 (selected years).

Year	Top-Bracket Income Tax Rate	Personal Rate of Saving
1980	70%	8.2%
1985	50	6.9
1988	28	5.2
1990	31	5.0
1993	39.6	4.5
1995	39.6	4.3

Source: Economic Report of the President, 1996, The Council of Economic Advisers, Washington, DC, p. 310; Robert Hall and A. Rabushka, *The Flat Tax,* Hoover Institution Press, Stanford, CA, 1995.

percent in 1985, which was a normal year for the economy. Then came the Tax Reform Act of 1986, in which the top-bracket income tax rate was pruned further to 28 percent. By 1988, as the tax rate declined, the saving rate had sunk further to 5.2 percent.

In 1990, President Bush raised the top-bracket tax rate to 31 percent. In 1993, President Clinton raised it to 39.6 percent, where it stood in 1995. However, the saving rate continued its relentless fall.

The evidence gives no support to the thesis that as the income tax rate is lowered, the saving rate climbs. On the contrary, the rate of saving has plummeted. Looking at the entire period from 1980 to 1995, the top tax rate was almost cut in half and the saving rate also fell by half.

Nor was the saving behavior of households in the 1980s exceptional in U.S. history. The other decade that supply siders wrongly cite as supportive evidence is the 1960s, which also witnessed a fall in top-bracket income tax rates.

Under a tax cut act passed in 1964, Congress trimmed the top tax rate from 91 percent to 70 percent, beginning in 1965. The tax rate went up somewhat because of a temporary tax surcharge of 10 percent enacted in 1967, then held steady at 70 percent during the 1970s.

How did the saving rate behave during this period? Take a look at Table 4.2, which shows a slightly upward trend after 1963. The saving rate rose at first when the tax rate fell, but then rose again when the tax rate went up because of the surcharge, which lapsed in 1970. During the 1970s, the top tax rate was constant and the saving rate in 1980 was basically the same as in 1970.

In 1975, the saving rate rose slightly to 9 percent, but 1975 was a recession year, and when people are afraid for their job security, they sometimes save more. In any case, the top tax rate had not changed after 1970, and the saving rate moved up in 1975.

From all this, we may conclude that the top-bracket income tax rate does not have a significant effect on household savings.

TABLE 4.2 **Top-bracket income tax rate and personal rate of saving: 1960–1980 (selected years).**

Year(s)	Top-Bracket Income Tax Rate	Personal Rate of Saving
1960–1963	91%	7.0%
1965	70	7.6
1970	70	8.4
1975	70	9.0
1980	70	8.2

Source: Historical Statistics of the United States: Colonial Times to 1970, Part 2, U.S. Department of Commerce, 1975, p. 1095; *Economic Report of the President,* 1996, The Council of Economic Advisers, Washington, DC, p. 310.

Even if taxes are constant, as they were in the 1970s, the saving percentage of the economy may fluctuate up or down.

Some people argue that the effective tax rates climbed sharply during the 1970s, which experienced exorbitant rates of inflation. As inflation pushed people into higher income brackets without raising their purchasing power, they had to pay increasing amounts in taxes. Millions of people then paid higher effective tax rates.

According to the Internal Revenue Service (IRS) figures, a single person with a $75,000 income paid an effective tax rate of 30.2 percent in 1970 and 39.1 percent in 1980.[3] This was a substantial jump in the tax rate for a person who, at the time, was certainly among the top 5 percent of income earners in the country. But even though the effective tax rate soared for the wealthy, the saving rate hardly budged from 8.4 percent in 1970 to 8.2 percent in 1980.

To summarize our discussion so far, low income tax rates from 1980 to 1995 failed to expand the personal saving rate, and rising effective tax rates in the 1970s did not discourage household saving behavior. During the 1960s, the tax rate fell somewhat (the top rate was still a hefty 70 percent), but the saving rate hardly budged. In other words, there is absolutely no historical backing for the supply-side idea that low income taxes stimulate personal savings.

Tables 4.1 and 4.2 reveal that, between 1960 and 1985, the personal rate of saving varied between 6.9 percent and 9 percent. After 1985, it just collapsed, dropping to 4.3 percent in 1995. What happened in 1985? After all, people normally like to put some funds away for their children, and for a rainy day in the future.

The answer can be found in the Social Security (SS) tax between 1980 and 1993 in current and constant dollars. This tax went through the roof. The Social Security tax is a direct tax on income but it carries a different label. And it falls most heavily on the backs of the poor and the middle class, because the same rate applies whether a person is earning the minimum wage or is a CEO earning thousands of dollars per hour.

If any tax has killed the saving rate in the United States since 1985, it is the SS tax. In 1980, the SS tax rate was 6.13 percent and applied to taxable earnings of $25,900. By 1993, the rate had jumped to 7.65 percent and the taxable threshold was set at $57,600.[4] The tax rate's climb at about 25 percent, is sizable, but it fails to reveal the full burden. In reality, the SS tax load soared by 97 percent by 1993.

Here's why. If we divide the SS tax actually paid by the consumer price index (CPI) and then multiply by 100, we get the *inflation-adjusted* amount of the increase in the SS levy. These calculations show that the real tax burden almost doubled, from 1,927 in 1980 to 3,826 in 1993. In the same way, we can calculate the maximum effective SS tax rate—the rate that would prevail if the real or inflation-adjusted taxable wage was constant at the 1980 level. When the wage base subject to taxation rises faster, the tax bite grows even more. Appendix Tables A.1 and A.2 show that while the actual SS tax rate was 7.65 percent in 1993, the effective maximum rate was 12.17 percent, which exceeded the actual 1980 rate by 97 percent. In other words, the amount actually paid after adjustment for inflation was not 7.65 percent but 12.17 percent if your taxable income was above $57,600 in 1993.

Soaring SS taxes have simply clobbered our rate of saving since 1980. The politicians, of course, blame the low saving rate on high taxes on the wealthy, but Figure 4.1 reveals the true culprit.

Never before in the history of the United States—not even during the Second World War—have taxes been raised so much on the poor. This is what has really destroyed the rate of saving in America. In 1995, the saving rate stood at a laughable 4.3 percent even though the top-bracket income tax rate, at 39.6 percent, was way below the 1980 rate of 70 percent.

So the logic behind supply-side arguments is hollow. The affluent are a very small minority, about 5 percent of the population. But their incomes are so high that, regardless of the income tax rate, they can achieve their target of saving. Thus, when their tax rate declines, they don't raise their savings, as

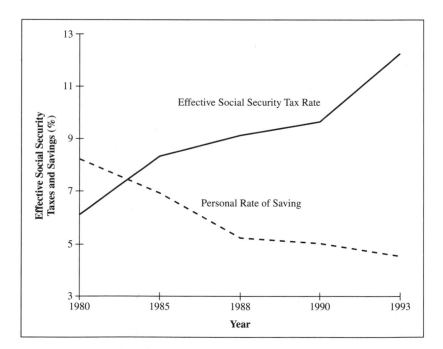

FIGURE 4.1   The effective social security tax rate and the personal rate of saving: 1980–1993. As the Social Security tax soared after 1980, the rate of saving collapsed. (*Source:* Appendix Tables A.1 and A.2.)

is clear from the evidence. They simply put their extra income into what the late Stanford Professor Thorstein Veblen called conspicuous consumption—gold and other precious metals, art objects, antiques, yachts, financial and commodity speculation, and so on.[5]

Similarly, if the top tax rate rises, it does not crimp the ability of the rich to meet their saving target. Thus, when the effective tax rate jumped during the 1970s and the 1990s, the household saving rate remained practically unchanged.

This conclusion is also confirmed by the saving performance of the economy in the 1950s. The top-bracket rate climbed from 84 percent in 1950 to 91 percent in 1959. Did the saving rate fall? No. It was unchanged at 7 percent. Of course, the SS tax was then negligible—a mere 2.5 percent applied to first $4,800 of wages. Some may argue that giant income taxes in the 1950s and the 1960s were associated with a lot of loopholes that reduced the effective tax rates. There is a grain of truth in this. But the IRS calculations show that the effective tax rate on top incomes exceeded 75 percent in the 1950s. Even in the 1970s, figures compiled by Pulitzer Prize winning authors Donald Barlett and James Steele show that the effective tax rates on top incomes exceeded 60 percent.[6]

THE INCOME TAX AND INVESTMENT

There are two sources of investment in a country: savings by individuals and savings by corporations. We have already seen that low taxes on the wealthy do not stimulate savings; nor do they encourage investment.

Since corporate savings depend on corporate income and taxes, the individual income tax has no direct link to corporate funds. In other words, there is no logical reason to expect a connection between low taxes on the wealthy and the economy's rate of investment.

However, Republican politicians and conservative economists constantly claim that the rich are natural investors while the poor and the middle class are natural consumers, so that

investment rises as the rich grow richer. They conclude that
the government should reward the wealthy with investment incentives in the form of investment tax credit, liberalized depreciation rules, and low taxes on capital gains and dividends.[7]
This is, of course, trickle-down economics or tricklism, whereby
prosperous rich people create a prosperous middle class.

But if the rich are natural investors, then why do they need
tax breaks to use their wealth for investment? They are also
natural speculators. Speculation means borrowing money to
buy assets for quick resale and earn a hefty profit. To the affluent, a small return means nothing. For multimillionaires,
an activity bringing in an extra few thousand has little at-
traction. Their goal is to earn millions of dollars more and
high returns are available only from speculation, not from
investment.

Investment requires patience and hard work. It often creates new jobs. Speculation feeds on impatience and mega
mergers that destroy good jobs.[8]

In Economics 101, we learn that there are three types of investment: business spending on plant and equipment, household spending on new homes, and business spending on
inventories.[9] To an economist, the money that people spend
on stocks and bonds is not investment, because that spending
may not result in increased production of goods and services.
Investment raises the GDP, but the purchase of financial assets
is not included in the measurement of GDP. Capital spending
that may result from IPOs (initial public offerings) is a drop
in the bucket of national investment. Therefore, economists
exclude all stock purchases from GDP estimates.

According to supply siders, low income taxes on the rich
stimulate business spending on plant and equipment. But
there is no earthly reason for this to happen, because most
business investment is done by corporations, and their behavior is affected by corporate profits and taxes, not by the individual taxes paid by the affluent. No businessperson would
risk money in a business unless he or she expects to sell a
product. If demand is inadequate, no amount of tax incentive

is enough for anyone to risk money in investment. To examine the effect of taxes, economists usually calculate investment as a percentage of GDP.

The final column in Table 4.3 lists business investment as a percentage of GDP, from 1980 to 1995. In 1980, when the income tax rate on the wealthy was 70 percent, the investment-to-GDP ratio was 12.6 percent. After the massive income tax cut of 1981, the investment ratio fell slightly, to 12 percent. When the tax rates were trimmed further after 1986, with the top-bracket rate no higher than 31 percent in 1990, the investment ratio, also called the rate of investment, tumbled to 10 percent and was essentially the same in 1995 when the top tax rate jumped to 39.6 percent. Figure 4.2 demonstrates this relationship graphically.

Does this demolish the investment myth spread by the rich and their hirelings? Ostensibly yes: Investment plummeted as the top tax rates fell. The reason again is the sharp jump in the SS tax rates. It is well known that investment is lubricated by savings, which, as we have seen before, were all but destroyed by the SS tax hike. Therefore, investment fell as the SS tax burden climbed.

TABLE 4.3   Business fixed investment as a proportion of GDP: 1980–1995 (selected years).

Year	Investment (billions)	GDP (billions)	Investment (Percent of GDP)
1980	$350.3	$2,784.2	12.6%
1985	502.0	4,180.7	12.0
1990	575.9	5,743.8	10.0
1995	735.0	7,214.0	10.2

Source: Economic Report of the President, 1996, The Council of Economic Advisers, Washington, DC, p. 280.

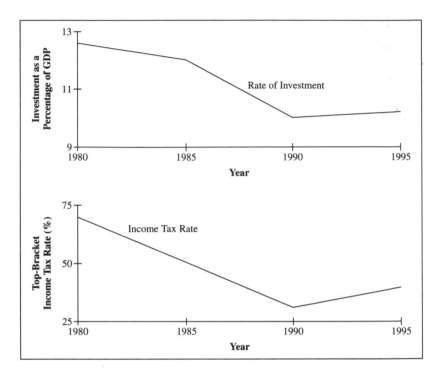

FIGURE 4.2   The rate of investment and the top-bracket income tax rate: 1980–1995. As the top-bracket income tax rate tumbled in the 1980s so did the rate of investment. In the 1990s both the income tax rate and the rate of investment rose slightly. (*Source:* Tables 4.1 and 4.3.)

TAXES AND THE WORK EFFORT

Another favorite one-liner of Reagan devotees is that low income taxes encourage people to work harder. This claim is just as specious as the others, on logical as well as historical grounds. Those who believe that unemployment is the same thing as leisure also maintain that low taxes encourage people to put in longer hours of work.

Robert Hall and Alvin Rabushka, senior Fellows at the Hoover Institution, argue that "higher tax rates reduce the demand to work, save and invest by reducing after-tax rates of return. Lower tax rates increase the demand to work, save and invest by increasing after-tax rates of return."[10] There is no logical support for this hypothesis. Indeed, history supports the contrary view: lower income taxes have either had little effect or have actually lowered the demand to work, save, and invest.

Do people have a choice between leisure and work? For most of us, work is a matter of life or death. As soon as a person graduates from high school or college, he frantically looks for a job. He or she has to pay off the college debt, and, with parents living from paycheck to paycheck, needs employment right away.

We live in a culture in which a person's identity and self-respect are defined by his or her employment. After finding a job at whatever wage the employer offers, the employee normally must put in eight hours of work, five days a week. There is no choice between leisure and the number of hours worked, at least up to a point.

There are, of course, jobs where people can make more money by working overtime. A rich person or someone with a large inheritance also has a genuine choice between leisure and employment. But these are exceptions, not a general rule. Yet, every textbook on economic principles treats the labor–leisure choice as a standard feature of economic behavior.

Those who argue that the high income tax, though not the high Social Security tax, hurts a person's incentive to work usually utilize the model of labor–leisure choice and then apply their analysis to the entire workforce. In reality, their conclusions describe only the behavior of the super rich. For others, the lack of employment is a matter of survival. They have to work to feed themselves and their children.

Let us now look at history. If low income taxes encourage work effort, we should expect the participation of people in the labor force to rise when taxes decline. But look at the government data on the civilian labor force participation rate in Table 4.4. In 1950, when the top-bracket income tax rate was 84 percent, 59.2 percent of the population participated in the labor force. When the tax rate was 91 percent, as in 1960, the participation rate was essentially unchanged at 59.4 percent. The higher tax had no effect on labor supply.

TABLE 4.4   Labor force participation rate: 1950–1995 (selected years).

Year	Labor Force Participation Rate
1950	59.2%
1955	59.3
1960	59.4
1965	58.9
1970	60.4
1975	61.2
1980	63.8
1985	64.8
1990	66.4
1995	66.6

Source: Economic Report of the President, 1996, The Council of Economic Advisers, Washington, DC, p. 316.

The tax rates dropped in the 1960s, but the labor force participation fell slightly in 1965 and then rose marginally by 1970. Again, the tax cuts of the 1960s had no visible impact on the labor force.

The participation rate began an upward trend in the 1970s when the top-bracket tax rate was constant; but the effective tax rate climbed for most people because of inflation. In the 1970s, rising taxes were associated with growing labor supply—just the opposite of what supply-siders preach. During the 1980s, the participation rate continued the upward trend that began in the 1970s; income taxes fell, but SS taxes soared. Here the outcome is inconclusive for Reaganomics.

During the 1990s, both the top-bracket tax rate and SS taxes have been rising without any effect on the participation rate. In other words, history fails to confirm the supply-side position that low income taxes induce people to work harder and join the labor force in growing numbers.

A better explanation for the rising participation rate since 1970 is that, as real wages fell during the 1970s, women in increasing numbers joined the workforce, in spite of rising taxes, to maintain their family income. The after-tax wage was clearly more important than the top-bracket tax rate. During the 1980s, the after-tax wage continued to fall for the vast majority of people. As a consequence, the participation rate also continued upward.

THE CORPORATE INCOME TAX

Hall and Rabushka also believe that low corporate taxes encourage the rate of investment. On the surface, this proposition seems more logical than their low-income-tax hypothesis. A low tax on their profits, after all, will leave corporations with more investable funds, and that should encourage capital formation. However, even this thesis is open to question.

If demand is insufficient, a company, just like an individual, will not usually risk its money on new projects. Conversely, if demand is adequate, then high taxes would not stop a business from investing, because it can always borrow money from a bank.

Suppose the corporate income tax is 30 percent. A company earns a profit of $100 and pays $30 as tax, keeping $70 for dividends to shareholders and investment. If the corporate tax increases to 40 percent, the company would be left with only $60. But if demand is adequate enough to make an investment project profitable, the corporation will borrow the extra money needed and will undertake the same amount of investment as before. In other words, corporate taxes affect dividends, but not the rate of capital formation.

As long as pre-tax profitability is unaffected, a high corporate income tax does not discourage investment. Similarly, a low business tax does not encourage capital spending if it fails to enhance the pre-tax profit. That is why we find that, historically, the corporate income tax has had no visible effect on the investment/GDP ratio.

Take a look at Table 4.5 and its graphic counterpart, Figure 4.3. In 1950, business or nonresidential investment as a percent of GDP (GNP, at that time) was 9.7 percent. In 1995, it was 10.2 percent—hardly a change. During these 45 years, corporate income taxes were changed time and again. Not only the direct taxes on corporate income, but corporate deductions were also altered frequently. As best-selling author William Greider remarks: "The corporate tax code was so thoroughly gutted in 1981 that hundreds of profitable corporations became free riders in the American political system—paying no taxes whatever or even collecting refunds."[11]

During the 1950s, the corporate income tax was 52 percent of profits. It was lowered to 48 percent in 1964, to 46 percent in 1978, to 45 percent in 1981, and then to 34 percent in 1986. In 1993, the corporate tax structure became more complex, with a tax rate of 35 percent on income over $10 million, 38 percent on income between $15 and $18.3 million, and reverting to 35 percent for income beyond that amount.

TABLE 4.5   Investment/GDP ratio and share of the corporate income tax: 1950–1995 (selected years).

Year	Investment (Percent of GDP)	Share of the Corporate Income Tax
1950	9.7%	26.4%
1955	9.6	27.3
1960	9.3	23.2
1965	10.3	21.8
1970	10.3	17.0
1975	10.4	14.6
1980	12.6	12.5
1985	12.0	8.4
1990	10.0	9.1
1995	10.2	11.6

Source: Economic Report of the President, 1987 and 1996, The Council of Economic Advisers, Washington, DC.

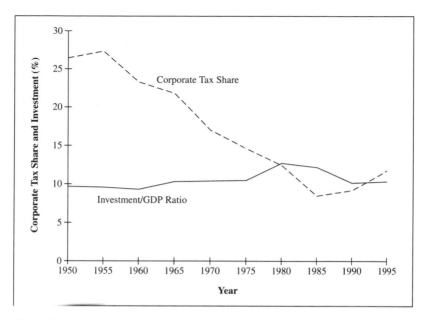

FIGURE 4.3 **Investment/GDP ratio and share of the corporation income tax in federal revenue: 1950–1995.** From 1950 to 1995 the corporate tax share fell by more than half, but the rate of investment in the economy changed little. Corporate tax breaks don't stimulate investment. (*Source:* Table 4.5.)

In addition, an investment tax credit, granted to businesses in 1962, was raised to 10 percent in 1975. The credit was repealed in 1986.

Through all this churning in the tax treatment of corporate profits, the rate of investment remained more or less fixed, as shown in Figure 4.3. This is because, as Professor Samuel Morley argues, "one significant determinant of profitability is the level of aggregate demand."[12] The point is simple: If an investment project is profitable before taxes, the firm will not abandon it just because of a high tax. Interest rates are likely to have a larger impact on investment than the corporate tax, because they influence the pre-tax rate of profit. In any case, the long history of capital formation shows that the business rate of investment has barely fluctuated since the Second World War ended 50 years ago.

It is then clear that all the tax breaks handed out to corporations since 1950 have been a colossal waste. Figure 4.3 reveals a dramatically declining trend in the corporate share of the total income tax receipts from 1950 to 1995, even though the rate of investment was basically unchanged. Where is the stimulus to investment? Big business pocketed one tax handout after another and offered only downsizing in return. The corporate share of tax revenue exceeded 25 percent in the 1950s. By 1985, after the Reagan tax cuts, it was down by two-thirds. In 1995, it barely exceeded 10 percent.

Multinational business did not return a penny in increased investment as a percent of GDP, even as it extracted billions from the U.S. Treasury in tax breaks. Whatever investments the companies made were going to be made anyway to meet the demand for their products. The rate of investment stayed constant while tax benefits were showered on companies.

Although the rate of investment generally hovered around 10 percent, there was one decade, 1975 to 1985, when it approached 12 percent. Why was the investment rate above average during these years? The answer lies in the roaring inflation or the force of demand. When prices soar, it means that national demand for goods and services is way ahead of national supply. The greater the gap between demand and supply, the larger the rate of inflation. Furthermore, the higher the gap, the higher the rate of investment.

When demand outpaces supply, businesspeople know that the products generated by their investment will find a ready market. This tends to reduce their risk of loss and thus stimulates capital formation. The decade of 1975 to 1985 is the only post-WWII period when persistent inflation generated strong inflationary expectations. That period stands out in the otherwise dull picture of investment that was more or less constant over the other four decades.

However, none of these discoveries has stopped conservative economists and politicians from pleading for even more corporate tax breaks.[13]

THE CAPITAL GAINS TAX

The capital gains tax is a major irritant among those who think prosperity trickles down from the rich to the poor. In their view, business investment responds negatively if taxes are high on individual income, corporate profits, and capital gains.

The supply siders add another wrinkle in their analysis of the capital gains tax: It discourages risk taking or entrepreneurship. In today's economic slowdown, Newt Gingrich continues to see the need for "capital gains tax cuts to increase economic growth."[14]

Let's examine this idea. Capital gains tax is a levy on the appreciation of any assets, including new investment projects, and the purchase of stocks and bonds in financial markets. Gingrich suggests that reducing or eliminating the capital gains tax will stimulate investment and make America competitive in global markets.

Even some conservative economists are tired of this argument. John Makin and Norman Ornstein, both of the American Enterprise Institute, a conservative think tank, argue that "little empirical evidence links a long series of impositions and demands of a differential tax rate on capital gains with either faster growth or more competitiveness."[15]

So why the constant harangue by politicians for a capital gains tax cut? The stock market has been soaring since August 1982, except for one major blip that occurred in the market crash in October 1987. The Dow Jones Index has jumped from about 780 in 1982 to over 5,600 in March 1996. In the process, a few hundred shareholders have earned billions of dollars in paper profits. They would like to see the maximum capital gains tax rate go back from the current 28 percent level to the 20 percent level enacted in 1981.

According to Kevin Phillips, a political analyst and best-selling author, as early as 1983, just a year after the long bull market began, "each of the fifty-three stockholders [profiled by *Fortune*] had already made profits of over $100 million!

One, David Packard, co-founder of Hewlett-Packard Inc., found himself richer on paper $1.2 billion. Nine others gained over $300 million. More and bigger gains would follow in the mid-1980s, augmented by reduced tax rates on these swollen unearned incomes."[16]

That was just in 1983. The spectacular gains of the early 1980s pale before those earned since then. But they remain mostly unrealized and will perhaps remain so until the Republican Congress passes the capital gains tax cut. This is the hidden agenda behind the tax cut proposal included in *Contract with America*.[17] Will it have any salutary effect on capital formation? You already know the answer from the 45-year history of investment behavior graphed in Figure 4.3. It will not.

The investment lesson of history is that investment is linked to demand, not to tax breaks for millionaires, corporations, and venture capitalists.

CHAPTER 5

High Historical Growth with a 90 Percent Income Tax

We have seen that low taxes on individuals, corporations, and capital gains do not promote saving, work effort, and investment. Four decades of history following the end of the Second World War revealed that the rate of investment barely budged, whether taxes on the wealthy rose during the 1950s or were lowered during the 1980s. Instead, saving and investment were crushed by the Social Security tax hikes of the 1980s.

In this chapter, I will show that economic growth was much greater when the rich paid high taxes on a variety of incomes. The much touted growth miracle of the 1980s, achieved in an environment of low income taxes, pales before the giant growth rates of the 1950s and the 1960s, when incomes were taxed at extraordinary rates. Even the much maligned 1970s, with their higher tax rates, had somewhat faster growth than the 1980s.

From its inception in 1913, the income tax in America has been a progressive levy: the tax rate increases with taxable income. The principle of progression has been considered fair throughout this century.[1] The flat tax, currently popular among Republicans, would, in one stroke, eliminate what many have regarded as the bedrock of the American tax system. Almost all other taxes—sales, excise, and Social Security taxes, for example—are regressive: that is their burden falls most heavily on the poor. The income tax, by contrast, is progressive.

Postwar history shows that, when the tax system was highly progressive, economic growth and real wages soared. But when the tax structure became regressive, trouble followed in the form of low growth and a decline in the living standard.

LOW GROWTH WITH A 28 PERCENT TAX IN THE 1980s

In Table 5.1 and Figure 5.1, look at the link between the top-bracket income tax rate and the average annual growth of real GDP. Economic growth fluctuates from year to year and is affected by a number of factors, including taxes. War normally stimulates growth, for example, but then recession or low growth follows the end of hostilities. During a war, government spending jumps to fuel demand, which invites increased production from businesses. Wars, therefore, generate above-average growth and inflation. Prices rise fast because of rising raw material costs, which affect supply adversely. In other words, demand grows faster than supply, leading to a rise in output as well as in the rate of inflation.

TABLE 5.1   GDP growth rate and top-bracket income tax rate: 1950–1995.

Decade	Average Annual GDP Growth Rate	Top-Bracket Income Tax Rate	
		Range	Average
1950s	4.0%	84–92%	89%
1960s	4.4	91–70	80
1970s	3.2	70–70	70
1980s	2.8	50–28	39
1990s (1990–1995)	1.7	31–39.6	35

Source: Economic Report of the President, 1988 and 1996, The Council of Economic Advisers, Washington, DC, pp. 251 and 283; Historical Statistics of the United States: Colonial Times to 1970, 1975, U.S. Department of Commerce, Washington, DC, p. 1095; Statistical Abstract of the United States, 1981 and 1995, U.S. Department of Commerce, Washington, DC, pp. 260 and 349.

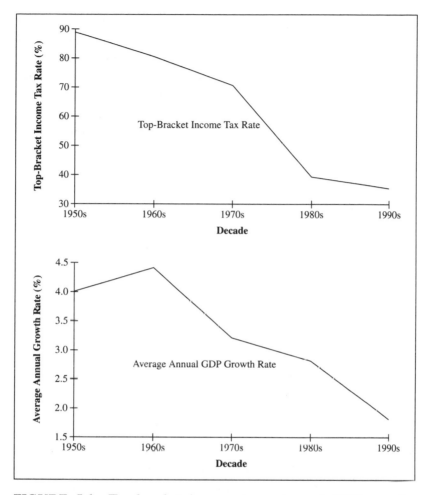

FIGURE 5.1 Top-bracket income tax rate and GDP growth: 1950–1995. As the top-bracket income tax rate tumbled between the 1950s and the 1990s, so did U.S. GDP growth. (*Source:* Table 5.1.)

When peace returns, government spending on arms and related materials plummets. Recession, with zero or negative growth, follows. The fast growth during wartimes is then balanced by the low-growth years. Similarly, the fluctuating international price of oil has had significant impact on GDP growth.

Table 5.1 lists average economic growth rates for five decades. These are obtained by adding annual growth rates, positive or negative, over a decade, and then dividing the sum by 10. Thus, the average growth of the 1980s equals the sum of the annual growth rates from 1980 to 1989, divided by 10.

The top-bracket income tax rate also varies every decade. The highest income taxes after the Second World War were levied in the 1950s—92 percent in 1953, and 91 percent between 1954 and 1963. The average of the tax rates on top incomes in the 1950s was 89 percent. Out of every dollar earned above $1 million, the taxpayer had to pay 89 cents to the government. Most people would call this confiscatory taxation, and with good reason. But did it kill economic growth? Hardly. Growth averaged 4 percent per year during the 1950s.

During the 1960s, the average top-bracket income tax charge fell slightly (to 80 percent), and the growth rate moved up a little (to 4.4 percent per year). The top-bracket income tax rate was still confiscatory, but growth was exceptionally high.

In the 1970s, the top-bracket rate was fixed at 70 percent, below the levels of the 1960s. Average growth tumbled during this decade of lower taxes on the affluent. Some may legitimately argue that the gargantuan jump in energy prices crushed growth during the 1970s, offsetting the lower taxes. They may be right, but let us examine the record of the next decade before we jump to this conclusion.

The top-bracket tax rate during the 1980s ranged from 28 percent to 50 percent, and the average plummeted to 39 percent after being 70 percent in the previous decade. Did the growth rate soar? No; just the opposite happened. Average growth sank to 2.8 percent in the 1980s. The international price of oil also fell sharply after 1985, yet the GDP growth rate fell below the rate in the 1970s. So much for the notion that low income taxes on the wealthy stimulate economic growth.

Energy prices have a significant impact on a nation's economic performance because energy plays a crucial role in virtually every economic activity. In factories, machines need energy to operate. In homes, it is used for heating, cooling, and lighting. A rise in the price of oil adversely affects the

U.S. economy in a variety of ways. First, it raises costs for the producers, who then have to reduce their supply of goods and services. Second, because the United States imports more than half its demand for oil, a rise in energy prices increases import costs and worsens the trade deficit, which is a major drain on the country's GDP.

When supply falls relative to demand, prices rise. During the 1970s, oil prices rose frequently. As a consequence, the country went through the wrenching experience of low growth and leaping inflation. One reason for mediocre economic performance of the 1970s was the sharp jump in the international price of oil.

But what is the excuse for the 1980s, when oil prices began to *fall* after 1982 and nosedived after 1985? The culprit for growth stagnation in the 1980s was the massive transfer of the tax burden from the rich to the poor. Payroll taxes soared, and the top-bracket income tax rate tumbled. If oil prices had been unchanged, the growth record would have been even worse. In spite of fortuitous aid from the oil cartel, OPEC, the Reagan decade could only produce what until then was the worst economic performance of the post-World War II period—an anemic average annual growth of 2.8 percent per year.

The champions of Reaganomics like to ignore the recession years, 1981 and 1982. Instead, they focus on the growth years between 1983 and 1988.[2] To be consistent, they should also ignore the recession years from other decades. If they did, supply-side economics would still deliver the worst performance.

In sum, the record of economic growth since World War II shows that low taxes on the wealthy hurt economic development. When the rich paid high taxes, as in the 1950s and the 1960s, the economy grew more than twice as fast as in the 1990s, when they paid low taxes. Reagan's growth record pales before the achievements of his post-WWII predecessors. In other words, a sharply progressive income tax system has been the lifeblood of the post-WWII U.S. economy. Once progressivity was abandoned, growth turned mediocre.

HIGH TAXES ON THE POOR AND LOW GDP GROWTH

The economic performance of the 1980s and the first half of the 1990s is so poor relative to prior decades that there must be some other culprits as well to share the blame. There are, and one of them is the giant Social Security tax. Let us examine the economic record within each decade and see how rising taxes on the poor and the middle class have hindered prosperity. Conversely, we should see how low taxes on the destitute and middle-income groups promote development.

Table 5.2 compares the first-bracket income tax rate and the Social Security tax rate over two decades. Both taxes fall heavily on the poor and the middle class. The first-bracket tax is the effective tax on the lowest income level subject to taxation, taking into account all the deductions and personal exemptions. It is the minimum rate applicable to taxable net income.

The minimum income tax rate ranged from 17.4 percent to 22.2 percent in the 1950s; in the 1960s, a significant reduction in the income tax rate, from 20 percent to 14 percent,

TABLE 5.2   First-bracket income tax rates and social security taxes: 1950s and 1960s.

Year(s)	First-Bracket Tax Rate	Social Security Tax Rate
1950	17.4%	1.5%
1951	20.4	1.5
1952–1953	22.2	1.5
1954–1963	20.0	2.0–3.6
1964	16.0	3.6
1965–1967	14.0	4.2
1968	14.0	4.4
1969	14.0	4.8

Source: Historical Statistics of the United States: Colonial Times to 1970, 1975, U.S. Department of Commerce, Washington, DC, pp. 335 and 1095.

occurred. Almost 90 percent of the tax break went to the poor and the middle class, and only 10 percent went to the affluent. Despite the sizable cut in the minimum income tax, GDP growth rose only slightly—from 4.0 percent to just 4.4 percent (Table 5.1). The reason: the concomitant rise in the Social Security (SS) tax rate. The jump in the SS rate is actually larger than shown in Table 5.2: first, it affects both the employees and the employers, especially small businessowners, and second, the taxable wage base also rose. The positive effect of a cut in the minimum tax rate was offset to some extent by the negative effect of the SS rate hike. Nevertheless, average growth rose somewhat as taxes fell overall for lower-income groups. In fact, the 1960s generated the best economic performance of the post-WWII era.

During the 1970s, inflation soared and, even though the tax rates did not change much, millions of people in the middle class were pushed into higher income brackets. Inflation slowed somewhat in the 1980s, but prices still rose faster than in the 1950s and the 1960s. To see the effects, examine the tax rates on inflation-adjusted income, in Table 5.3, where the first-bracket or minimum tax rates apply to the lowest taxable income expressed in 1988 dollars.

TABLE 5.3   First-bracket tax rates on income in constant (1988) dollars, and the Social Security Tax: 1970–1993 (selected years).

Year	First-Bracket Tax Rate	Social Security Combined Tax Rate	Wage Base
1970	15.0%	9.6%	$ 7,800
1980	14.0	12.3	25,900
1985	11.0	14.1	39,600
1990	15.0	15.3	51,300
1993	15.0	15.3	57,600

Source: Statistical Abstract of the United States, 1981, p. 328; 1991, p. 328; 1995, p. 379; U.S. Department of Commerce, Washington, DC.

We already know that growth slowed sharply in the 1970s and more acutely in the 1980s, even though the top-bracket income tax rates fell. We also know that one reason for the slowdown in the 1970s was the big jump in the price of oil. As the minimum (first-bracket) tax rate barely budged, another cause of the slowdown was the giant leap in the SS burden, which rose from 9.6 percent in 1970 to 12.3 percent in 1980, and continued to rise thereafter. This is the combined tax rate paid by the employer and the employee. Note that while the rate itself increased slightly, the wage base to which it applied more than tripled within 10 years (1970 to 1980). Thus, inflation caused by rising oil prices and Social Security hikes combined to destroy economic growth in the 1970s.

Even though oil prices tumbled during the 1980s, the growth blight continued with increasing virulence. Here, the SS tax hike is the only culprit. Not only did the SS rate jump, but the government almost doubled the wage base it could tax in the 1980s. The first-bracket income tax rate also climbed in 1990. In the early 1990s, the minimum tax rates were unaltered, but the SS tax bite worsened via yet another rise in the taxable wage base. The conclusion is unavoidable: *The poor performance of the economy in recent decades stems from confiscatory taxation of the poor.*

PROGRESSIVE VERSUS REGRESSIVE TAXATION

Why does progressive taxation improve economic performance and regressive taxation worsen it? In advanced market economies, demand is at the center of productive activity. Investment, profit, output, employment, and the federal budget all revolve around consumer spending, which accounts for more than two-thirds of national demand. In capitalism, where the employer holds all the cards, top incomes tend to rise much faster than bottom incomes (as indeed they have been doing lately). Since the rich spend a much smaller proportion of their income for consumption than the poor do, consumer spending and hence demand generally fail to grow as fast as output. In other words, because of rising inequality, demand lags supply. Output then has to fall to the level of demand, and growth slows down.

Growth is still positive because a rising population generates some rise in demand. But that growth becomes anemic with rising inequality. Keynes discovered this weakness of capitalism as early as 1936 and, under his influence, the governments in North America, Europe, Japan, and Australia designed a highly progressive tax system from the 1940s to the 1960s. The idea was to finance government spending by taxing the rich heavily, while sparing the poor from any taxation. In this way, money could be kept rolling in the economy—from production to consumption and then back into production.

Money must be kept rolling in any economy. If money sits idle in the checking accounts of the rich or in their speculative financial activities, then demand becomes inadequate.

The poor spend all their income because they have so little of it. The middle class saves only a small fraction of total income. The rich save a lot more than others, but if their funds sit idle in banks or are used mostly in financial speculation, then money stops rolling from rich households to producers, and the circular flow breaks down. This breakdown generates recessions and depressions.

The progressive tax system siphons off a large portion of the idle funds of the rich and uses them in government spending. Government demand then makes up for the shortfall in national demand caused by the high savings and speculation of the affluent. For that reason, when the tax system was progressive, economies operated smoothly and growth was high around the world.

Fissures in the system appeared when Social Security taxes began to rise not just in America, but in most other advanced economies, which we will examine in Chapter 11. The rich, the poor, and the middle class were all now taxed heavily. As long as the government returned the money to households in the form of Social Security benefits, there was no net loss of spending in the economy. In the 1970s, for example, the economy still grew at a respectable rate, even though oil prices soared.

In the 1980s, however, the Social Security tax was so high that it created a growing surplus in its trust fund. The money taken by the government from lower-income classes, the real consumers, was not fully returned to households. Demand could not grow as fast as before. Hence, investment grew slowly and so did output.

What killed growth in the 1980s and the 1990s? The giant Social Security taxes on the destitute and middle-income groups, and the fact that the promised investment from the low-taxed rich never materialized. How could it? Why would a rich person risk money on an investment project when its subsequent output might not find demand? Investment is always lubricated by demand, not by low taxes on the wealthy.

From the 1950s to the 1970s, the administrations had heavily taxed the wealthy and then spent the resulting revenues. During the 1980s, income taxes fell, federal budget deficits soared, and the government increasingly borrowed money from the wealthy and spent it. So Borrow-and-spend policies replaced tax-and-spend policies. This was a major change, but it kept the circular flow alive. Growth continued for a while, but at a low rate because of the heavy taxation of the poor.

However, a new headache developed because of massive federal deficits. Government borrowing raised the interest rates above what they would have been without the deficits. High interest rates, just like high taxes on the poor, discourage consumer spending, especially on durable goods such as cars, appliances, furniture, and similar big-ticket items. They also stifle the purchase of new homes, because high interest rates raise monthly mortgage payments. The rise in interest rates generated by government deficits effectively slowed the growth in demand.

We all know that the interest rate we pay on a loan rises with inflation. For this reason, economists have introduced the concept of the *real rate of interest*—the actual rate paid for a loan minus the prevailing rate of inflation. When companies and individuals borrow money for investment, their behavior is determined by the real rate. The reason is simple: People are more likely to pay a higher market rate of interest if inflation rises, because they expect to sell their assets later at higher prices.

The real rate of interest averaged 1.24 percent in the 1950s, 2.68 percent in the 1960s, 1.32 percent in the 1970s, and a high 6 percent in the 1980s.[3] The reason: the big federal deficits. Such a high real rate naturally discouraged home buying and led to a decline in home ownership in the 1980s.[4]

It must be clear by now that mediocre U.S. growth since 1980 arose from two reasons—a growing surplus in the Social Security trust fund, and extremely low income taxes on the rich, which created huge budget deficits and generated high interest rates. Since 1992, the budget deficit and interest rates have declined, but the SS tax bite has continued to rise, and growth is still anemic.

SMALL BUSINESS OWNERS

The big increase in Social Security taxes, along with the simultaneous jump in self-employment taxes, practically broke the back of small businessowners in the 1980s and the 1990s. In addition to paying a tax of 7.65 percent on the wages of each worker they hired, they had to part with a self-employment tax of 15.3 percent on their own income. Furthermore, they were obligated to pay the regular income tax on their profit.

The folly of the current tax structure is that small businesses have been the most prolific job creators in America.[5] Yet most of the tax breaks have been showered on big corporations, leaving ministores and shops with the tax bill. Suppose a small businessowner also owns a home and earns $60,000 in 1996. Current tax law imposes a self-employment tax of 15.3 percent, a federal income tax of 20 percent, a sales tax of 8 percent (in most major cities), and a property tax equal to 4 percent of the homeowner's income, or a total of 47 percent of gross income. In high-tax states that have their own income and gasoline taxes, the tax bite would exceed 50 percent.

Smaller firms, started by middle-class owners, have been the real entrepreneurs and investors. The affluent merely speculate on existing large companies through mergers, which generate mega debts and downsizing in the process.

With the present immense tax burden on minicompanies, workers lose out in pensions and health insurance. Small firms can no longer afford them. As employment shifts from giant corporations to undercapitalized companies, a growing fraction of the workforce is without fringe benefits, which, prior to the 1980s, were taken for granted.[6]

The agony of small business also means slow growth for America. How can a minifirm raise wages when it has to pay confiscatory charges to the government month after month? Low wages mean low consumer spending, which eventually translates into mediocre economic growth.

To recapitulate, America's anemic growth since 1980 can be traced to two factors: puny taxes on the rich and on giant corporations and high taxes on the poor and on small companies. The results are a growing Social Security trust fund and the concomitant loss of consumer spending, sharply higher real interest rates that choke home buying, and an increasingly burdened small-firm sector unable to afford higher wages and employee benefits.

CHAPTER 6

Are Income and Social Security Taxes Better Than Tariffs to Fund the Government?

The love affair of modern economists and politicians with income taxes goes back to 1913, when President Woodrow Wilson prodded Congress into passing the 16th Amendment to the Constitution, permitting the income tax. An income tax had first been introduced in the North during the Civil War to finance the enormous rise in government spending. But after the conflict, in 1872, the tax was repealed on grounds of supposedly socialistic leanings. Great fortunes had been made in the North during the war, and the Democrats were anxious to tax them and to trim other taxes at the same time. However, the Republicans decried the income tax on the wealthy as a move toward socialism, and would not allow it to continue.

During the Civil War, the income tax, born out of an emergency need for new sources of revenue, was not popular, especially with the affluent Northerners who had to bear the brunt of it. Introduced in 1861, it granted an exemption of $600 and imposed a 5 percent fee on incomes above $10,000 and a 3 percent fee on incomes below that amount. The exemption was large enough to spare much of the population from the tithe. In 1864, the tax rates increased to between 5 percent and 10 percent, and the tax revenue soared to as much as a quarter of federal receipts.[1]

Until 1861, the principal source of federal revenue had been customs duties—tariffs or taxes on goods imported from abroad. Even in 1866, when the income levy accounted for 25 percent of the revenue, tariffs produced a 32 percent share. After the income tax was repealed, duties accounted for more than half of the federal receipts.[2]

The income tax had shown its capability in generating revenue, but it lacked popular support. Between 1873 and 1973, some 68 income tax bills were introduced in Congress, and they were all defeated.

The main support for the income tax came from farmers, factory workers, and economists who had become enamored with the doctrine of free trade. In 1816, a businessman named David Ricardo showed, with the help of numerical examples, that all countries benefited from the removal of tariffs. Leave aside for the moment the author's ludicrous assumptions—for example, that capital was not needed in production, or that labor was fully employed both before and after trade, ignoring the reality of frequent recessions.[3]

By comparing two goods, one exported and the other imported, Ricardo demonstrated that both trading partners enhanced their labor productivity by specializing in their export product and by importing the other good. The power of the numerical example was so strong that the economic profession came to regard free trade as its gospel.

There was one practical problem, however. The tariffs in question raised a lot of revenue for the government. The free traders were willing to offset this revenue through the income tax, even though there was no such element in Ricardo's model. Economists loved the income tax, but politicians and the newspapers were not convinced until the 1890s. At that time, Republicans believed in protectionism requiring high tariffs, and Democrats advocated low customs duties. C. H. Jones, editor of the *St. Louis Republic,* has been cited by historians as an influential voice behind the so-called tariff reform that preferred the income tax to import duties. In a letter written in 1893 to the Ways and Means Subcommittee, Jones had this to say:[4]

> The income tax is one that ought to be levied at the next session of Congress. Some way of increasing the revenues must be found, especially if we are to redeem our pledges of tariff reform.

The result was the Wilson-Gorman Act of 1894, a small step toward trade liberalization. According to historian James Davidson and his colleagues, the tariff act "reduced some schedules, raised others, and enacted a modest income tax to *make up for lost revenues.*"[5] (Italics added.) A year later, however, the Supreme Court held the income tax provision unconstitutional, and the tax bill died.

Even though the Wilson-Gorman Act went nowhere, it strengthened the resolve of the economists and Democrats to bolster free trade by means of an income tax. Ever since the end of the Civil War, consumer and wholesale prices had been declining. Their decline had spawned depressions during the 1870s, 1880s, and 1890s, with high levels of unemployment. To inflation-weary consumers of today, deflation may not appear a problem, but, in the late 19th century, falling prices were considered a scourge that repeatedly caused business bankruptcies and mass layoffs.

In this environment, one might think that tariff reduction would be the last thing on people's minds, since prices could fall more, at least in the short run. Even some Republicans were believers in free trade and favored replacing tariffs with the income tax. To enact a tariff bill in 1909, President William Taft accepted some protectionist amendments he disliked. As Davidson et al. point out: "Taft, who wanted tariffs lowered, caved in so that the tariff bill would pass. . . . Taft's support of a constitutional amendment permitting graduated income taxes was sometimes ardent, sometimes tepid, but in the end proved decisive."[6] In economist William Gill's words: "The focus of the battle in Congress became not so much the

tariff per se as the income tax which was to replace it."[7] However, the 1909 Act was so peppered with amendments that the
tariff rates hardly budged.

Free traders finally succeeded in 1913, when the 16th
Amendment was added to the Constitution, permitting the
income tax. The same year, with the blessings of President
Woodrow Wilson, the Underwood-Simmons Tariff was enacted, reducing the average tariff but adding an income tax
at the same time. According to Davidson et al.:[8]

> The Underwood-Simmons Tariff of 1913 marked the first down-
> ward revision in 19 years and the biggest since before the Civil
> War. It lowered most rates from 40% to 20% and placed many
> new items on the free list. *To compensate for lost revenue,* Congress
> enacted a graduated income tax, permitted under the newly
> adopted Sixteenth Amendment. It applied solely to corporations
> and the tiny fraction of Americans who earned more than $4,000
> a year. It nonetheless began a *momentous shift* in government rev-
> enue from its nineteenth century base—public lands, alcohol
> taxes and customs duties—to its twentieth century base—per-
> sonal and corporate incomes. (Italics added.)

Free traders had won a great victory by promising modest income tax rates. Initially, the rates ranged from a low of 1 percent to a high of 6 percent on the wealthiest. Soon, however,
tariffs were lowered further, and to make up for lost revenue
and finance the needs of the First World War, the top marginal income tax rate was raised to 70 percent by 1918 and the
lowest one to 6 percent. Falling tariffs went hand in hand with
climbing income taxes.

Tariffs and the Roaring '20s

Then came a serious recession in 1920. Warren Harding, a Republican, won the presidency. He had been appalled by the
tax policy of his Democratic predecessor. He considered it
bizarre that taxes had been repeatedly reduced on foreign

goods and transferred onto the American people, who could avoid the tariff by avoiding imports, but could not elude the income tax.

So Harding began to lower the income tax and raise the tariff rate. His successor, Calvin Coolidge, continued in the same vein. By 1929, the top income tax rate had fallen to 25 percent and the lowest one to 0.4 percent—even lower than the inaugural rate of 1 percent. At the same time, the average tariff on imported goods rose from 16 percent in 1920 to 40 percent by 1929. Needless to say, economists were extremely worried by the Harding tariffs. During the recession of 1920–1921, doomsday forecasts flowed freely from free traders. How wrong they were. Instead, the nation got the "Roaring '20s." As Davidson et al. put it:[9]

> If anything roared in the "Roaring Twenties," it was industry and commerce. America was in the midst of a *productivity revolution,* turning out more goods with less labor. Manufacturing output rose 64 percent, output per worker by 40 percent. Between 1922 and 1927, the economy grew by 7 percent a year—the largest peace time growth rate ever. (Italics added.)

Where free traders had gone wrong was in arguing that protectionism destroys the innovative spirit and national productivity of the nation. As the average tariff more than doubled during the 1920s, the United States enjoyed a productivity revolution and the largest peacetime growth ever, despite the extraordinary jump in protectionism.

There are two varieties of protectionism: in one, intense competition exists at home; in the other, it does not. The first may be called *competitive protectionism,* in which a large number of protected companies offer a serious challenge to one other on their home turf. The second may be called *monopolistic protectionism,* in which a small number of domestic firms are shielded from foreign rivals. The monopolistic variety destroys an economy, but the competitive variety has been a great success wherever it has been tried. (I will return to this matter in Chapters 8 and 12.) Needless to say, the secret of rapid U.S. economic growth in the 19th century and then in the 1920s was intense domestic competition unhindered by foreign competition.

GIANT INCOME TAX RATES AND THE GREAT DEPRESSION

But protectionism's resurgence would prove to be temporary. In 1929, the stock market crashed and a deep slump began. Congress passed another tariff bill in 1930, the infamous Hawley-Smoot Tariff Act, which raised the average tariff to 59 percent.[10] But this time, instead of reducing the income tax, as was done in 1921, lawmakers opted to raise it. In 1932, the income tax experienced the largest rise ever. The top rate jumped from 25 percent in 1929 to 65 percent in 1932, and the lowest one, from 0.4 percent to 4 percent. As a consequence, the recession of 1929 turned into a depression.

Free traders blamed the new higher import tariff for the depression. To them, the ensuing trade war that lowered U.S. exports was the real culprit. But closer scrutiny of facts and figures reveals something else.

Gross national product (GNP) is defined as domestic demand (or absorption) plus net exports, or exports minus imports. From 1929 to 1933, GNP fell from $104 billion to $56 billion, a loss of $48 billion. However, net exports fell by only $700 million, and domestic spending declined by $47.3 billion. In other words, net exports decreased by 1.5 percent of the fall in GNP, and domestic demand fell by the remaining 98.5 percent! It is patently absurd to fuss over the 1.5 percent fall and overlook the other 98.5 percent. (See Appendix Table A.3.)

According to free traders, the Hawley-Smoot tariff was responsible for the depression because the ensuing trade war around the world sharply lowered American exports. But this charge is nonsense. Even if the tariff had completely eliminated the U.S. export sector, which it did not, all it could have destroyed was 1.5 percent of the total fall in production. Statistically, 1.5 percent is like zero. There is absolutely no way that the Hawley-Smoot tariff could have caused or contributed to the depression. Stanford University Professor Krugman, no friend of tariffs, confirms this emphatically: "The claim that protectionism caused the Depression is nonsense; the claim that future protectionism will lead to a repeat performance is equally nonsensical."[11]

The huge rise in the income tax rate, passionately advocated by free traders, crushed domestic demand and caused the Great Depression. One might call it the Hoover-Roosevelt tax: Herbert Hoover signed the bill in 1932, and Roosevelt welcomed the new tax in 1933.[12]

INCOME TAXES REPLACING TARIFFS

Influenced by free traders, FDR began a systematic policy of tax switching. He renewed Wilson's policy of tariff reduction, and, although the income tax rates had already skyrocketed, he raised them even higher. By 1940, the top rate had climbed to 81 percent and the bottom rate rose a little, to 4.4 percent.

In Figure 6.1, we see the history of the tariff and top-bracket income tax rates from 1912 to 1963. Whenever tariffs went down, income taxes went up; and whenever import duties rose, the income tax rate fell.

Under FDR, the average tariff fell from 54 percent in 1933 to 36 percent in 1940. In contrast, the top-bracket income tax rate soared. This was the height of lunacy. Both of these were deflationary policies and were pursued while prices had already sunk 25 percent.

Even the poor could not escape. In 1942, according to Davidson et al., "the administration agreed to a 5 percent tax on incomes over $624 a year."[13] The new Act expanded the taxable population caught in the IRS net from 13 million people in 1941 to 50 million in 1942, while tariffs continued to fall.

Meanwhile, in 1935, another tax had been imposed on Americans' incomes—the Social Security (SS) or payroll tax. At the start, it was just 2 percent on the first $3,000 of income and was shared equally by employer and employee. No wonder

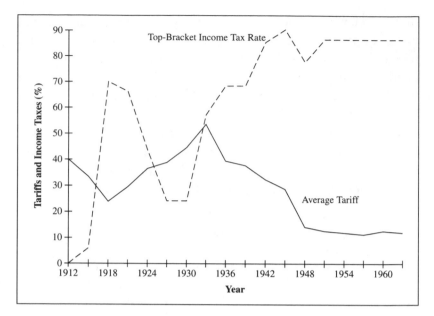

FIGURE 6.1   Average tariff and top-bracket income tax rate: 1912–1963. Between 1912 and 1963 whenever tariffs fell, the income tax rate went up; whenever tariffs rose, the income tax rate fell. (*Source: Historical Statistics of the United States: Colonial Times to 1970,* 1975, U.S. Department of Commerce, Washington, DC, Series U 212 and Y 439.)

the depression went on and on. Every time domestic demand recovered from the onslaught of an earlier tax, a new tax was introduced or an old one was raised, all inspired by the acolytes of free trade.

After FDR's death in 1945, the free trade policy of transferring taxes from foreign goods to Americans' incomes continued. However, the top income tax rate was already so high that some other revenue source had to be found to make up for the lost tariff revenue. So the SS tax rate was doubled in the early 1950s and then nearly doubled again by 1969. By 1994, the payroll tax had climbed above 15 percent and the average tariff had fallen to just 5 percent.

In 1964, the U.S. tax policy took another turn. For the first time, income taxes and some business taxes were cut to fight the recession, reflecting the Keynesian view of fiscal expansion. Another era had now begun. (That is why Figure 6.1 stops at 1963.)

With the ascendance of Keynesian economics, the income tax rates were repeatedly lowered, but because of changes in exemptions and the upward bracket creep during the inflationary 1970s, the actual share of total revenue contributed by the tax changed little over time. As shown in Figure 6.2, income and SS tax shares rose relentlessly while free trade advanced via a continued decline in the average tariff rate.

Indeed, the tax burden of free trade policies was mostly transferred to the SS tax; since 1960, the tax share of the SS levy has increased steadily, reaching 37 percent in 1993; the share of the income tax has been steady around 45 percent. In Figure 6.2, the top line measures the aggregate tax burden on Americans' income, counting the SS tax as a tax on income, even though half of this amount is paid by the employer. There

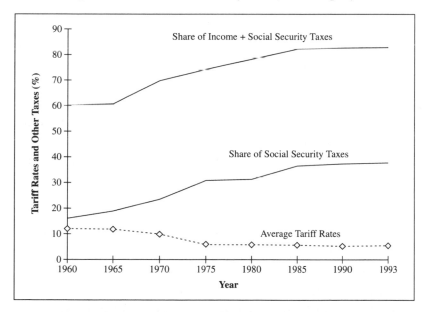

FIGURE 6.2 Income and social security tax shares, and average tariff rates: 1960–1993. After 1963 as tariffs fell the tax burden was transferred to the Social Security taxes because the income tax was already too high to raise any further. By 1993 the Social Security tax was 37% of the total tax receipts. The American tax structure thus became ultra regressive. (*Source: Statistical Abstract of the United States,* 1981 and 1994.)

has been a dramatic rise in the aggregate income tax burden, which reached an all-time high of 82 percent of the federal tax revenue in 1993. The tax share of import duties that year was just 1 percent, down from 44 percent in 1913. Thus, even in the Keynesian era of economic policy the tax burden on Americans' income went up despite periodic cuts in the income tax rates, and tariffs continued to fall.

In sum, the historical conflict between protectionists and free traders in the United States has really been over tariffs and personal taxes. Protectionists prefer taxes on foreign goods, and free traders favor taxes on Americans' incomes. The monumental tax shift introduced in 1913 was reversed during the 1920s but reappeared in the 1930s and has continued to this day.

FREE TRADE AND FREE LUNCH

The appeal of free trade policies is obvious: No matter what the economic system—capitalism, communism, or socialism—how can tax reduction, unmatched by a replacement, not please the consumer and apparently improve his or her welfare? Hundreds of books and articles have been written since 1913 on the theory of gains from trade, but I cannot find a single study where the author found it necessary to provide for government services, as tariffs were reduced or eliminated. This is exactly what a free lunch is: you get your food without having to pay for it.

Free traders argue that the government returns the tariff revenue to the consumer. This is not a bad assumption, because the government spends what it collects, and then some. But when the tariff revenue is eliminated to make room for free trade, where does the government get its funding?[14]

Some free trade models do replace tariffs with lump-sum taxes, but they never identify any country where such taxation is in vogue; nor do they specify the nature of such taxes; nor do they offer an analysis of their effectiveness. In short, their theories are incomplete and misleading.[15]

If tariffs can be shown to be inferior to an equivalent income tax or the SS tax, in a realistic economy suffering from myriad imperfections, then, of course, free trade is superior to protectionism. But to my knowledge, no one has done this so far.

PROFESSOR SAMUELSON ON GAINS FROM TRADE

MIT Professor Paul Samuelson won a Nobel Prize in 1970 for demonstrating, among other things, that free trade benefits all nations. He took Ricardo's theory several steps forward by introducing many commodities, as well as productive resources, into his analysis. Like any economist, he made several implicit and explicit assumptions. Here are some of them:

1. There is no government in the economy.
2. Gainers compensate the losers from trade.
3. Capital or industry stays at home and does not chase low wages abroad.
4. Wages at home are equal in all industries.
5. The country has no trade deficit.

Assuming these conditions, Professor Samuelson demonstrated in a rigorous mathematical model that some trade is better than no trade for every nation, rich or poor, large or small.[16] Harvard Professor Richard Caves explained it this way:[17]

> With *ideal cooperation,* after the introduction of trade everyone who has suffered thereby could be compensated to leave him as well off as before without taxing away all the gains of the people who have benefited. (Italics added.)

The five assumptions presented above remind me of a joke about a scientist and an economist stranded on an island with nothing but cans of peaches to eat. They had lost everything else in a shipwreck. The scientist looked for a sharp and large

stone to break open the cans but couldn't find one. The economist stayed calm, enjoying the view on the beach. "Don't
worry," said the economist. "We will open the cans when we're
hungry." "How can we do that without a hammer or a sharp
object?" asked the scientist. "Let's assume we have a can
opener, and the rest is easy," replied the economist.

Samuelson's five assumptions are like the economist's non-
existent can opener. These conditions simply assume away the
problems that the United States has faced as tariffs have been
gradually replaced by income and SS taxes. In the real world,
is there any economy without a government or is there any government that does not need taxes? Do we have gainers that
would compensate the losers from trade?

The assumption about U.S. industries not chasing low wages
in Mexico, Malaysia, India, and other parts of the Third World
is equally laughable. So is the precondition that wages are the
same in all industries. In 1994, the average wage in manufacturing was more than twice that in retail trade. Finally, the assumption that the country has no trade deficit is a big joke;
the United States has had horrendous foreign deficits since
1983.

Still, the vast majority of economists believe in the gospel
that a nation should remove import barriers regardless of
what others do. As Milton Friedman, another Nobel laureate,
puts it: "Economists often do disagree, but that has not been
true with respect to international trade."[18] Elsewhere, he continues in the same vein:[19]

> A fourth argument, one that was made by Alexander Hamilton
> and continues to be repeated down to the present, is that free
> trade would be fine if all other countries practiced free trade
> but that so long as they do not, the United States cannot afford
> to. This argument has no validity whatsoever, either in principle
> or in practice.

No? Within the United States, there is free trade. No state
has any tariff on products coming from another state. According to free traders, all states should be equally prosperous,

because they can all export and import whatever they want, each specializing in doing what it does best. Then why are some states much poorer than others? In 1994, Connecticut had a per-person income of $24,732 after deducting all federal, state, and local taxes, whereas Mississippi's per-capita income, in spite of lower state taxes, was only $14,362, or 59 percent of Connecticut's income. Both have free trade within America. Why is one so much poorer than the other? Both states have equal access to productive resources. Yet Connecticut must have something that really makes the difference. Trade is completely insignificant here. The crucial factor is manufacturing, which we will examine in another chapter. Other high-income states are Massachusetts and New Jersey, while Utah and New Mexico are in the pits. Again, manufacturing is the crucial difference.[20]

Since Professor Samuelson wrote his masterpiece in 1939, economists have written hundreds of articles and books, confirming and refining his conclusions. But only one of the five assumptions has been abandoned—that gainers compensate the losers. This condition has been replaced by another hypothesis that only an economist could devise. If tariffs were replaced by income taxes on the gainers from trade, and the government returned the revenue to the losers, some people would still gain and no one would lose.[21]

Imagine the task of estimating the gains and losses of millions of people affected by trade and then taxing or subsidizing them. The tax code, a madhouse already, would become a monster.

Then, in an article coauthored with Wolfgang Stolper, Professor Samuelson argued that if a high-wage country imports labor-intensive products from a low-wage country, the removal of tariffs would hurt wages in the developed nation while benefiting the owners of capital.[22] This conclusion is now well known as the Stolper-Samuelson theorem and is part of any standard text on international economics. In spite of this new revelation, Samuelson and his followers continued to insist that even if free trade hurts labor in an advanced nation such as the United States, the country is still better off with trade than without it.[23] All you need is that elusive compensation scheme whereby executives offset the losses of laborers.

In most countries, less than 10 percent of the population can live on capital income alone. The rest of the people survive on labor or earned income.[24] If trade raises the income of the 10 percent group and lowers that of the 90 percent group, it must destroy the country's well-being, even if the income gains of the rich are so large that they more than offset the losses of the workers.

Free trade doctrine has become religion for economists today. The theology, noted as the fourth commandment of modern economics in Chapter 3, says that unilateral tariff reduction raises the well-being of the entire country. The level playing field, wherein countries play by the same rules, is of no consequence, because, as economists Krugman and Obstfeld put it: "The fundamental reason why trade potentially benefits a country is that it *expands the economy's choices.* This expansion of choice means that it is always possible to redistribute income in such a way that everyone gains from trade."[25]

However, the authors are candid enough to admit that "everyone *could* gain from trade unfortunately does not mean that everyone actually does"[26] (italics added). This is double talk. If the 90 percent who are wage earners lose and the 10 percent who are wealth holders gain from trade, the country is a vast loser even if the gains of the winners are so large that there is an overall gain, because, in practice, there is no redistribution of income related to trade.

According to Milton Friedman, "protection really means exploiting the consumer."[27] There is not an iota of explanation here. It just assumes that consumers suffer from tariffs. Let me demonstrate why this is impossible.

Suppose the United States imports a Lexus for $20,000 and has an auto tariff of 50 percent. The U.S. consumer pays $30,000, of which $10,000 goes to the government as tax revenue. If the tariff is removed, the U.S. consumer then pays $20,000, and the economists and politicians loudly trumpet the benefits of free trade in terms of the lower price. They forget that the government has now lost the tariff revenue and must collect it from the same consumer in the form of income and/or Social Security tax.

The consumerism argument for free trade is valid only if the government can run without money. Otherwise, when the tariff is removed, the consumer pays an equivalent fee in the form of other taxes. Indeed, to collect tariffs, you do not need the IRS, which exists only to collect internal levies. There is no benefit to the consumer from the replacement of the tariff with the income or payroll tax. Abraham Lincoln was aware of this fact, when he argued that "the consumer does not usually pay the tariff."[28]

The consumer is also a worker. He or she loses a lot from Samuelson's own argument that laborers in rich nations are hurt while capital owners benefit from trade with the labor-abundant Third World. How can trade then be beneficial to America when the vast majority suffers losses in earnings?

The Krugman-Obstfeld premise that trade potentially benefits everyone by expanding consumer choices is feeble because most people would prefer expanded income to expanded choice. Consumers can use extra income for improved education, housing, and medical care, none of which is imported. In fact, imports still constitute less than 15 percent of America's total consumption; fully 85 percent comes from domestic production. Therefore, to most Americans, who derive earnings from wages, expanded income means a lot more than expanded choice from imports.

WAGE EQUALITY BETWEEN THE FIRST WORLD AND THE THIRD WORLD

In 1948, Professor Samuelson offered a rigorous proof of what would be later celebrated as the "factor price equalization" theorem. Using the Stolper-Samuelson thesis, he demonstrated that free trade alone, under certain conditions, would equate real wages between the First World and the Third

World. This startling claim would have been summarily dismissed had it not sprung from the pen of a luminary like Samuelson.[29]

Economists specializing in international trade wasted the next 25 years debating the pros and cons about the theorem; so it is worth exploring the gist of Samuelson's thought. He argues that wages are linked to prices and technology. With free trade, international prices of traded goods come close to each other, the small difference being in transportation costs, which have been falling throughout this century. If technology is the same among countries, it then follows that their wages must also be the same.

The theory offered great hope to impoverished nations. They only had to open their markets to the developed world and their real wages would rise to the levels enjoyed in rich countries.[30] What more could they ask for? Real wages would, of course, fall in developed nations, but that was a small price to pay for global harmony and prosperity, because, remember, free trade is supposed to benefit all nations if rising capital incomes are taken into account.

There was no need for industrialization. The Third World should use the best agrarian technology available from advanced nations, export farm products and minerals, and the rest would follow from the magic of free trade. Unfortunately, the facts do not support this thesis. Real wages have been falling in America, and those in Mexico, India, Pakistan, and China have lagged further behind. Capital owners, of course, have prospered in both areas, but that also contradicts the theory. Capital was supposed to benefit only in countries like America and suffer in labor-abundant nations.

Consider Samuelson's theory from another perspective. All states within America have equal access to capital and technology. Product prices are also close to each other because of free interstate trade. Are real wages then the same in different regions of the country? In 1993, the average annual salary in San Jose was $38,040; in Los Angeles, within the same state of California, it was only $31,760—a difference of more than

$8,000. In Cincinnati, Ohio, the salary was $26,465, more than $12,000 below that in San Jose.

If real wages are not the same or even close among states inside the United States, what chance do they have of being equal between the First World and the Third World? The preconditions of the factor price equalization theorem are clearly satisfied inside America. But even there, the theory does not seem to work. From the commonsense viewpoint, the whole idea is worthless. Yet it offered a partial rationale for the North American Free Trade Agreement (NAFTA) that went into effect in 1994.

What has rising trade between the United States and Mexico done to Mexican wages? Since 1985, when our Southern neighbor began to open its markets, many U.S. companies have moved factories to Mexico. Technology between the two nations is now more similar than before; so are their product prices, thanks to trade liberalization in 1985 and again in 1994 because of NAFTA.

From 1985 to 1988, real wages in Mexico fell 6 percent. They fell another 25 percent by 1995.[31] In the United States, however, the real hourly wage fell only 2.5 percent, and the weekly wage declined 5.5 percent in the same period. Real wages fell in both countries as markets opened, but the gap between their wages went up sharply. So much for the wage equalization theorem.

The wage equalization theory is just as loony as the Lucas idea of voluntary unemployment. Imagine the living standard in India and China, each with close to a billion people, rising to the U.S. level or the Japanese level just through free trade. The economics profession wasted 25 precious years on this theory while many more pressing problems went begging. Does excess population have no impact on wages? Not according to the wage equalization hypothesis.

Many economists defend this proposition by looking at its assumptions, which, if valid, do logically lead to equalization. But there precisely is the rub—the assumptions of the economist. When the assumptions are as preposterous as the can opener on the desert island, how can the theory be sound?

The five assumptions made by Samuelson in defense of trade liberalization are all outrageous, as is the whole idea of free trade.

INCOME-RELATED TAXES VERSUS TARIFFS

A monumental shift in U.S. tax policy occurred in 1913 when the individual income tax began to replace the tariff in financing government spending. The shift was reversed for a decade in the 1920s and then resumed in 1933. Today, the tariff is all but gone, and its place has been taken by a multitude of largely regressive taxes. Few have explored the economic effects of what must have sent shock waves through the production system, at least in the early years of the epochal switch from taxing foreign goods to taxing American goods and incomes.

Comparative analysis of income-related taxes versus tariffs is crucial in deciding the appropriate tax system to finance the federal budget. In order to do this analysis, let us first settle on the main criterion. To my mind, a tax structure is desirable if it raises the living standard of everybody—or at least of the vast majority of people—without destroying the environment. And the best way to measure the living standard is to examine the inflation-adjusted real wage of non-supervisory workers who constitute as much as 80 percent of the labor force. Other economic statistics such as the real GDP growth or per-capita GDP are also important, but they are not the best measures of prosperity. They are highly aggregated, and if the rich get richer and the poor get poorer, the GDP figures may distort the true picture. Real GDP may rise while the real wages fall.

For all practical purposes, gross domestic product (GDP) is the same as gross national product (GNP). GDP is the aggregate value of production inside a country's borders, whereas GNP is the production value by a nation's citizens regardless of where they live in the world. The United States switched to

GDP from GNP in 1992. But the two concepts are virtually the same in the American context.

When tariffs are high, the country does not import much, because high tariffs make foreign goods expensive relative to home goods. Similarly, the country also does not export much, because foreign countries have their own tariffs. In the world of tariffs, few nations are dependent on trade. Trade as a fraction of GDP is then low.

The tariff-oriented tax system, then, has three effects: it produces revenue; foreign goods are expensive; and the trade/GDP ratio is low. The income-oriented tax structure, by contrast, has a high trade/GDP ratio and cheap foreign goods; of course, it also generates revenue.

Although tariffs began a long downward march in 1933, their price and trade effects were not felt in the United States until the late 1960s. Much of the world was in depression in the 1930s, and most countries were too preoccupied with domestic troubles. Then came the Second World War, in which the bulk of Europe and Japan was all but destroyed. These nations were too feeble to make any inroads into the U.S. economy, in spite of the steadily declining tariffs.

After the war, it took Western Europe and Japan about two decades to recover and stand on their own feet. America helped them to fight the Cold War against the Soviet Union. By 1965, both Western Europe and Japan had regained their former industrial status, while U.S. industry had become monopolistic and overconfident. That is when low U.S. tariffs generated the full effects of foreign competition, and American imports began to outpace exports.

Until 1965, the tariff decline mainly produced a revenue loss that was made up primarily through the highly progressive income tax and the slowly rising Social Security tax. The trade effect was not felt yet, because the foreign countries were not strong enough to challenge American corporations at home. Thus, the full effects of the tariff cuts, whether salutary or harmful, were first felt in the late 1960s, when imports, exports, and trade began to rise faster than GDP. That is why we should divide U.S. economic history into two main time periods—pre-1965 and post-1965.

After World War II, 1967 was the first year when the real wage of nonsupervisory workers actually fell. It recovered the next year and grew again until 1972. After that, it began a long period of decline that has not yet been reversed.

Unfortunately, we lack historical data about all nonsupervisory workers; for manufacturing workers, however, records go all the way back to 1909. The manufacturing real wage can be obtained by dividing the weekly earnings by the consumer price index (CPI). In this way, we can obtain the inflation-adjusted wages in manufacturing for 85 years, from 1909 to 1994.

From 1909 to 1970, when the trade/GDP ratio was low, either because of high tariffs or because of their delayed effects on the U.S. economy, the inflation-adjusted wages rose every decade. This occurred because of rising productivity: the index of national productivity jumped from 65.6 to 137.2.[32] However, since 1972, for the first time this century, the real wage has been falling, as tariffs have declined further and the trade/GDP ratio has soared. The decline in the real manufacturing wage occurred in spite of the rise in another productivity index from 75.2 to 101.0.[33] Thus, even though productivity climbed 35 percent, real earnings in manufacturing between 1972 and 1994 fell by 9 percent before taxes. Note that the earnings rose between 1930 and 1940, even during the Great Depression. Such has been the wage carnage of rising trade and declining tariffs. In some ways, the absence of the tariff has done what even the depression could not do to the U.S. economy. (See Appendix Table A.4.)

The history of the previous century reveals that real wages never sank in America until the early 1970s, even though the nation passed through three depressions and the convulsion of the Civil War. Millions of immigrants—some literate, others unskilled—came to the United States; prices went up and down; the country went through myriad storms of automation, downsizing, bankruptcies, and bank failures; but the real wage kept rising with growing productivity.[34] This is what gave birth to the mystique of the American Dream. Those were the good old days when the government budget was primarily financed through tariffs, and trade was low.

When federal financing switched gradually from customs fees to income-related taxes, and as exports and imports soared, the real wage blight began, while productivity continued its relentless forward march.

If tariffs destroy a nation's efficiency and productivity, as the free traders contend, how come the United States became the world economic leader at the end of the 19th century with giant tariffs? Citing Professor Krugman, reporter Bob Davis says that "the link between tariffs and economic growth is so tenuous," that it may not be worth exploring.[35] This position confirms the professor's earlier view: "A protectionist country is usually less productive and thus poorer than it would have been under free trade."[36]

If this is true, then why did rising productivity always raise real wages and thus make people richer when America had high tariffs, and now why is rising productivity not doing the same under free trade? Why is poverty growing with expanding foreign commerce?

TARIFFS AND ECONOMIC GROWTH

Until recently, and perhaps not until Pat Buchanan sirened the wake-up call, economists have not focused on the U.S. real wage. They have always been more concerned with GDP growth. Let us see how our growth rate performed before and after trade began to soar in the early 1970s. From 1869 to 1970, per-capita GDP growth was 2.1 percent; between 1970 and 1995, in the presence of roaring trade, the corresponding growth rate has been 1.5 percent, a half percentage point below the pre-1970 level.[37]

One half percent of deficient growth may seem inconsequential, but when repeated year after year, it can mean a huge difference over decades. In fact, the pre-1970 record is a gross understatement, because female participation in the labor force was much lower at that time, and whatever work women did at home was not included in the GDP. The per-capita growth rate prior to 1970 could be as high as 2.5 percent, a full percentage point higher than the subsequent economic performance.

Figure 6.3 displays the connection between trade and growth in the post-World War II era. It is divided into two parts; the upper part reveals the behavior of trade as a percentage of GDP, and the lower part displays the trend of GDP growth. (The data underlying Figure 6.3 are presented in Appendix Table A.5.) Trade is defined as the sum of exports and imports. From 1950 to 1970, the ratio of trade to GDP was fairly

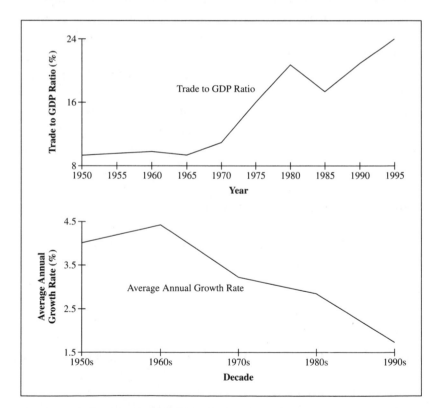

FIGURE 6.3   Trade and GDP growth: 1950–1995. As the contribution of trade to GDP soared after 1970, economic growth plummeted. (*Source: Economic Report of the President,* 1996, The Council of Economic Advisers, Washington, DC, p. 283.)

constant, rising only from 9.4 percent to 10.9 percent over 20 years. After 1970, both exports and imports expanded briskly, and so did the trade ratio, which rose to a record high level of 23.7 percent in 1995.

Now take another look at Figure 6.3. When the trade/GDP ratio was low, insignificant, and fairly constant, as between 1950 and 1970, real GDP grew annually at an average rate of 4 percent or more; as soon as trade shot up, the growth rate plummeted and reached a postwar low of 1.7 percent in the 1990s, just as trade reached a peak. The trade pickup was clearly associated with the growth slowdown.

What can free traders say about this association? Not much. A lot of excuses can be made for soaring trade, but without the knowledge of history, the free traders usually contradict themselves.

The usual excuses are that oil prices jumped in the 1970s, productivity growth has declined because of falling standards in education, regulations have gone up sharply, budget deficits are too high, and so on. The free traders blame the slowdown on everything but rising trade. Some even say that the economy has been in transition ever since the 1970s and, in the long run—when all of us are dead—growth would return to the historical norm.

Yes, oil did become expensive in the 1970s, but it then became cheap in the 1980s and the 1990s. Productivity growth has indeed declined, but isn't rising trade supposed to be good for efficiency? How come productivity growth fell with expanding international commerce?

American higher education is still the best in the world. Why else would thousands of foreign students be enrolled in American universities? With respect to regulations, three consecutive Republican administrations, led by Reagan and Bush, who were lax in regulatory enforcement, produced sharply lower growth after the war. Regarding budget deficits, first the deficit soared after 1981, whereas the growth stagnation began in the early 1970s; secondly, the budget deficit has been falling under Clinton, whereas the wage and income stagnation, as demonstrated in Chapter 10, is worse.

None of the culprits commonly cited by free traders and their friends, the supply-siders, is responsible for the growth blight that has afflicted America since 1970. The stagnation, in the historical perspective, is so bad that there must be several reasons responsible for it. There are. Two culprits were described in the previous chapter—low taxes on the rich, and high taxes on the poor and the self-employed. Now we see that there is another culprit as well—low tariffs or soaring trade.

CHAPTER 7

Are Tariffs Inflationary?

O ne common complaint of voodoo economics is that tariffs are inflationary because they stifle competition, innovation, and entrepreneurship. Professor Samuelson, for instance, argues that tariffs make labor less productive and raise the cost of living.[1] In support of their thesis, free traders usually cite the experience of Third World countries like India, Brazil, Mexico, and Argentina.

This logic is inconsistent. To see whether tariffs would cause inflation in America, one should look at past U.S. experience with customs duties, not at countries that don't have developed markets. Free traders also argue that trade may lower real wages and raise the return to capital;[2] yet, they believe that rising trade always augments a nation's well-being even though workers outnumber executives ten to one. It seems clear to me that if 90 percent of the population loses and the other 10 percent gains from trade, the nation as a whole loses.

HIGH-TARIFF DECADES AND INFLATION

Free traders point to two potential problems associated with tariffs: the rising cost of living and lower labor productivity. The inference is that tariffs generate inflation as well as worker inefficiency. Let us look at U.S. history (Table 7.1 and Figure 7.1).

The tariff data go back to 1821, when the average tariff on dutiable imports was at 45 percent. By 1830, it had jumped to

TABLE 7.1   High-tariff decades and the consumer price index (CPI): 1821–1840; 1870–1910; 1920–1929.

Year	Average Tariff	CPI (1967 = 100)
1821	45%	40
1830	62	32
1840	34	30
1870	44	38
1880	44	29
1890	45	27
1900	49	25
1910	42	28
1920	16	60
1929	40	51

Source: Historical Statistics of the United States: Colonial Times to 1970, 1975, U.S. Department of Commerce, Washington, DC, pp. 210 and 888.

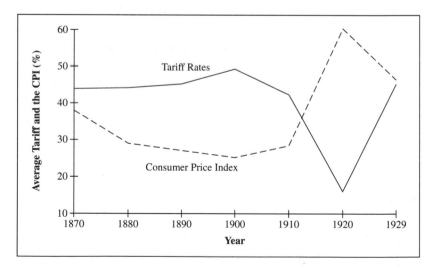

FIGURE 7.1   High-tariff decades and the consumer price index: 1870–1929. Whenever the tariff rates fell the Consumer Price Index soared; whenever the tariff rate soared the Consumer Price Index tumbled. (*Source:* Table 7.1.)

62 percent, an all-time high.[3] Yet, as the tariff rate soared and reached an all-time high, the CPI fell from 40 to 32—a huge 20 percent. Then tariffs plummeted all the way to 34 percent. This, according to free traders, should have given a bonanza to consumers, but the index fell a limp 2 points or just 7 percent over 10 years. Thus, prices fell sharply in spite of a huge jump in customs, and then fell slightly in spite of a major fall in duties.

The next era of high tariffs began in 1865, when prices were already beginning to fall. The CPI fell dramatically after 1865 as the average tariff soared. But free traders may object to the choice of the Civil War decade, because, during wars, prices first skyrocket and then plummet. So, in Table 7.1, we ignore the Civil War decade. The analysis begins in 1870 and goes on until 1910, when the average tariff was above 40 percent. The CPI was 38 at the beginning of the period and 28 at its end. Consumer prices fell about 26 percent. Where is the inflation resulting from high tariffs?

You may recall that President Woodrow Wilson sharply lowered the customs in the decade following 1910. They were raised again in the 1920s. To avoid potential contention that the Great Depression distorts the analysis, I have stopped at the year 1929. During the 1920s, the average tariff more than doubled, but the CPI fell from 60 to 51. Again, where is the inflation in the decade of high tariffs? In fact, the opposite happened. The consumer was the major beneficiary of giant tariffs.

Indeed, a century of U.S. history from 1821 to 1929 shows that whenever tariffs jumped, consumer prices tumbled; when tariffs fell, prices hardly budged.

Low-Tariff Decades and Inflation

Next let's examine the trends in consumer prices since 1950 when tariffs have been exceptionally low. (See Table 7.2 and Figure 7.2.)

TABLE 7.2 Low tariff decades and inflation: 1950–1995.		
Year	Average Tariff	CPI (1982 = 100)
1950	13%	24
1960	12	30
1970	10	39
1980	6	82
1990	5	131
1995	4	152

Source: Historical Statistics of the United States: Colonial Times to 1970, 1975, U.S. Department of Commerce, Washington, DC, p. 888; *Statistical Abstract of the United States, 1995,* U.S. Department of Commerce, Washington, DC, p. 824; *Economic Report of the President, 1996,* The Council of Economic Advisers, Washington, DC, p. 343.

Prior to 1930, tariffs were generally above 35 percent; in most decades, they exceeded 40 percent. Notice that the inflation performance of the free-trade years is ugly compared to that of protectionist decades. How can anyone claim that tariffs will cause inflation in the United States, when in the past they were always associated with declining prices? By contrast, as Figure 7.2 demonstrates, there is not a single year in which prices declined in the post-WWII free-trade era.

HIGH-TARIFF DECADES AND LABOR PRODUCTIVITY

Professor Samuelson asserts that the tariff gives rise to worker inefficiency so that labor productivity declines. Actually, in most advanced economies around the world, labor productivity has been rising for more than a century, with or without free trade. The reason lies in investment, new technology, and capital formation. To see what trade does to labor productivity, let's explore what the rate of productivity growth was in high-tariff decades and then in low-tariff or high-trade decades.

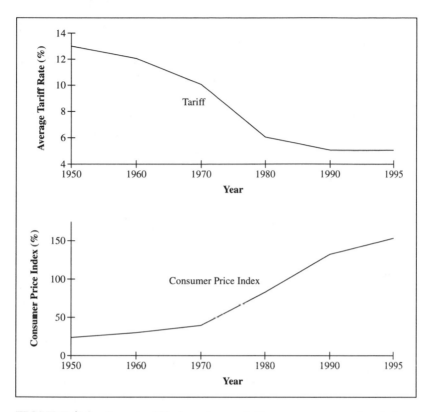

FIGURE 7.2   Low-tariff decades and the consumer price index: 1950–1995. After the Second World War, as the tariff rate fell steadily, there was a relentless rise in the Consumer Price Index. (*Source:* Table 7.2.)

Productivity is measured by national output per hour. If you spend two hours mowing your lawn, and, two weeks later, someone else spends four hours mowing the same area, then you are twice as productive as the other guy. But we know that productivity grows in most years anyway, with or without trade. So, to test the effect of tariffs or trade on hourly output, we have to explore the response of productivity growth— the rate at which hourly national output rises per year.

Unfortunately, productivity data only go back as far as 1889. Let's look at the high-tariff decades from 1890 to 1929, in Table 7.3. During the 1890s, labor productivity grew at an annual rate of 2 percent per year. Then the rate fell to 1.3 percent during the decade 1900–1910. All this time, tariffs were above average. During the decade 1910–1920, the tariff tumbled while productivity growth climbed back to 2 percent. Does this mean that low tariffs stimulate productivity? Hardly. The 1910–1920 decade included World War I, and anything can happen during wartime. The result is inconclusive. But see what happens next. In the 1920s, the tariff rate soared from 16 percent to 40 percent, and so did labor productivity growth—to 2.8 percent per year. From all this, we can conclude that high tariffs have generally been associated with high productivity growth in America, not low productivity growth.

Professor Samuelson also claims that rising trade stimulates labor productivity. In fact, this is the logic behind the idea that trade benefits all nations. Let us examine this claim for post-WWII decades in America, as the nation gradually moved toward a global economy. During the 1950s and the 1960s, the contribution of trade to GDP was about 10 percent, but productivity growth was exceptionally high—above 2.5 percent in both decades. In fact, the 3.1 percent rate in the 1960s was the highest for any decade in U.S. history. When trade began to

TABLE 7.3   High-tariff decades and productivity growth.

Year	Average Tariff	Annual Productivity Growth[1]
1890	45%	
1900	49	2.0%
1910	42	1.3
1920	16	2.0
1929	40	2.8

[1] Calculated as the compound rate of growth.

Source: Historical Statistics of the United States: Colonial Times to 1970, 1975, U.S. Department of Commerce, Washington, DC, p. 948.

soar from the 1970s to the 1990s, productivity growth hit rock bottom. (See Table 7.4.)

How do we explain these findings? Prices are determined by supply and demand. When demand falls relative to supply, product prices fall. Whenever a business is stuck with excessive inventory, it marks its prices down to boost demand. This is how supply and demand work.

High tariffs in America created a dynamic manufacturing sector; the supply of products increased so much that prices tumbled. When tariffs fell and trade soared, U.S. manufacturing suffered, and so did the dynamism of the economy. On this point, even some free traders agree. According to the World Bank, for example, "manufacturing is generally the most dynamic part of the industrial sector."[4] With the fall of American manufacturing, the economy became stagnant, and supply fell relative to demand in most industries. When supply declines relative to demand, inflation is the inevitable result. That is why, without exception, when tariffs escalated, prices always fell in America, and when tariffs vanished, inflation soared. There are, of course, other reasons for constantly rising prices since World War II, but the absence of the tariff is one of the main culprits.[5] From another viewpoint, tariffs

TABLE 7.4 High trade decades and productivity growth: 1950–1995.

Decade	Trade GDP	Annual Productivity Growth
1950s	9.6%	2.7%
1960s	10.0	3.1
1970s	15.8	1.9
1980s	19.5	1.3
1990s	22.2	1.2

Source: Economic Report of the President, 1996 and 1991, The Council of Economic Advisers, Washington, DC.

led to strong productivity growth and hence to declining prices. Free trade, by contrast, generated productivity stagnation and hence rising prices or inflation.

FREE TRADE AND BUDGET DEFICITS

One distinguishing feature of the post-WWII era, compared to the prewar period around the globe, is the constant presence of government budget deficits, especially in the United States. Most Americans today realize that the debt-and-deficit colossus of the federal government is the handiwork of just one president and his Congress, out of a total of 43 administrations. The government largesse, of course, didn't begin with Reagan. There has been a budget deficit almost every year since 1929. Between 1930 and 1946, the deficit tended to be high for two reasons: First, the Great Depression depressed tax receipts and raised spending on public works projects; then came the war in 1939, and war-related government spending soared. Thus, the culture of federal deficits was inaugurated in the 1930s and then continued with vehemence in the 1940s. But the budget deficit vanished after earlier wars and even evolved into a surplus. This time, however, the happy outcome of the past was not repeated. Figure 7.3 reveals that, following the Truman presidency, the deficit became a permanent feature of American life. (See Appendix Table A.6.)

At the end of World War II, Harry Truman was in office for six years, and his administration produced a peacetime surplus of $18 billion or about 1.2 percent of GDP. Dwight Eisenhower generated a cumulative deficit of $19 billion during his eight years in office, enough to erase Truman's surplus. The average annual deficit in Eisenhower's term was $2.4 billion, which doubled to $5 billion under John F. Kennedy, and nearly doubled again to $9 billion per year under Lyndon Johnson. The annual deficit escalated to $26 billion in the Richard Nixon–Gerald Ford era, rose to $57 billion under Jimmy Carter, and then nearly tripled to $167 billion during Ronald Reagan's tenure. George Bush produced annual red

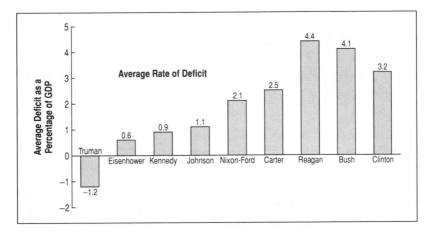

FIGURE 7.3 **Average deficit as a percentage of GDP.** After the war, the peacetime budget deficit first emerged under Republican administrations in the 1950s, and then soared again under Republican administrations in the 1980s. (*Source:* Appendix Table A.6.)

ink of $233 billion per year. Of the nine postwar presidents who preceded Bill Clinton, Truman was the only one to produce a surplus. Presidents Reagan and Bush generated the worst deficits: over 4 percent of GDP per year.

It is interesting to note that the peacetime deficit began under Eisenhower, a Republican President, and reached its zenith under Republicans Reagan and Bush. History is full of irony. Republicans constantly rail against deficits, yet their leaders have been most responsible for the country's red ink.

Let's examine the cumulative federal debt at the start of each administration after World War II. The debt was $271 billion in 1946 and came down to $259 billion by the time Eisenhower was sworn into office. By 1980, the debt was still below $1 trillion. Reagan added $1.7 trillion to the red ink, more than the cumulative debt of all the presidents who preceded him. He sought to cut taxes for wealthy individuals and corporations, raise defense spending, and balance the budget at the same time. But the debt and deficits mounted, even though he presided over the largest tax rise ever imposed on the poor and on small business owners, in the form of the Social Security and self-employment taxes.

In terms of the deficit, this outcome suggests that the mix of taxes is just as important as the overall tax rates. *Compared to a progressive system, a regressive tax system tends to generate a greater deficit.* I will return to this point later. First, let us see what others say about debt and deficits.

THE POPULAR VIEW OF DEBT AND DEFICITS

The popular view is that the twin evils of debt and deficits have sprung from the huge rise in government spending since the late 1960s, when President Johnson established many new programs to aid the poor and the handicapped at home while defense spending continued high during the Vietnam War. The overall purpose was to create a "Great Society" free from poverty. To this end, an omnibus bill, The Economic Opportunity Act, was enacted in 1964. The Act created Medicare and Medicaid, scholarships for college students, aid to education, and programs for consumer protection. As a result, social spending began to rise. At first, the programs did not cost much; later, spending on Medicare and Medicaid grew apace. Doctors, hospitals, and drug manufacturers took advantage by increasing their prices. Life spans rose and so did the use of health care because of its ready availability. As the former chairman of the Council of Economic Advisers, Herbert Stein, wrote:[6]

> In 1965, the last year before the Vietnam War dominated federal finances, social programs cost $30 billion, 25 percent of the budget and 4.5 percent of the GNP. By 1980 these programs cost $280 billion, 48 percent of the budget and 11 percent of the GNP. In constant dollars, the increase was 310 percent, more than five times as large as the percentage increase of real GNP.

In addition to federal aid for health care, social spending was stretched to cover antipoverty programs, of which some were purely welfare fraud. As Stein documents, "In 1980, only about 20 percent of federal benefit payments went to raise people who were otherwise below the poverty line toward it or to it. The remaining approximately 80 percent went to people who even without it would have been above the poverty line."[7]

There are others who believe that the source of today's budget dilemma goes as far back as the 1930s, when the nation was in the midst of vast unemployment and poverty.[8] Millions of the elderly, who were without federal pensions, had lost their life savings in bank failures. The government responded to the mass misery with an unprecedented program called the New Deal, which established new agencies to reassure the public and restore prosperity. The FDIC (Federal Deposit Insurance Corporation), the SEC (Securities and Exchange Commission), and the NLRB (National Labor Relations Board), among other agencies were inaugurated to stabilize the banking system, the stock market, and the economy.

As usual, the new programs did not cost much at their inauguration; but others were soon added. In 1935, the Social Security Act was passed to ensure that the elderly would never be homeless and hungry again. For the first time in U.S. history, the government became committed to offering life's basic necessities to needy retirees.

The Social Security Act provided for a payroll tax of 2 percent—1 percent each on the employer and the employee—on the first $3,000 of income earned. The idea was to build a substantial trust fund that would be invested in Treasury Securities and pay benefits out of interest and continuing payroll contributions.

The social programs that started under the New Deal and then under the Great Society are today lumped together under the umbrella of entitlements or transfer payments. Entitlements have the most voracious appetite of all the federal programs today, and are growing apace. In 1972, the Social Security benefits were indexed to the rate of inflation, which soared in the 1970s. Inflation cooled after 1983 but did not disappear completely, and prices have continued to rise. Benefits thus increase automatically; according to some, the CPI formula overstates the rate of inflation, so that the benefits grow even faster.[9]

Today, it is fashionable among the elites to blame the budget deficit entirely on entitlements.[10] This, as we shall soon see, is only one side of the story. The other, more important side is the slow economic growth because of government bungling of the tax system to favor the rich.

SOARING TRADE AND THE BUDGET DEFICIT

In the popular image of the federal debt and deficit, Great Society programs are devouring tax revenues. Vast growth in government since the mid-1960s is thus to blame, in this view, for the continuing red ink. Closer scrutiny, however, discounts this image.

Look at the trend in the growth of inflation-adjusted spending by the federal government from 1950 to 1995. The fastest growth of real government spending occurred in the 1950s, during the Truman and Eisenhower administrations. In 1950, government spending as a percentage of GDP stood at 16 percent; by 1959, it had jumped to 19 percent, which was not much lower than the 19.8 percent rate in 1969.[11] Government spending rose by $50 billion during the 1950s, but half the rise had occurred by 1952, under Truman's tenure. This was spurred by the Marshall Plan to aid Western Europe and by the Korean War, which began in June 1950. Even after the war ended, the defense buildup continued as the country embarked on the era of Cold War with the Soviet Union and China. Defense outlays as a fraction of GDP doubled during the 1950s to 10 percent, although the Korean War itself was over by 1952.

Government spending after inflation slowed a bit in the 1960s, even though America was caught in the throes of the Vietnam War. In fact, in spite of the Great Society programs, real government spending failed to grow as fast as in the 1950s and the 1960s, as shown in Figure 7.4. The spending growth then slowed to 3.6 percent annually in the 1970s, to 2.9 percent in the 1980s, and to a paltry 0.7 percent so far in the 1990s. In fact, real federal expenditures in the 1980s grew at half the pace of the 1950s, even though both decades saw a major jump

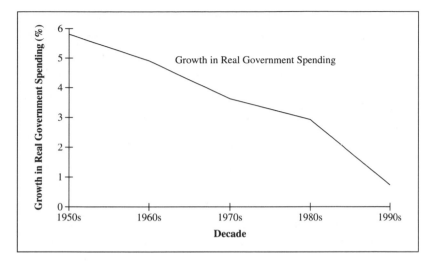

FIGURE 7.4   Growth in real government spending: 1950s–1990s.
There has been a steady decline in the growth of real government
spending. The government spending growth in the 1990s has been
less than ⅛th of the level in the 1950s. (*Source:* Appendix Table A.7.)

in defense spending. In the 1990s, there is practically no rise
in real government spending, even though population has
continued to rise. Government spending growth is clearly not
responsible for the federal debt mountain of today. (See Appendix Table A.7.)

Since 1980, federal outlays have averaged 23 percent of
GDP. Why is this percentage much larger than in the 1950s
and the 1960s, if real government spending in recent years has
grown at less than half the level as before? The reason lies in
paltry GDP growth.

The real cause of the giant debt and deficit is slow economic growth engendered by unwise federal policies. Is it a coincidence that soaring trade has coexisted with growing
deficits? Not at all. When President Johnson launched his war
on poverty, he and his advisers were very optimistic about the
nation's prospects for economic growth. And why not? The
country had been growing at an average annual rate of nearly
4 percent ever since 1890, and that performance had been duplicated more recently in the 1950s and the 1960s. The end of
World War II had made no dent in growing prosperity.

True, tariffs had been gradually reduced since 1933. But the competing economies of Europe and Japan had been destroyed in the 1940s. In spite of low U.S. tariffs, other nations lacked the products to penetrate U.S. markets. They did not have the infrastructure and industries to challenge American firms on their own turf.

But this was about to change just when the Great Society programs were launched. As soaring trade and slow growth coincided in the 1970s, the growth of tax revenue fell. During the 1950s, the real tax receipts, after adjustment for inflation, grew annually at a torrid rate of 6.7 percent (see Figure 7.5). This was the result not only of high growth but also of a sharply progressive tax system that levied giant taxes on wealthy individuals and corporations. When taxes were cut in the 1960s, GDP growth moved up a notch, but the annual tax revenue grew slowly at a rate of 4.7 percent, which was still healthy and kept the deficit in check. (See Appendix Table A.8.)

Then came soaring trade, and growth slowed both in real GDP and revenues. The process was duplicated in the 1980s.

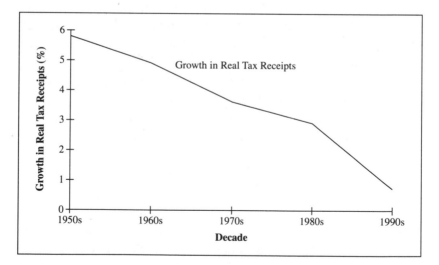

FIGURE 7.5   Growth in real tax receipts: 1950s–1990s. There has been a relentless decline in the growth of real tax revenue. Real revenue growth in the 1990s has been ⅛th of the level in the 1950s. This is the main cause of the persistent federal budget deficit. (*Source:* Appendix Table A.8.)

In the 1990s, the real revenue growth has been the most sluggish since World War II. Low taxes on the rich do not stimulate revenue growth, as we have seen. Indeed, the revenue growth of the Reagan–Bush 1980s, the crown jewel of supply siders, was less than half that in the 1950s and the 1960s, when taxes were truly progressive. The lesson postwar history teaches us is that progressive taxation and low trade are essential for America's prosperity and for balanced budgets.

CHAPTER 8

Low Manufacturing, Low Wages, and Low Growth

F ree traders look upon every industry equally when they analyze a country's standard of living. No one area of the economy is of special significance to them; manufacturing, agriculture, and services all play equivalent roles. A predominantly agrarian country, such as India, can then in theory enjoy the same living standard as an industrial nation such as Japan, as long as the two have comparable levels of technology in their economies. Michael Boskin, Chairman of the Council of Economic Advisers during the Bush Administration, has been quoted as saying, "It doesn't make any difference whether a country makes potato chips or computer chips."[1] We will see, however, that the nature of the chips makes a lot of difference to national affluence.

It should not come as a surprise that the idea of free trade first sprang from the writings of British businessmen and economists. Britain wanted its colonies to supply raw materials for British industry, and its intellectuals perpetuated the myth that the colonies would gain from the arrangement. What was essentially a colonial economic strategy was later popularized by Professor Samuelson as a general principle.

Few agrarian nations free to determine their destiny have followed the path of free trade. Instead, they have focused on industrialization, especially manufacturing. One of these countries was the United States. The administrations of the young republic knew that exporting wheat, cotton, and corn was no way to riches.

If wages were the same in every industry, free trade would make some sense. If each country were to specialize in the production of goods where it has an efficiency advantage and export these products in exchange for imports in which it has a disadvantage, then its productivity would be maximized. Its living standard would rise with expanding foreign trade.

In the real world, however, wages are remarkably different from sector to sector. A person with same skills usually earns more in large firms than in small companies. Some industries are, by nature, more productive than others. Manufacturing, for instance, has higher productivity than most service industries. A secretary working for International Business Machines (IBM) may earn $50,000 annually, whereas she may earn only $25,000 working at a university.

Today, most countries export and import the same goods. America exports computers to Japan and also imports them from Japan. The old Ricardian idea wherein a country exports and imports different products no longer applies.[2] Nor does the rhetoric of free traders. Take, for example, the oft-cited words of Milton Friedman:[3]

> As a homely illustration, should a lawyer who can type as fast as his secretary fire the secretary and do his own typing? If the lawyer is twice as good a typist, but five times as good a lawyer as his secretary, both he and the secretary are better off if he practices law and the secretary types letters.

Friedman's logic is very appealing. But it envisions a world without change. Friedman has not allowed for the low-paid secretary choosing to become a lawyer in the future if she has the capability to do so. The free trade idea condemns a nation to doing endlessly what it does best in the present. If America, Japan, and Canada had followed this idea, they would now be prominent agrarian economies supplying raw materials to the

European nations of Britain, Germany, and France, the colonial masters. Free trade would have kept America and Canada specialized in farming, because that is what they did best at their birth.

The fastest growing occupation in the nation since the early 1980s has been residential care (some call it janitorial service).[4] I once asked my students if any of them would like to join today's biggest growth industry. Not a single hand went up. They all wanted to have high-paying careers in business, banking, and medicine. Nations face a similar choice.

If wages are unequal in different industries, then some countries must lose from international trade. Trade leads to an expansion of export industries and a shrinkage of import-competing sectors. Export-related jobs rise, and import-related occupations fall. If a country's export-related jobs have higher wages than its import-related jobs, the country gains from trade. Otherwise, it loses.

In most countries, wages in manufacturing are much higher than those in services. In 1994, for example, U.S. weekly earnings in manufacturing were $507 compared to $360 in services.[5] America imports more manufactured goods than it exports. Therefore, the nation is a net importer of manufactures. Similarly, the United States is a net exporter of services. Expanding trade then creates service jobs in the United States and destroys some manufacturing jobs. Result: since exports generate low-paying jobs and imports eliminate high-paying jobs, soaring trade is bad for the United States.

On the other hand, rising trade is beneficial for all those countries, such as Japan, China, and South Korea, that export manufactured goods to America, because in these nations trade produces high-wage jobs at the expense of low-wage jobs. Thus, so long as wages are sharply unequal, trade benefits the exporters of manufactures and hurts the exporters of services. In the real world, wages are very different between exported and imported goods, and some countries must lose from trade.[6]

Manufacturing and the Standard of Living

The growth experience of most countries reveals that prosperity lies in the development of manufacturing rather than services. Agriculture is also important, but only to an extent. In the absence of a thriving farm sector, prosperity is, of course,difficult to achieve. But there is a limit to how much farm output a country can consume. If your income doubles, your food consumption will not normally double. You may switch to a better and more expensive diet, but your calorie intake is unlikely to jump.

Once a country has a developed agrarian sector, its further prosperity can come only from an expansion of manufacturing, which is really the foundation of advanced economies today. In manufacturing, a country builds something tangible; in the service sector, products are repaired or relocated, packaged properly, and then sold by savvy salespeople in retail shops and malls. The service sector cannot thrive without a developed manufacturing sector. Retailers, of course, could sell imported goods, but they would need the high-paid workers of manufacturing industries as customers.

Other service industries, such as banking, insurance, and real estate, also depend crucially on a healthy manufacturing industry, where productivity and wages tend to be high. People receiving high wages can afford to save money, which then creates a need for banks and savings associations. Savings, in turn, enable people to put a down payment on a house and borrow a mortgage from a financial institution. Banks and savings associations lend money not only to home buyers, but also to various industries, which all thrive on the foundation of manufacturing.

Manufacturing also assists agriculture, where the use of machinery may raise productivity. Tractors, harvesters, and combines are all manufactured products that are essential to operating a competitive farm. Hence, a healthy manufacturing industry leads to a rich farm sector, and vice versa. In fact, industrialization and prosperity are difficult to achieve without affluent agriculture.

Manufacturing is the locomotive that pulls most enterprises. In its absence, even new technology fails to flourish. New ideas and innovations cannot be developed without a healthy manufacturing sector at home. Otherwise, a country will invent new products, but their production will occur in other countries. New technology industries normally enjoy the fastest growth, because the demand for new products generally outpaces the demand for old products. That is why high-tech companies pay higher wages. But if the manufacturing sector is not robust, then the actual production of new inventions usually occurs abroad. The inventor benefits, of course, but people in his or her country do not. Two economists, Stephen Cohen and John Zysman, professors at the University of California, Berkeley, and members of the Council on Foreign Relations, have noted:[7]

> Manufacturing matters mightily to the wealth and power of the United States and to our ability to sustain the kind of open society we have come to take for granted. If we want to stay on top—or even high up—we can't just shift out of manufacturing and into services.

The history of the G-7 countries (United States, Canada, United Kingdom, France, Germany, Japan, and Italy) only underscores that economies should be built on the foundation of manufacturing. None of the G-7 group heeded the advice of free traders to specialize in agriculture and raw materials. The North American and European G-7 nations gave that advice to the Third World and Japan, but for their own prosperity they relied on the time-tested idea that manufacturing, not free trade, is the main source of prosperity. They protected their industries from foreign competition through high tariffs. Table 8.1 shows how pervasive protectionism was in earlier times, in some of today's advanced economies, notably in the United States. The fact that the developed countries had exorbitant tariffs on manufactured goods and not on all products shows that they understood the importance of manufacturing in the development process.

TABLE 8.1   Manufacturing tariffs in industrial countries.

Country	1875	1902	1913
Canada	NA	17%	26%
France	12–15%	34	20
Germany	4–6	25	13
Italy	8–10	27	18
Japan*	6	10	20–35
United States	40–50	73	44

*Average tariff on dutiable imports.

Source: *World Development Report,* 1991, The World Bank, Washington, DC, p. 97; Ryoshin Minami, *The Economic Development of Japan: A Quantitative Study,* second edition, Macmillan, London, 1994, p. 194; Ravi Batra, *The Myth of Free Trade,* Macmillan, New York, 1993, p. 178.

The United States tended to be self-sufficient in most products and could afford to impose one of the largest tariffs in the world. In the process, the country became the global economic leader by the end of the 19th century. Such was the crucial role that the manufacturing tariff played in the affluence of the United States. As explained in Chapter 12, protectionism hurts an economy only when it generates monopolies at home, as is happening in some developing countries today. In the midst of intense domestic competition, however, tariffs have led to fast growth wherever they were tried.

AMERICAN EXPERIENCE WITH TARIFFS

How did America escape from the clutches of economists and think tanks who supported the colonial relic of free trade? Britain, France, and Germany were happy to receive raw materials and farm products from the United States in exchange for their manufactures. Their economists had already sung the melodies of laissez faire, which resonated with the earlier governments of the free American Republic.

How did the young nation manage to escape the stranglehold of free trade?

The escape was almost providential; it occurred a quarter century after the end of the revolutionary war in 1783. At that point, America was predominantly an agrarian economy, with 90 percent of its people engaged in farming. A small manufacturing sector in the Northeast, supplied local handicrafts such as linens, shoes, and furniture. For much of its industrial needs, however, the country depended on imports, mostly from England.

Soon after gaining its independence, the United States became embroiled in European intrigue and commerce. In 1793, England, France, Spain, and Holland were locked in a bloody war that drained their naval resources. This provided an opening for New England shipping merchants to haul goods on the transatlantic route between Europe and the United States. Besides benefiting the shipping magnates, the war accentuated the agrarian bent of the U.S. economy. Europe relied increasingly on American wheat, flour, and cotton, but British manufactures also penetrated deep into the American market.

There were some duties at the time, on imports of glass, iron, and textiles, but they ranged between 5 percent and 15 percent and were imposed to collect revenue and not to protect domestic industries.[8]

Then a fortuitous development forced America to develop industry at home. Both England and France were perturbed by America's participation in oceanic shipping. They began to seize American ships in their waters. In response, in 1807, Congress passed the Embargo Act, which prohibited exports. Trade came to a screeching halt. Although the embargo was eased somewhat in 1809, America itself went to war with England in 1812. All these developments greatly stimulated American industry.

The Embargo Act raised the prices of local goods overnight. Profits soared, attracting new capital into domestic industries. Cotton and woolen textiles flourished; so did glass, iron, shoes, furniture, and handicrafts. However, the industrial development was limited to the Northeast—New York, New Jersey, Massachusetts, New Hampshire, Connecticut, and Vermont. The number of new factories in these states jumped from 4 in 1807 to 128 in 1815.

The South, however, remained untouched by the industrial frenzy of the North. Southern producers heavily relied on slave labor, which was thought to be unsuited for factory operations.

The fortuitous developments that led to the birth of new factories in America, however, also created the seeds of conflict between the North and the South. Emerging industries and their workers now had an interest in protecting their wages and jobs from low wage competition from Europe. America was a vast expanse of unmolested land with a small population. Labor shortages and thus high wages were common even in American agriculture. Compared to American wages, European salaries were low.

The South wanted free access to European markets for its farm products. The New England shipping interests also favored freer trade in order to haul as many goods as possible across the oceans. Thus, after the war of 1812, two opposing factions emerged to control American trade policy. The first test came in 1815, at the end of the conflict with England.

British manufacturers resumed their exports to the United States after the war, and that low-wage competition drove many American industries out of business. In fact, the British dumped their goods into America and sold them at inordinately low prices in order to regain their lucrative market. The outcry among American businessmen and workers quickly forced Congress to double the tariff rates to a range of 15 percent to 30 percent in 1816,[9] and industrial calamity was avoided.

American historians, handicapped by their bias for free trade, have been quick to slight the role of U.S. tariffs in economic development. But raw evidence reveals something else. Look at the development of the cotton industry in the early 19th century. In 1805, only 46 thousand yards of cloth were produced in New England and in 1807, 84 thousand. Then the industry took off: by 1815, production was 2.3 million yards. As peace returned and foreign supplies rushed to American shores in 1816, the U.S. output plummeted to 840,000 yards, about one-third of the output just a year before. Congress responded with a protective tariff in 1816, and the cotton industry resumed its frenzied growth.

Without Congressional intervention, the nascent American industry was decimated, but the tariff quickly revived it. The colossal increase in textile output from 1816 to 1860 shows that the tariff could not have done any harm to the economy (see Table 8.2). The output climbed from less than a million yards in 1816 to almost a billion yards in 1860. In addition, the tariff generated revenue that obviously kept other taxes low. How could it have possibly hurt the U.S. consumer—as free traders would argue—when the consumer paid few other taxes and earned much higher wages in mushrooming industries?

TABLE 8.2   Cotton industry output in New England: 1805–1860 (selected years).

Year	Yards of Cloth (thousands)
1805	46
1807	84
1810	648
1815	2,358
1816	840
1820	13,874
1830	141,616
1840	323,000
1860	857,225

Source: Robert Zevin, "The Growth of Cotton Textile Production After 1815," in Robert Fogel and Stanly Engerman (editors), *The Reinterpretation of American Economic History*, Harper & Row, New York, 1971, Table 1, pp. 123–124.

As the 1816 tariff succeeded in reviving dying industries, there were calls for expanding the umbrella of protection. Alexander Hamilton was the most vocal supporter of this view. He offered what is known as the "infant industry" argument: the young American industries should be protected until they became strong enough to compete with older established British companies that payed lower wages.

Tariffs were raised in 1824 and then again in 1828, when the highest average rate in U.S. history, 62 percent, was imposed on foreign goods. By this time, the South had begun to fight back against huge tariffs. Southern farmers felt that customs tended to raise the prices of industrial goods. A compromise was reached, and import duties were reduced in 1833. Thereafter, the average tariff remained below 35 percent until the onset of the Civil War.

Under the umbrella of tariffs, U.S. manufacturing enjoyed remarkable growth even though real wages were twice as high as in Europe. We've already mentioned the wildly successful story of the cotton industry. Many other industries—iron, lumber, coal and gold mining, fishing, whaling, and fur trapping—also grew apace.

Industrialization also helped agriculture, which was increasingly mechanized through machines produced at home. American agriculture became the most productive in the world. Prosperous agriculture in turn supplied abundant raw materials to home based industry, so that manufacturing and farming complemented each other.

With soaring productivity, workers were freed from agriculture to be employed in industries. In spite of vast numbers of arriving immigrants, labor was constantly in short supply. American industry absorbed the immigrants, along with laborers from agriculture, at ever-increasing wage rates.

The development of manufacturing also promoted local discoveries of new technology, which had initially been imported from Europe—mainly England. American industry had to cope with high wages and new minerals—anthracite and molybdenum, among others—not found in Europe at the time. The principle of interchangeable parts, the foremost

American invention of the pre-Civil War period, was one result. By standardizing various components of a product, labor requirements were substantially reduced in factories. As a result, in some industries, one American could do the job of 25 British workers.[10]

Other American inventions of the time include the steel plow, developed by John Deere in 1837, and the mechanical reaper, invented by Cyrus McCormick. These were invaluable in enhancing farm productivity.

Large scale production of goods required efficient transportation to distribute them over long distances. People living in different states spread out in a large country also needed facilities in communication. The growth of manufacturing facilitated the use of steamboats, railroads, and the telegraph, which together linked the continent into one economy and one nation.

The American economic boom, protected by tariffs, attracted vast amounts of foreign capital. In fact, without European investment, the spectacular growth of U.S. industry would not have been possible. In spite of high American wages, the return on capital was impressive, and foreign capital came into the United States in search of the higher return. Today, some people equate foreign investment with free trade. They are mistaken. More foreign capital is attracted with the umbrella of tariffs than without. The 1880s were the last decade to see substantial inflow of foreign capital into America for investment and production (see Table 8.3). The United States has also attracted foreign capital in the 1980s and the 1990s, but that is primarily to finance American consumption, not investment. We'll discuss this in the next chapter.

In the 1800s, when manufacturing was stagnant, foreign capital inflow was zero. It jumped to $97 million in the next decade, after the tariff of 1816 sparked the industrial boom. The 1820s were marked by depression in Europe and foreign investment virtually vanished, only to jump to $253 million in the 1830s. The U.S. depression of the 1840s eliminated the inflow, which resumed in the 1850s.

TABLE 8.3 Foreign investment in America per decade: 1800–1890.

Decade	Foreign Investment (millions)
1800s	$ 0
1810s	97
1820s	−6
1830s	253
1840s	−5
1850s	322
1860s	786
1870s	247
1880s	578
1890s	−629

Source: Historical Statistics of the United States: Colonial Times to 1970, 1975. U.S. Department of Commerce, Washington, DC, p. 868.

During and after the Civil War, tariffs jumped again, and so did foreign investment, which financed the import of machines and technology. In the 1890s, capital inflow from abroad ended. America by then had become the world industrial leader. The inflow turned into an outflow as the United States began to invest abroad. Tariffs do not discourage foreign investment. In fact, they have the opposite effect. The United States today has a high level of investment in many tariff ridden countries, which normally offer a lucrative return on capital.

To sum up, there are many facets of America's spectacular development before and after the Civil War, but the tariff played the foremost role. Population growth, immigration, technology, education, and the banking system also spurred the process of development, but without the protective tariff, the country would not have experienced the boom that catapulted it into the planet's economic leadership with the highest real wage.

We must remember the event that triggered America's remarkable growth: the Embargo Act of 1807, which practically destroyed foreign trade. The next big event in the growth process was the tariff of 1816, which neutralized the British dumping of manufactures, and allowed all that followed. First, manufacturing developed, requiring raw materials from farms, which in turn needed machines from the manufacturers. They in turn created new technology that facilitated transportation and communication. Rising wages in manufacturing then created the demand for housing, and the banks that financed the housing became the conduit for workers' savings. This is a long chain of events in the developmental process, but the trigger for the chain reaction was the destruction of foreign trade and the subsequent tariff, without which America's budding industry would have withered away. This is precisely why Abraham Lincoln championed protectionism: "the abandonment of the protective policy . . . must result in increase of both useless labour, and in idleness; and so, in proportion, must produce want and ruin among our people."[11]

If America had followed the path of free trade, the country today would be the foremost agrarian economy. That is exactly what British economists had prescribed for the United States both before and after independence.[12] They championed their self-interest in the name of objective analysis and world economic development. But America was fortunate to have a fortuitous event that killed its foreign trade, allowing the country to discover its true potential.

THE AMERICAN CENTURY: 1870–1970

Some writers have described the 20th century as the American century, because of America's domination of the world economy during this period. In terms of the living standard and poverty, however, America's century essentially ended in 1970. The average real wage peaked in 1972, and if rising Social Security taxes are taken into account, for the vast majority of Americans the real wage crested in 1970 or just before that year.

Manufacturing employment peaked in 1979 at a little over 21 million. Ever since then, the new entrants in the job market have gone primarily to service-producing industries. In 1995, manufacturing employment stood at 18 million, about 15 percent of the total nonfarm employment. However, the share of manufacturing jobs as a fraction of employed labor began its rapid decline after 1965, when this number stood at 31 percent, roughly the same as in 1930. In the interregnum of 35 years, the world went through the Great Depression, World War II, and the Korean War, among other events, but the U.S. employment share in manufacturing was essentially unchanged. The United States remained the industrial leader and continued to enjoy the highest living standard.

Soon after the decline in the manufacturing employment share, however, the U.S. living standard peaked and began a long-term decline. Is this a coincidence? No, not at all.

First, real wage growth fell. During the 1950s, real wages grew at an average rate of 3 percent per year. From 1960 to 1965, wage growth declined but it was still a healthy 2.2 percent per annum. But between 1965 and 1972, when the real wage peaked, average wage growth was a puny 0.7 percent.[13] Following 1972, wage growth became negative, and its direction has yet to be reversed. Is it a coincidence that declining real wages and wage growth coincided with the sharp decline in the percentage of the labor force employed in manufacturing? Of course not. America's economic history, and that of all advanced nations, confirms that manufacturing nourishes all other industries and a country's well being. Manufacturing decline has been associated with sinking real wages in all sectors, including those dependent on highly skilled labor.[14]

Why did this happen? America became the world economic leader in the 1890s, when it switched from being an importer of capital to an exporter. Even as early as 1870, the nation had come to dwarf Europe in terms of industrial production and real wages, but the long depression of the 1870s masked the nation's affluence until the end of the century. By then, millions of agriculture workers had moved into a vast multitude of factories producing goods and services. Farm employment had dwindled to less than 40 percent of the labor force; manufacturing commanded a third, and the rest was in services, mining, and construction.

The landscape of employment remained more or less unchanged until 1960. Manufacturing still employed about a third of the work force, but services commanded about 60 percent. During the 19th century, labor moved out of agriculture and into goods and services. After 1930, farm labor moved primarily into services, so that the share of the manufacturing workforce was mostly unaltered. Then the labor share of manufacturing began to fall, at first slowly as in the 1970s, and then rapidly after 1980, when giant corporations began an orgy of mergers and downsizing.

The seeds of the employment decline in manufacturing were sown in the 1930s, when President Roosevelt revived the onslaught on the tariff. But foreign producers were unable to take advantage of the lucrative American market until about 1965. First, they were trapped by the Depression and then by World War II. Europe and Japan were all but destroyed during the 1940s, and it took them about two decades to recover enough to challenge America's industry at home.

During these 20 years, Americans were busy shooting themselves in the foot. They expanded competition from abroad, but smothered competition at home by allowing giant corporations to gobble up smaller businesses with impunity. The government did little to stop the wave of mergers. As companies turned into regional monopolies, their unions became arrogant. Big Business and labor combined to ignore the customer. They turned out shoddy products and neglected the repair aspect of their operations.

Small but efficient foreign corporations, battle-tested in the intensely competitive arena at home, easily vanquished the corporate behemoths in the United States. During the 19th century, tariffs protected American industry and wages from low-wage competition from abroad. But American companies tended to be small, and they faced intense rivalry with other local firms. In short, America followed a policy of competitive protectionism, wherein businesses face little pressure from abroad but intense competition at home. Now, in contrast, the country adopted the policy of monopolistic free trade. It exposed regional monopolies to tough foreign competition.

Just as the destruction of foreign trade that accompanied the raising of the tariff started a long chain of industrial development after 1807, the delayed effects of the tariff abandonment since the 1930s triggered a chain reaction that stifled almost all facets of the economy. First, light and labor-intensive industries such as textiles and shoes took a beating from foreign producers. Then came the turn of consumer electronics—cameras, radios, TVs, VCRs, camcorders, and watches, among hundreds of other small items. Finally came the retreat in big and expensive items—autos, tractors, air conditioners, appliances, and so on. One by one, bloated American industries fell prey to corporate conquerors from abroad.

Unable to cope with competition from Japan, Taiwan, Hong Kong, and South Korea, American corporations began to move factories into low-wage countries. This development accelerated the deindustrialization process that had been sparked by cheap imports. The low tariff also encouraged this trend because now American companies could build products abroad, paying pennies per hour in wages, and then bring these products back home at low taxes. High tariffs in the past had discouraged this practice because anything manufactured abroad was taxed at hefty rates. American wages had been always high, but punitive tariffs had kept American industry at home. The country retained its industry and collected revenue at the same time, thereby keeping other taxes at paltry levels. All it needed was an activist government to maintain intense domestic competition so that companies would remain efficient while paying generous wages.

Today, economists and others blame automation for the loss of high-paying jobs, forgetting that labor-saving innovations have been a constant fact of American life.[15] When tariffs were high, automation created only minor troubles, because those downsized could find equally productive jobs in new-product industries. Workers from contracting industries would move into expanding sectors at the same or higher salaries, because new technology not only economized on labor but also created new products and services.

When the railroads ceased to be the primary mode of transportation, workers switched to the auto industry. When radio listenership fell, they went into television production. When textiles shrank, those laid off migrated to appliances. Americans invented new technology and, because of the tariffs, they also translated it into production on American soil. Therefore, the victims of downsizing could find jobs in new-tech industries. Today, America still copiously generates new inventions, but the resultant production occurs in low-wage countries. Most Nobel prize winners in the sciences are still Americans, but American companies rush out to materialize these ideas in the Third World, because the import of goods is mostly free from taxation. Hence, those laid off from one industry are unable to find equally lucrative jobs in emerging industries. They just swell the ranks of part-timers, the self-employed, or service workers.

Facsimiles, photocopiers, VCRs, and robotics are all post-war American inventions. America should be exporting these new products. Instead, they are all imported into the United States in vast quantities. One by one, either these industries have come under the dominance of foreign producers, or U.S. corporations have relocated them to other countries. The United States has the largest market in the world, so the high American tariff was a great incentive to American and foreign companies to locate some of their plants on American soil. Automation or downsizing was never a serious problem in the past.

With tariffs mostly gone, trade began to soar after 1965, and American economists confidently predicted a surge in U.S. productivity, growth, and real income. They helped President Johnson design his war on poverty, assuming that the 4 percent average annual growth would continue well into the future.[16] Instead, the opposite happened. Faltering manufacturing retarded productivity growth in all other sectors and created unintended repercussions.

As labor demand fell in manufacturing, workers were laid off, and the wages of those who remained increased at a lower rate than prices. Their inflation-adjusted wages tumbled. Those fired could not move into export industries because these industries were downsizing to be able to export to low-wage countries. The fired workers and new entrants to the labor force had to work in the localized or non-trading service sectors. The influx of a large number of workers depressed service wages as well.

The development process was now moving in reverse. Labor moved from a high-productivity sector (manufacturing) into a low-productivity sector (services). Productivity growth had to fall. With this came a fall in the rate of GDP growth and the resulting decline in tax revenue growth. The budget deficit was bound to rise.

Until 1980, tariffs were primarily replaced by income related levies, so that the tax system was at least progressive. Idle funds of the rich were largely collected by the government to finance its spending and maintain an adequate level of demand. Rising imports crimped the growth rate in the 1970s, but it still averaged 3.2 percent per year in an environment of exploding oil prices.

In the 1980s, however, the entire tax structure became ultraregressive, retarding the growth of demand. GDP growth tumbled again. The budget deficit soared. Real rates of interest skyrocketed. And real wages continued their inexorable fall—in spite of rising productivity.

The economic performance of the 1990s has been the worst since the 1930s. Soaring trade and regressive taxes continue their onslaught on the American economy, with no end in sight. The unemployment rate in April 1996 plummeted to a low of 5.4 percent, a rate rarely seen since 1974. But instead of celebrating, Americans were increasingly worried about job security, shrinking paychecks, and the ever-increasing bite of the payroll tax. Such is the legacy of the tariff repudiation for the American consumer.

Today, the official line is that exports are creating a lot of jobs. According to the 1996 *Economic Report of the President,* "twelve million American workers now owe their jobs to exports."[17] The question is: What would have happened if exports had remained at the low levels of the 1950s and the 1960s? Would we then have enormous unemployment, as the official line seems to predict? Figure 8.1 shows otherwise. From the 1950s to the 1980s, exports as a percentage of GDP surged, and so did the average rate of unemployment in every decade—from an average 4.5 percent in the 1950s to 7.3 percent in the 1980s.

Average joblessness has declined somewhat in the 1990s, to 6.2 percent, but today's figures are not comparable to the old

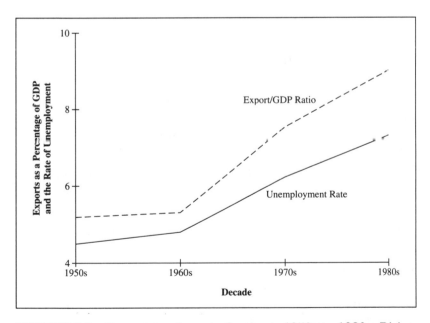

FIGURE 8.1   Exports and unemployment: 1950s to 1980s. Rising exports in the U.S. have been associated with a steadily rising rate of unemployment since the war. (*Source: Economic Report of the President,* 1996, The Council of Economic Advisers, Washington, DC.)

data, because nearly 15 percent of the workforce is now under-employed. The myth that exports create myriad jobs is thus demolished under closer scrutiny.

THE REGIONAL ECONOMIES

In spite of free trade within U.S. borders, regional incomes have always been vastly different.[18] Many forces, in addition to commerce, affect state incomes: location, education, soil fertility, availability of minerals, climate, racial discrimination, unionization, and, above all, the degree of industrialization.

Historically, the thirteen English colonies established along the Atlantic coast of North America had a great location advantage. Initially, New England and the Mid-Atlantic states attracted much of the industry and were the richest regions in the nation. Still, by 1860, only 10 percent of the labor force was engaged in industry. The rest was mostly in agriculture, which was a niche of the South. When gold was discovered in California in 1848, the pendulum of affluence quickly swung toward the West, which began to excel in mining. The entire coast along the Pacific Ocean grew rich from its plentiful mineral and extractive industries.[19]

In 1860, industrial production was ten times the amount in 1810, yet the nation was predominantly agricultural. After the Civil War, industry grew rapidly but still was not large enough to overcome the advantage that minerals gave to Western states. In 1880, some Western states were the richest in America, enjoying per-capita incomes at least 64 percent above the national average. Table 8.4 compares per-capita personal income in various regions.

The Northeast region, with its manufacturing, had an affluence level 29 percent above the national average in 1880. The Midwest was about par with the nation, and the agricultural South was the poorest region. Within the South, the subdivision of East South Central was destitute. The main reason for its poverty was employer discrimination directed against Black workers. The East South Central area includes the states

TABLE 8.4   Personal income per-capita in U.S. regions: 1880–1920.

Region	1880	1900	1920
United States	100	100	100
Northeast			
New England	129	120	111
Mid-Atlantic	129	125	123
Midwest			
East North Central	99	101	104
West North Central	92	98	84
South			
South Atlantic	45	47	61
East South Central	50	48	52
West South Central	60	58	68
West			
Mountain	191	142	105
Pacific	164	149	126

Source: R. A. Easterlin, "Regional Growth of Income: Long-Term Tendencies," in S. Kuznets et al., *Population Redistribution and Economic Growth, United States, 1870–1950,* Vol. II, *Analyses of Economic Change,* American Philosophical Society, Philadelphia, 1960, p. 146.

of Kentucky, Tennessee, Alabama, and Mississippi. Of the four, the last two had the largest percentage of African Americans. Even today, 35 percent of the population of Mississippi is Black. In spite of the backbreaking work required of them as farm laborers, the Black people received the lowest wages. That is why the East South Central region was one of the poorest areas of the United States. After 1880, industry moved to the Midwest, and that region gained at the expense of the Northeast and the West. Within the West, a remarkable shift occurred. The mountain states exported the bulk of their minerals to the rest of the country, especially to California, which had attracted immigrants, capital, and industry from other states as well as from Europe. As the mineral industries of the

Pacific sector could not maintain their torrid growth, that area lost relative to the nation. The regional income trends between 1880 and 1900 remained more or less unchanged until 1920, although parts of the South gained at the expense of the West North Central area. A slight industrial shift, from New England into the South, also contributed to the southern gain.

There was free trade within the United States, yet industrialization showed its strengths relative to specialization in exports. If the mountain states had fully utilized their raw materials in their own industries, they would have grown faster. Instead, they lost considerable ground to other regions, especially to the Pacific states.

This phenomenon is reminiscent of modern Japan, which imported raw materials from foreign countries, protected its industry but maintained intense competition at home, and, in the process, became the fastest growing nation from 1950 to 1990. Japan's rapid rate of growth, maintained over such a long period, has not been duplicated by any other country in the world in 5,000 years of recorded history. Modern Japan manifests the triumph of competitive protectionism.

MANUFACTURING IN U.S. REGIONS SINCE 1950

Most economists concede that rapid industrialization was indeed the key to differential affluence within regions of the United States in the pre-World War II period. But things are different now. In their view, America today is in a postindustrial stage where the living standard depends less on manufacturing than on services.[20] This is a bogus claim. We have already shown that the manufacturing blight has been associated with the real wage debacle for 80 percent of the workforce. Also, within regions, the loss of manufacturing has hastened decline as recently as the 1990s.

Let's take a look at Table 8.5. It makes sense to compare per-capita income within regions because contiguous states reflect great similarities in terms of taxation, technology,

TABLE 8.5   Regional per-capita income and manufacturing employment: 1994.

Region	Employment Share in Manufacturing	Per-Capita Income
Northeast		
New England	17.6%	$25,319
Mid-Atlantic	14.9	25,260
Midwest		
East North Central	21.3	21,952
West North Central	16.6	20,965
South		
South Atlantic	14.9	21,279
West South Central	14.2	19,024
West		
Mountain	10.3	19,755
Pacific	14.6	22,418

Source: Statistical Abstract of the United States, 1995, U.S. Department of Commerce, Washington, DC, pp. 425 and 461.

education, work ethic, unionization, and so on. Market conditions in Texas are far different from those in California, but Texas and Oklahoma are likely to have many similarities.

As shown in the table, within every region, the area with a larger fraction of employment in manufacturing has a higher per-capita income. In some areas, the income differentials are small; in others, they are substantial. But in every region, manufacturing advantage confers a better living standard. Within the West, the Pacific states, with a larger employment share in industry, earned $2,663 more per person than the mountain states in 1994. For a family of four, the income difference was significant: more than $10,000. Within the South, the income advantage for greater industrialization was also large: $2,255 per capita. In the Northeast and Midwest, regional incomes were closer, but the manufacturing premium was still present. The Mid-Atlantic states of New York and New

Jersey, despite hosting mega-banks and the stock exchange in their vast financial centers, were unable to dwarf the manufacturing benefit accruing to New England. Clearly, manufacturing matters as much in the 1990s as in the distant past.

In Table 8.5, we omit the East South Central (ESC) sector, which has historically lagged behind the rest of the nation because of employer discrimination against African Americans, who are a large percentage of the population in this area. But even here, manufacturing has played a vital role in raising the per-capita income relative to the U.S. average. Manufacturing employment has declined everywhere in the United States, but the decline has been smaller in the ESC area. As a result, the ESC employment in manufacturing, relative to U.S. employment in manufacturing, has been rising since 1950. (See Table 8.6.) Not surprisingly, the ESC per-capita income has been moving closer to the U.S. average, and reached the highest level in 1994. Manufacturing makes a difference for depressed areas in spite of racial discrimination—even in the 1990s.

It also makes a difference for affluent states such as California, which by itself has the seventh largest economy in the

TABLE 8.6 Per-capita personal income and manufacturing employment in the East South Central (ESC) region: 1950 to 1994 (selected years).

Year	ESC Per-Capita Income as a Percentage of U.S. Per-Capita Income	ESC Manufacturing Employment as a Percentage of U.S. Manufacturing Employment
1950	60	4.6
1960	68	5.1
1970	75	6.3
1980	78	6.7
1990	79	7.4
1994	83	8.2

Source: Statistical Abstract of the United States, various issues, U.S. Department of Commerce, Washington, DC.

world. It has 12 percent of U.S. population and 13 percent of U.S. GDP. Manufacturing matters a lot in California, as demonstrated in Figure 8.2. In 1960, California had 27 percent of its labor force employed in manufacturing. The percentage fell to 14.6 in 1994. Its income advantage over the rest of the nation, 23 percent in 1960, fell to 3 percent in 1994. Because of the growing manufacturing blight, a state that was among the richest in the nation for more than a century had virtually lost that advantage by 1994. There is no doubt that manufacturing makes as much a difference today as in the past, for poor as well as affluent regions of the country. (See Appendix Table A.9.)

The moral here is that a country should adopt policies that stimulate manufacturing within its borders. Even the World Bank, a bastion of free trade policies, believes that manufacturing is the most dynamic sector of the economy.

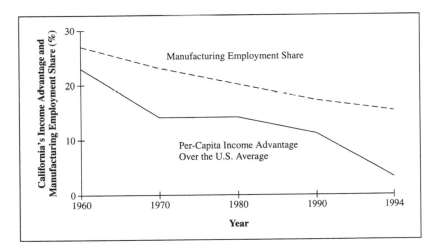

FIGURE 8.2   California's manufacturing employment share and per-capita income advantage over the U.S. average: 1960–1994. As the manufacturing share of employment fell in California, its per capita income advantage over the U.S. steadily declined. By 1994 this advantage all but disappeared. (*Source: Statistical Abstract of the United States,* various issues, U.S. Department of Commerce, Washington, DC.)

CHAPTER 9

The Hangover of NAFTA

I n the memorable debate between Vice President Al Gore and billionaire Ross Perot in 1993, Al Gore argued that Mexico was one country with which the United States had a trade surplus, and that he and most economists expected NAFTA to enhance that surplus by billions more and thus create thousands of new American jobs. Ross Perot scoffed at the proposed treaty, which he described as sucking away American jobs south of the border. Gore's optimistic views prevailed. The trade agreement among Canada, America, and Mexico was overwhelmingly passed by Congress in November 1993, and went into effect on the first day of 1994.

Today, few politicians like to talk about NAFTA, perhaps because the 1992 U.S. trade surplus of $5 billion turned into a $15 billion deficit in 1995. They shy away from these facts, yet they claim that NAFTA has still generated new employment opportunities in the United States.[1] Their reasoning is simple: NAFTA has raised U.S. exports to Mexico, creating more jobs in exporting industries, and hence more jobs in the United States. The first two points of this argument are valid. The final conclusion, however, is not.

Few businesses hire more people without a prior increase in orders. Employment rises nationwide only with expanding national output. Did NAFTA increase national output in 1994 or 1995? It could have done so in only one way: by raising exports more than imports. Since our trade surplus has turned into a deficit—a downturn of $20 billion between 1992 and 1995—the output could not possibly have risen.[2]

Amazingly, free traders are just as defiant in their support for NAFTA today as they were in 1992. They are truly the masters of double talk: If the U.S. has a trade surplus, it is good for America. If the U.S. has a trade deficit, it is still good for the nation.

At base, NAFTA was one way for American bankers and businesspeople to recover the billions they had earlier lent to the Mexican government and to some Mexican companies. The loans had their origin in the 1970s, when OPEC raised the price of oil fourfold. The immediate result was a major transfer of wealth from oil-importing countries such as the United States, Germany, and Japan to the oil exporting nations of Saudi Arabia, Iran, and Kuwait. The oil exporters could spend only a fraction of their newfound riches at home and abroad. The rest they deposited with multinational banks located in America, Europe, and Japan.

All of a sudden the banks were awash with petro-dollars. Idle funds accumulated at a rapid rate, and bankers felt increasing pressure to find borrowers. After all, deposits do no good to a bank if it cannot lend them and earn lucrative fees and interest from the loans.

As oil prices soared, inflation began to rise and so did interest rates, which in turn cramped loan demand in advanced economies, just at a time when the multinational banks had a surfeit of funds. Setting aside their customary caution, bank officials rushed to extend loans to the Third World. It didn't matter that the developing countries were not creditworthy and did not have good collateral to offer. What the bankers saw were the million dollar fees that they could charge hefty borrowers.[3]

Mexico was one developing economy that had valued property. In 1977, vast quantities of offshore oil were discovered, and Citicorp, Chase Manhattan, and Bank of America eagerly lent money against the new oil wells that were yet to be developed. Mexican officials proved avid borrowers. The state-owned petroleum company, Petroleos Mexicanos (PEMEX), borrowed $20 billion to expand its facilities.

Today, Mexico has at least 24 billionaires, excluding drug lords and corrupt officials.[4] Much of their loot was siphoned off from the loans made by American banks. Other companies owned by the government also borrowed billions to finance hasty and ill-conceived projects. Between 1977 and 1981, Mexico's real GDP climbed by nearly 38 percent. Hundreds of office holders became millionaires overnight, but the vast majority of people became poorer because of the onslaught of inflation. The real wage index, in fact, fell from 140 to 136, because fast-paced growth created massive demand for investment and consumption goods, and their prices soared, generating vast inflation.[5]

The new rich had a stake in foreign trade and investment. They were natural allies of the U.S. multinational banks, which had lent almost $60 billion to Mexico by 1981. But that year the massive lending of petrodollars slowed sharply as the price of petroleum began to fall. The latest Mexican miracle, founded on borrowed money, came to an abrupt halt. The declining price of oil hurled Mexico into a recession; in less than a year, the country was on the verge of default. Panic spread among the bankers, and President Reagan, setting aside his customary penchant for free enterprise, came to their aid. He authorized a rescue of $2 billion so that Mexico could pay the interest on its loans.[6]

Foreign money was no longer available to finance imports, so demand for the peso fell sharply, resulting in a collapse of the currency. Whenever the peso collapsed in the past, chronic inflation followed because of the capital outflow from Mexico's own prominent citizens, who habitually keep funds in dollar-denominated accounts in foreign banks. With a growing capital shortage, the Mexican government was forced to print more money to pay its bills. Inflation was already strong between 1977 and 1981, but after 1981, as the currency printing presses rolled, it turned into hyperinflation. The consumer price index jumped from 12 in 1981 to 100 in 1985, nearly an 800 percent climb. Not surprisingly, real wages fell sharply.[7]

Ordinarily, Washington would have left Mexico alone, but billions of dollars of American funds were involved in loans. Mexican default hung in the air, and American administrations could not just stay aloof in spite of their professed love for free markets.

In 1985, the Reagan Administration prodded Mexico to open its markets to American goods, and offered debt rescheduling as a bait. Mexico obliged and lowered its tariffs on some products. By 1988, some of Mexico's maturing debt was rolled over into long-term bonds, and the country received new funds from its lenders.

A new era of cooperation then began between the two neighbors. American bankers were eager to link the two economies, so that the peso could be convertible into dollars in the foreign exchange market. The whole idea was that if the U.S. economy were opened to Mexican suppliers, then the Mexicans could easily pay off their loans from export earnings. Thus was born the grand design called NAFTA.

The proposal was presented to Americans as a free trade agreement. It took three years to finalize, and about 2,000 pages of rules and regulations now govern the movement of goods and capital across the borders. Later, Canada, for fear of being left out, joined the party.

PROS AND CONS OF NAFTA

Once the words "free trade" were added to the proposed agreement, it was very difficult for most officials and economists to withhold their support. Few read the proposal, but the name was too good to attack. Almost everyone in office supported NAFTA—Clinton and Gore, senators, most representatives, governors, mayors, and local council members.

That narrowed opposition to the proposal to the American workers, environmentalists, import-competing industries, some journalists, Dick Gephardt, Pat Buchanan, and Ross Perot.[8] The workers, already reeling from tough competition from Japan and the low-wage countries of Asia, felt threatened by the vast pool of impoverished and unemployed labor across the southern border. Mexico had already lured some 1,800 American companies in what is called the Maquiladora program, with great loss of high-paying American jobs.[9] Even so, only large corporations—General Motors, Ford, IBM, and General Electric, for example—were attracted by the tax and tariff concessions offered by Mexican authorities. These companies had established big plants just south of the American border, hiring Mexican workers for low wages. They then brought their products back to the United States, unconcerned about the convertibility of the peso into the dollar because they earned huge profits from American sales of their Mexican made goods.

Small to medium companies, in contrast, had not been ready to accept the convertibility risk. But once that risk was eliminated by NAFTA, American labor worried about a loss of jobs. Small businesses have been the only job creators in the United States in recent years, and if they were to move their operations, wholly or partly, to Mexico, their wages would sink again.

NAFTA backers conceded that American workers could lose *initially*. But Mexicans would become rich so quickly, they argued, that before long they would buy U.S. goods in vast quantities, despite the fact that Mexico's market was just 4 percent of the American market, and then everyone would prosper.[10]

This was the main premise of NAFTA backers. Did state governors really believe it? Of course not. In 1993, when General Motors proposed to close its plant near Dallas and move it back to Michigan, Governor Ann Richards of Texas pleaded with the GM hierarchy and succeeded in retaining the factory. She shuddered at the thought of GM moving out of Texas and back into Michigan; but it suited her fine if GM moved some plants out of Michigan into Mexico.

Governor Pete Wilson had been doing his best to retain industry in California. Yet he was happy to let U.S. industry *elsewhere* move south of the border. As governor of Arkansas in the 1980s, Bill Clinton offered tax concessions to attract businesses into his state. But as president, he rejoiced at the thought of American companies moving to Mexico.

MEXICO IN DEPRESSION

What good did NAFTA do for Mexico? In the entire debate, almost everyone took it for granted that our southern neighbor would be a major beneficiary of the agreement. When I raised my voice in the debates that NAFTA would practically destroy Mexico, even NAFTA opponents shrugged. In 1992, in *The Myth of Free Trade,* I wrote:[11]

> Like East Germany, Mexico suffers from backward technology and bloated state monopolies. The trauma of exposure to giant northern firms could be fatal to Mexican manufacturing. True, NAFTA proposes to open Mexican markets to its neighbors gradually, and to that extent the foreign onslaught would be contained. *Yet the suffering would be massive in the short run,* especially since Mexico, which has already been mired in a deep slump since 1982, will not, unlike East Germany, receive huge financial aid. I hope the Mexicans will take a closer look at East Germany's plight before endorsing NAFTA. In fact, the plight of East Germany offers a precious lesson to the United States as well, namely, that free trade can cripple an economy if manufacturing erodes. (Italics added)

This statement says in the clearest possible terms that the Mexican "suffering would be massive in the short run." Yet the governments of both Mexico and America ignored this warning. In just two years after the inauguration of NAFTA in January 1994, the Mexican economy collapsed.

What happened was entirely predictable. With their money supply surging from NAFTA-induced euphoria, the Mexicans went on a buying spree, leading to a huge trade deficit of $30 billion.[12] At the same time, the bankers and investors from America poured money into short-term Mexican bonds paying higher interest rates. This inflow of capital temporarily financed the Mexican deficit. Then came a rebellion from the long-suffering army of unemployed Mexicans, and political instability. Meanwhile, Allan Greenspan, the Fed Chairman, had raised short-term interest rates in America, blunting the lure of Mexican bonds.

Investors fled the Mexican markets, and the peso collapsed in December 1994. Poor Mexico. It hadn't learned a lesson from its American connections in the late 1970s. It trusted the same bankers who had ditched it before in its hour of need. The result was nearly fatal this time. President Clinton, just like Reagan in 1982, had to mount a quick rescue of the southern neighbor. He pledged $20 billion and had the International Monetary Fund (IMF) pledge another $30 billion to escape the danger of Mexican default.[13]

But Mexico needed what West Germany gave to East Germany in another free trade link in the early 1990s. The paltry $50 billion in aid could not arrest the Mexican collapse. The real GDP in Mexico fell 7 percent in 1995. The Mexican free traders and bankers tried to put a positive spin on the disaster, but Jose Luis Mastretta, an officer at Monterrey's National Chamber of Commerce, knew better: "In reality these numbers are not good news. How can you be happy or even encouraged when you have an annual contraction of 6.9 percent? These numbers prove what we have been saying all along, and that is that thousands of business and factories are failing and many people have lost their jobs."[14]

Following the devaluation in late 1994, the peso lost half of its value, the annual inflation rate jumped to 52 percent, and more than a million people were laid off. Thousands lost their cars and homes because of soaring interest rates. Taxes went up sharply, gasoline prices skyrocketed, and the minimum real wage plummeted by 34 percent.[15] But no free trader in America or Mexico calls this a depression.

Did American banks lose money in the latest fiasco? No. As usual, the administration and its free market economists came to their rescue by lending funds to Mexico. In a year when the poorest Mexicans lost their shirts and homes,

Citibank managed to earn $81 million from its Mexican operations. J. P. Morgan came up with a profit of $40 million, Bank America with $10 million, and Chase Manhattan with $7 million.[16]

LOST AMERICAN JOBS AND WAGES

President Clinton has insisted that NAFTA has created 340,000 new American jobs. Let's dissect this claim. American exports to Mexico went up by $10 billion in 1994, and by another $8.5 billion to Canada. It takes about $54,000 of production to create one manufacturing job. Divide $18.5 billion by $54,000, and you get about 342,000 jobs.[17]

But the 1996 *Economic Report of the President,* on page 281, defines net exports as exports minus imports. Net exports, not just exports, are added to personal consumption expenditures, gross private domestic investment, and government expenditures to arrive at the estimate of GDP or national output. Every first-year economics student knows this. Every economist is aware of it, too. Yet some choose to disregard it.

America had a trade surplus with Mexico of $1 billion in 1994; by 1995, it had turned into a net deficit of $15 billion. Our country suffered negative net exports of $16 billion in Mexican trade. Divide this by 54,000, and you get the number of jobs *lost* to NAFTA—296,000.

When this many potential jobs are lost, real wages have to fall. As you already know, inflation-adjusted salaries in America have been generally on the decline since 1972. But they had bottomed by 1992 and were starting to turn up. Now look at what happened to U.S. and Mexican real wages after the adoption of NAFTA in January 1994. The U.S. real average earnings had bottomed in December 1992 at $253.68, and rose to $257.21 by the day NAFTA went into effect. Immediately, they started to fall, even as the rate of unemployment inched down. (See Figure 9.1 and Table 9.1.)

Ross Perot and Pat Buchanan were right when they suggested in 1993 that NAFTA was a conspiracy of American and

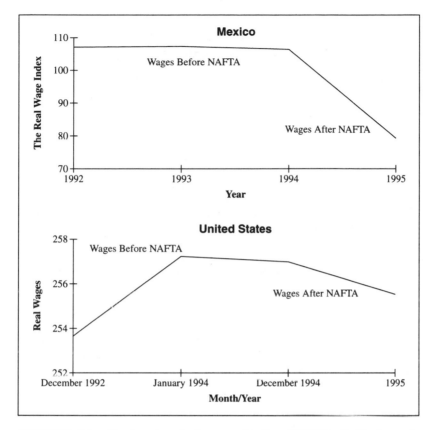

FIGURE 9.1   Real wages before and after NAFTA. Inflation adjusted wages were constant in Mexico and rising in America prior to the adoption of NAFTA in January 1994. After NAFTA, it didn't take long before real wages fell in America and collapsed in Mexico. (*Source:* Table 9.1.)

Mexican elites to fill their own pockets regardless of what happened to others. Just before the adoption of NAFTA on the first day of 1994, real wages had been constant or rising in both countries; soon after, American real earnings inched down and those in Mexico crashed. Thea Lee, an economist with the Economic Policy Institute, says: "NAFTA supporters were wrong in virtually every prediction they made about the agreements of short-term impact: The U.S. jobs they promised have not materialized, and free trade has fostered neither stability nor prosperity in Mexico."[18]

TABLE 9.1   Real wages in Mexico and the United States (1982 = 100) before and after NAFTA.

Month/Year	United States (Weekly Earnings)	Mexico* (Wage Index)
December 1992	$253.68	107
January 1994	257.21	106
December 1994	256.94	104
December 1995	255.49	79

*Obtained by dividing the wage index by the CPI and multiplying by 100.
Source: Economic Report of the President, 1994 and 1996, The Council of Economic Advisers, Washington, DC; International Financial Statistics, 1995 and February 1996 (section on Mexico), International Monetary Fund, Washington, DC.

Prior to the passage of the agreement, American economists and government officials were euphoric about NAFTA's success. Gary Hufbauer and Jeffrey Schott, writing for the Institute of International Economics, predicted that by 1995 NAFTA would create 600,000 new jobs in Mexico and 170,000 in the United States, while boosting Mexican real earnings by 9 percent and leaving American incomes unchanged.[19] The Undersecretary of Commerce for International Trade, Geffrey Garten, was more sanguine: "Our range of estimates for Mexican GDP growth is between a supercharged six percent a year, worthy of Asia's tigers, and a startling 12 percent a year, comparable to China's recent growth."[20]

Soon after the inauguration of NAFTA, the two-way trade between America and Mexico soared, and the NAFTA boosters were quick to take credit for it. Now that NAFTA has backfired for both countries, free traders everywhere in the world are busy denying that the agreement has anything to do with the fiasco.

Thea Lee of the Economic Policy Institute again: "NAFTA advocates who promised economic prosperity and trade-related job creation for the three North American partners have quietly changed the subject; they now talk about the long term, while still praising Mexico's 'fundamentals.'"[21]

You would think that NAFTA backers have learned their lesson. Think again. In June 1995, even as Mexico was crashing and U.S. wages were tumbling, the Clinton Administration announced its plans to invite Chile, a Mexican clone, to join the trade agreement.[22]

In fact, the Administration has plans for a mega-NAFTA. It is called FTAA or the Free Trade Area of the Americas. "In December 1994 in Miami, leaders from 33 Western Hemisphere countries joined with the President in embracing the goal of achieving free trade in the Western Hemisphere by 2005," says the 1996 *Economic Report of the President.*[23]

THE PERSISTENT TRADE DEFICIT

NAFTA's debacle is not the only failed prophecy of free traders. They have been predicting the end of the U.S. trade deficit through a devalued dollar since the early 1970s. Through numerous dollar depreciations, they have tried to balance the foreign account, but all such efforts have failed. The official line now is that in a global economy trade shortfalls don't matter—in fact, they may even be healthy for our economy. According to the 1996 *Economic Report of the President,* "The trade balance is a deceptive indicator of economic performance and of the benefit that the United States derives from trade. Trade policy is neither responsible for, nor capable of significantly changing, the overall trade balance."[24]

Every American administration since 1970 has tried the policy of dollar depreciation to balance foreign merchandise trade and failed. From Nixon to Ford to Carter to Reagan to Bush and then to Clinton, every president has attempted to bring down the foreign currency value of the dollar (see Figure 9.2 and Table 9.2). And now the 1996 *Economic Report of the President* (ERP) says that all this was a waste of precious time, because trade policy cannot generate an "overall trade balance."

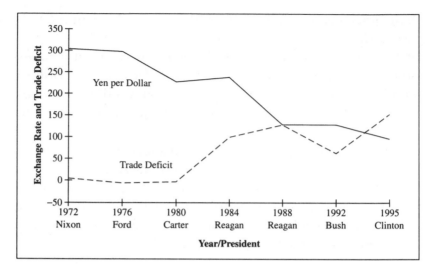

FIGURE 9.2   Trade deficit and the yen–dollar exchange rate: 1972–1995. The relentless fall in the value of the dollar has not eliminated the trade deficit. Every President tried the policy of dollar depreciation after 1972, but failed to balance the merchandise trade. Small surpluses under Ford and Carter arose from trade in services, but under other Presidents even services did not help. (*Source:* Table 9.2.)

TABLE 9.2   U.S. trade deficit and the yen-dollar exchange rate in the last year of each presidential term: 1972–1995.

Year	President	Yen per Dollar	Trade Deficit (billions)
1972	Nixon	303¥	$ 5.8
1976	Ford	296	−4.3 (surplus)
1980	Carter	226	−2.3 (surplus)
1984	Reagan	237	99.0
1988	Reagan	128	127.0
1992	Bush	127	61.6
1995	Clinton*	94	151.0

*One year remaining in term.

Source: Economic Report of the President, 1996, The Council of Economic Advisers, Washington, DC, pp. 392 and 400.

Has the Clinton Administration forgotten that the December 1994 devaluation of the peso turned the Mexican trade deficit into a surplus almost overnight? There must be some reason why an impoverished country like Mexico can transform its foreign account with devaluation in 6 months, something the United States could not do for 13 straight years from 1983 to 1996. That reason, I submit again, is manufacturing—or the lack of it.

The foreign currency value of the dollar has fallen under every presidency, starting with Nixon. A dollar bought 303 yen in 1972, 296 yen in 1976 under Ford, 226 yen in 1980 under Carter, and 237 yen in 1984 under Reagan. By that time, the U.S. trade deficit (called "current account deficit" in the data) had soared from a surplus of $2.3 billion under Carter to $99 billion under Reagan.[25] Alarmed at the unprecedented shortfall, officials of G-7 countries met in New York in 1985 and decided to bring the value of the dollar down. The currency had already depreciated a lot with no success. The dollar fell to 128 yen in 1988, but the deficit only went up. During Bush's term, the dollar remained stable and the deficit declined somewhat. Clinton pursued the failed policy again, and, again, it led to a soaring deficit.

How many times have free traders parroted the official line that trade balance is just one devaluation away? This line appears over and over on the media money shows, in newspapers, and radio talk shows.

And now the 1996 ERP declares this was all worthless to begin with. Professor Milton Friedman even goes a step further: "There can be no balance of payments [trade deficit] problem so long as the price of the dollar in terms of the yen or the mark or the franc is determined in a free market by voluntary transactions. It is simply not true that high-wage American workers are, as a group, threatened by 'unfair' competition from low-wage foreign workers."[26] There is more: "Our gain from foreign trade is what we import. Exports are the price we pay to get imports . . . the citizens of a nation benefit from getting as large a volume of imports as possible in return for its exports, or equivalently, from exporting as little as possible to pay for its imports."[27] In other words, the larger the trade deficit, the better for the country, according to Milton Friedman.

When production rises, businesses hire more; when it falls, employment shrinks. If exports rise, output and employment increase. If imports rise, GDP and jobs sink. Ignoring imports is like ignoring costs, and neglecting exports is like neglecting sales. Costs must not exceed sales, or the company will lose money and eventually go bankrupt. The trade deficit is like a company's loss, and should not be permitted forever.

This is not to say that a company should not borrow money to finance investment projects that expand future production, which will then pay for its loans. But a successful businessperson does not borrow to augment consumption, for that is the sure way to insolvency.

Similarly, a country may appropriately borrow money from abroad to finance its trade deficits if the imports go mostly into investment projects. All through the 19th century, the United States imported technology and machines for investment projects at home and ran up huge trade deficits in the process. But by the end of the century, these investments paid off and the country began to show a small trade surplus decade after decade.

Since the 1980s, however, much of the deficit has been caused by the excess of home consumption over home production. Imports are not going primarily into investments. This type of trade deficit is almost suicidal, because future production still remains stagnant. In other words, *investment-driven trade deficits are beneficial, but consumption-driven deficits are damaging.*

In consumption-driven trade deficits, such as those since 1983, domestic demand is wasted on foreign products. In 1995, for instance, the deficit was $151 billion, which means that American demand for consumption goods exceeded American production of such goods by that amount. To put it another way, if this deficit were zero, then American output would be larger by $151 billion. Allowing that every $54,000 of output creates one good job, U.S. labor demand would be greater by 2.8 million workers.

In the absence of the trade deficit, labor demand would be larger and American real wages would be much greater. In other words, the low-wage competition that generates a consumption-driven deficit means lower wages and fewer jobs for American labor.

If the trade deficit is driven by capital investment, then a different logic applies. Eliminating this investment-driven trade deficit in the 19th century made no sense because the United States at the time was not industrialized enough to meet its requirements for machine tools. But today's consumption-driven deficits should be ended as quickly as possible, because the country has all the factories and technology it needs for production, but consumption is partly wasted on foreign goods.

MANUFACTURING AND TRADE DEFICITS

Why did Mexico's devaluation in late 1994 end the trade deficit almost overnight, whereas the United States has been unable to do this at least since 1983? The answer lies in the lack of U.S. manufacturing. The relocation of many American companies to Mexico has given Mexico a large base that is geared primarily for industrial exports to the United States. Not so, with the U.S. manufacturing base, which is now puny relative to the size of the economy.

In general, we find that countries that export manufactured goods usually have surplus trade, and those that export services and/or farm products have deficits. This pattern holds with certainty in free markets undisturbed by trade barriers; but it is also usually valid in the case of tariff driven economies. In the 19th century, the United States imported manufactured goods in exchange for farm goods and raw materials. The country's trade was generally in deficit that was usually financed by foreign investment. At the turn of the century, America began to export more manufactured goods than it imported. As a net exporter of manufactured goods, its foreign account turned into a surplus that lasted until the early 1970s, when the country again became a net importer of manufactures. In the 1970s, the foreign shortfall was meager and did not adversely affect growth. But in the 1980s, the red ink turned into a gusher with no end in sight so far.

The U.S. experience with trade deficits is also confirmed by that of other countries. Table 9.3 compares three countries with persistent deficits in merchandise trade between 1983 and 1995: the United States, the United Kingdom, and Spain. They are all net importers of manufactured goods, and the United States was the leader with an all-time-high deficit in goods trade in 1995.

Now look at the other side of the coin: the trade performance of OECD countries that are net exporters of manufactures. This group includes Japan, Germany, and the Netherlands (Table 9.4). Of these, Germany and Japan were virtually destroyed during the Second World War. Once they regained independence from war victors in the late 1940s, they launched a vigorous program of industrialization. Initially, they imported investment goods in large quantities from the United States and endured large deficits in foreign commerce. But after 1970, both began to enjoy the fruit of thriving manufacturing. They became net exporters of manufactures and achieved a positive balance of trade.

Currency depreciation can eliminate a trade deficit for a country that has a growing base of manufacturing. Otherwise,

TABLE 9.3   Merchandise trade deficit in manufactures-importing countries (expressed as billions of dollars): 1983–1995.

Year	United States	United Kingdom	Spain
1983	$ 67	$ 2	$ 8
1985	122	4	4
1990	109	33	30
1995	186	17	19

Source: Economic Outlook, Organization for Economic Cooperation and Development (OECD), December 1995, p. A50.

TABLE 9.4   Merchandise trade surplus in manufactures-exporting countries (expressed as billions of dollars): 1983–1995.

Year	Japan	Germany	Netherlands
1983	$ 32	$19	$ 4
1985	56	28	5
1990	64	69	10
1995	138	74	16

Source: Economic Outlook, Organization for Economic Cooperation and Development (OECD), December 1995, p. A50.

it works only for a while. The United States and the United Kingdom have frequently tried depreciating their currencies, but with little lasting success.

Devaluation of the dollar means that a dollar buys less in foreign exchange. This tends to raise prices of foreign goods sold here, and American consumers then buy fewer imports. But we may still spend more on foreign goods because their dollar-denominated prices have risen. On the other side, other countries get more dollars for their currency, so that U.S. goods become cheaper abroad. Foreigners then buy more American goods, but that does not mean American exporters receive more foreign exchange, as prices of U.S. goods abroad have fallen. Currency depreciation, in other words, may or may not succeed in eliminating the trade deficit.

When a country constantly exports low-ticket items such as farm products and raw materials and imports expensive products like cars, air conditioners, televisions, and computers, it is bound to have large deficits no matter how often it devalues its currency. That is why U.S. devaluations have always failed, whereas the 1994 Mexican devaluation was a resounding success. Thanks to our own corporations, Mexico is now a big exporter of manufactures to the United States, and U.S.-based companies have vastly boosted their imports of cheaper but still big-ticket items.

In Washington, the official position is that U.S. trade deficits result from low savings and high budget deficits. But this is only partly true. In the 1990s, Japan has had one of the largest budget deficits in the world. Yet it also has the largest persistent trade surplus. Low savings indeed create a high foreign trade shortfall, but the responsibility for this lies with the regressive U.S. tax system. In the 1950s and 1960s, the U.S. saving rate was higher, but it still paled before the saving rates in other nations. Yet America had a trade surplus at the time. In the end, the state of manufacturing, and little else, determines the foreign account. To eliminate our persistent deficit, we have to reindustrialize America.

CHAPTER 10

Inequality and Depressions

H istory shows that extreme inequality is the bane of all economic systems and civilizations. In ancient Egypt, Mesopotamia, Rome, India, China, Europe, and Japan, gross disparities of income and wealth demolished what were once rich and cultured societies. At best, enormous inequality spawns peaceful rebellions; at worst, bloodshed and violence.

In medieval times, feudalism vanished because of inequality. Later, so did Tsarist Russia and Imperialist China. The poor and the middle class, reeling under decades of tithes and oppression, finally dethroned and annihilated the rulers. In modern eras, wealth disparity has engendered speculative bubbles, poverty, and depressions.

In 1978, in a book entitled *The Downfall of Capitalism and Communism,* I predicted that growing inequality between the elites and the masses would destroy Soviet Communism and modern-day monopoly capitalism around the year 2000.[1] One of them has already collapsed. The other is gasping for breath.[2] Such is the scourge of wealth disparity.

In 1985, in *The Great Depression of 1990,* I warned the public again that rising inequality would soon generate speculative manias in real estate and the stock market, and then create a global crisis reminiscent of past depressions.[3] Some of my readers have thought this view extreme. I will now demonstrate that we have been in a global depression ever since 1990, but, unlike the big bang of the 1930s, it has been quiet yet more pervasive. What is worse, this time there is no light at the end of the tunnel.

Conventional economics almost totally neglects the impact of wealth disparity on the health of an economy. Its focus is on the components of GDP—consumption, investment, government spending, taxes, and the balance of trade. This is unfortunate because, in any country, national wealth is usually four to five times the level of GDP, so even a small increase in the concentration of wealth can seriously hurt the economy. This oversight is perhaps the reason why conventional macromodels have generated faulty predictions again and again.

Despite their extensive theories and vast computer models, economists have lately had a dismal forecasting record. The consensus view at the beginning of the 1980s was that high inflation and interest rates had become permanent features of the U.S. economy; bond and stock markets were predicted to repeat their stagnant performance of the 1970s. Another, albeit a minority, view belonged to the supply-siders, who predicted a balanced budget by 1984 because of extraordinary economic growth to be generated by the tax cuts of 1981. By contrast, toward the end of 1983, Milton Friedman foresaw a serious recession in the first half of 1984 and a roaring inflation in the second half.[4] Many others predicted that the "prosperity" of the 1980s would continue into the 1990s. Markets, however, have been very unkind to most economists, forecasters and their complex econometric and computer models. All the predictions mentioned above have turned out to be wrong. In fact, as *New York Times* columnist Peter Passell points out, most large corporations have fired their forecasters.[5]

A critical summary of my own forecasting record is presented in Table 10.1. I believe that forecasts should be made long before an event is expected to occur, so that there is enough time to counteract possible negative trends. I also believe that forecasts are a true test of economic ideas, and that, if the prophecies are repeatedly wrong, the theories underlying them deserve to be cast aside. Free traders have frequently predicted that soaring trade would boost America's productivity growth, efficiency, living standard, and GDP growth. Since

TABLE 10.1   My forecasting record: 1978–1992.

Forecasts Made in 1978

1. Communism will collapse around the year 2000.
2. There will be a revolution in Iran in 1979, and priests will come to power.
3. There will be a seven-year war between Iran and Iraq, starting in 1980.
4. The rule of the wealthy will collapse in America around the year 2000.
5. Army officers will become popular prior to the fall of monopoly capitalism.
6. Crime, divorce, and promiscuity will soar until the end of the rule of money in politics.
7. Wealth disparity and poverty will climb.
8. Women will become increasingly active in business and politics.
9. The end of monopoly capitalism will be followed by a global Golden Age.

Forecasts Made Between 1980 and 1983

10. There will be seven years of prosperity in America between 1983 and 1989.
11. Inflation will gradually decline and then stabilize in the 1980s.
12. Interest rates will decline and then stabilize in the 1980s.
13. Stock markets will break records every year between 1983 and 1989.
14. Oil and farm prices will decline in the 1980s.
15. Concentration of wealth will rise every year until 1989 leading to a seven-year-long global depression.
16. Bond prices will first rise and then stabilize in the 1980s.
17. Merger mania will occur in the 1980s.
18. European countries such as Britain and France will experience a serious recession in 1986 and will face postwar peaks of unemployment.
19. After a correction in 1987, the stock markets will crash in 1989/1990.

(Continued)

TABLE 10.1   (*Continued*)

---

20. After the influence of money in politics ends, traditional values will make a comeback.

Forecasts Made in 1988 for the 1990s

21. The dollar will collapse by 1994.
22. Inflation and interest rates will be lower in the 1990s.
23. Real estate prices will sharply fall in many parts of the country.

Forecasts Made in 1991

24. Every year of the 1990s will be a dramatic year, full of unprecedented shocks in politics, economy, or religion.
25. President Bush will lose in a landslide to a Democrat.
26. There will be a third political party in the United States.
27. Japan will go through a major political upheaval.

Forecast Made in 1992

28. NAFTA will first destroy the Mexican economy and then the U.S. real wages.

---

the opposite has happened virtually every time, the idea of free trade should be abandoned. A listing of predictions I made in recent years appears on pages 157–158.

Of the 28 predictions listed in Table 10.1, only two have been partially or totally wrong: Contrary to my prediction, the Dow Jones Industrials Average of the New York Stock Exchange was at an all-time high in May 1996, and there has been no repeat of the joblessness of the 1930s. The table also lists forecasts for which some time remains. I will return to this subject shortly and will show that even the errors in my forecasts fit into the pattern of all that has come true and all that appears to be on the horizon.

The accuracy of most of the predictions indicates that something must be right about the theories underlying them. Soviet Communism has collapsed before our eyes, and my forecast excluded the Chinese variety, which is likely to vanish in the next century in an evolutionary rather than a revolutionary way. Iran, under the dominance of its priesthood since 1979, fought an eight-year war with Iraq, starting in 1980. Army officers like Generals Colin Powell and Norman Schwartzkopf have become extremely popular. Women have become very active in politics, and greed, crime, divorce, and poverty have soared.

The seven years of seeming prosperity did materialize between 1983 and 1989. Inflation, interest rates, and oil and farm prices plummeted in the 1980s from their levels in the 1970s. The stock market broke records every year from 1983 to 1987, but then plunged in a shocking crash. Wealth disparity climbed during the 1980s; so did bond prices and mergers. Britain, France, and Germany experienced mounting joblessness in 1986 and have suffered high unemployment ever since.

Thanks to the peso devaluation, the dollar did collapse in December 1994, and then hit an all-time low of 80 yen in April 1995. Inflation and interest rates have been tumbling since 1990; by 1995, they were at their lowest point in the past three decades. Real estate crashed in many prominent states—New York, California, and Florida, among others.

So far until May 1996, the time of this writing, every year of the 1990s has been full of drama and intrigue. The drama began when Saddam Hussein invaded Kuwait in August 1990, only to be engulfed in an unprecedented Gulf War of 1991 in which hapless Iraq was pitted against a coalition of nations. The conflict took President Bush to the height of his popularity, but he lost anyway, in a landslide, in the 1992 election. Right after Saddam's invasion of Kuwait came the reunification of East and West Germany in October 1990. In 1991, a military coup led to the subsequent breakup of the Soviet Union. A third party movement emerged in 1992, spearheaded by Ross Perot. He won an unprecedented 19 percent of the votes in the presidential election and has continued to be a persistent force since then. In 1993, the LDP government, which had ruled Japan since 1950, collapsed and paved the way for subsequent political disarray. In 1994, Nelson Mandela put an end to apartheid in South Africa and became its first Black president. Then came peace treaties between ancient enemies, Jews and Palestinians, with continued progress in 1995. The dollar, as stated above, reached its all-time low in April 1995. This plunge was followed by U.S. history's longest government shutdowns in November and December 1995, and well into January 1996.

Epoch-making events normally occur once in a century, but ever since the fall of the Berlin Wall on November 9, 1989, the world has witnessed a series of them. The destruction of the Wall itself was a once-in-a-lifetime occurrence. Many more such events can be expected in the near future.

Regarding my forecast about NAFTA, we have already witnessed a slow-motion Mexican crash, ongoing since December 1994. Mexico is in the worst depression in the past sixty years. At the same time, U.S. real wages have resumed their descent after bottoming out in December 1992 and rising in 1993. As soon as NAFTA was adopted in January 1994, real wages responded in the predicted fashion and tumbled in spite of falling unemployment.

When readers have asked me why some of my forecasts have failed to materialize, I have confessed to being human. I now realize that there is a deeper reason.

Cycle theory suggests that the current age of acquisitors in the West, or the system of monopoly capitalism, will soon come to an end. According to the inexorable law of social cycles, authored by the late philosopher P. R. Sarkar and borne out by 6,000 years of recorded history, when the ruling elites become tyrannical, when they burden the poor and the masses with exorbitant taxes, when they flourish on the sweat and toil of others, nature casts the elites aside and starts a new age. The law of social cycles enabled me to foresee the downfall of Soviet communism 13 years before it happened. Today, there are many signs of the impending doom of monopoly capitalism.

One of them is the sky-high stock market in the midst of downsizing and the wage blight. No system falls as long as the public is content with it. Few people want change for the sake of change, even if it might improve their lives. Only when their backs are pushed to the wall will people turn against the incumbents and cast them aside. That is where a booming stock market in the midst of rocketing executive compensation and sliding wages comes in. The grinding poverty that coexists with unprecedented opulence in America today is creating a climate of widespread distrust and backlash against the system. Unless timely reforms are undertaken to salvage the American living standard, the backlash will lead to class warfare.

Hear what journalist Jason DeParle, a staff writer for the *New York Times Magazine*, says: "Call it what you will, but class anger is back. Who could have imagined that a win in New Hampshire would come to a man who called the stock market 'un-American?' Or that Bob Dole would pose, even fleetingly, as a critic of corporate America."[6]

The anger in America is real. One target for it is Wall Street, which rejoices at every turn of a weak economy and has a vested interest in mediocre growth and stagnant wages. The irrational upward spiral of the stock market fits well into my prophecy that the rule of money in politics will collapse around the year 2000. The interests of the rich, more than ever before, now conflict with those of the rest of the people.

What about the depression that I predicted would start as a recession in 1990? In some ways, the depression is already here; in others, the threat of its deepening remains. The official line is that 9.5 million new jobs have been created since Bill Clinton took office. Never mind that about half of them are part-time opportunities, or that many people must have two or three jobs to survive. Moreover, millions of workers have been downsized in status, salaries, and fringe benefits.

Professor Galbraith has called the 1990 slump a recession cum depression.[7] Others, such as economist David Levy, call it a "contained depression."[8] Peter Peterson, U.S. Secretary of Commerce in the 1970s, describes it as a "middle class meltdown";[9] Lawrence Hunter, Deputy Chief Economist for the U.S. Chamber of Commerce, regards it as a "never-ending recession."[10] Wallace Peterson, a distinguished professor at the University of Nebraska, uses the most emphatic terms in his

1994 book, *The Silent Depression:* "Fashionable or not, the appropriate term for the economy today is 'depression,' even if it is a silent one."[11] Following Massachusetts Senator Ted Kennedy, I call it the quiet depression.[12]

Here's why I believe the 1990s may already be a decade of depression. Three features usually characterize a depression: paltry growth, tumbling family income or real wages over five or more years, and high unemployment. Figure 10.1 reveals that GDP growth in the 1990s, at 1.7 percent, has been the worst since the 1930s, when it was a minuscule 0.8 percent per year. No other decade since the 1880s, as far back as the data permits, displays a worse performance than the 1990s.

To modern-day economists, a recession occurs only if GDP growth is negative over two consecutive quarters. But this is absurd. Even in the 1930s, overall growth for the decade was positive, but the unemployment rate was 15 percent as late as 1939. According to voodoo economics, the depression was long over in 1934 because GDP growth picked up smartly. But

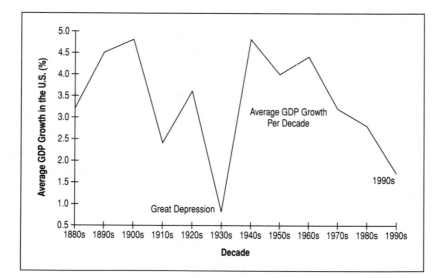

FIGURE 10.1   Twelve decades of economic growth in the United States: 1880s to 1990s. Average GDP growth in the U.S. in the 1990s at 1.7% has been the lowest since the Great Depression of the 1930s when it was at 0.8%. (*Source:* Appendix Table A.10.)

the average American would not have agreed. What really matters, in other words, is the extent of economic misery in society; how widespread and protracted it is. Some of the poorest countries in the world have low unemployment and fast-growing economies, but, compared to the United States today or even in the 1930s, they are in depression because of their overwhelming poverty.

Another feature of a depression is a sharp and prolonged downturn in real family income (RFI) or wages. Even though real wages have been declining since 1972, with more women working, the RFI has displayed a positive trend, dropping only in a slump. As long as family finances are steady or improving, the slow erosion of wages does not hurt that much. The real pinch comes when the RFI also drops.

Let's review the numbers for real family income, in 1994 prices, between 1947 and 1995. Officially, there have been eight recessions since the Second World War. In each recession, the family income fell. In Figure 10.2, the income amounts start with 1947. In every slump, the income fell for one to three

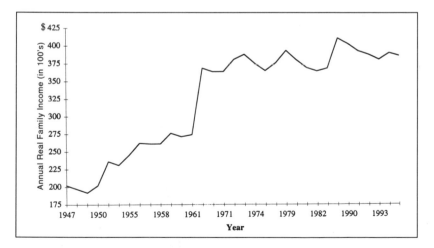

FIGURE 10.2 Median real family income (in 1994 prices): 1947–1995 (selected years). For the first time since 1947, real family income in the 1990s has dropped for five out of six years between 1990 through 1995. Such declines occur only in depressions. (*Source:* Table 10.2 and Appendix Tables A.12 and A.13.)

years. During most downturns, the fall lasted for two years. The worst pair of recessions occurred in the 1970s, when soaring oil prices ignited inflation as well as large drops in family finances. Between 1979 and 1982, the income figure fell during three straight years, creating the longest postwar recession. In 1989, however, real family income reached its peak. (Also see Appendix Tables A.12 and A.13.)

Incomes have been tumbling generally since 1990, with one minor reversal in 1994. (See Table 10.2.) Five of the six years from 1990 through 1995 have seen a decline in family fortunes. After the sixth year, family income had dropped by 6 percent. Now compare these data to the 1930s. Family income figures are not available, but the real wage fall was initially so severe that income must have fallen sharply. The acolytes of voluntary unemployment say that if only the unemployed would accept salary cuts, there would be no joblessness. Not so. Table 10.3 shows that, from 1929 to 1933, money wages or salaries in manufacturing fell nonstop; yet by 1933 the rate of unemployment was as high as 24 percent.

TABLE 10.2   Median real family income during the quiet depression of the 1990s (in 1994 prices): 1989–1995.

Year	RFI	Percentage Change	Years of Decline
1989	40,890		
1990	40,087	−2.0	
1991	39,105	−2.5	
1992	38.632	−1.2	
1993	37,905	−1.9	4
1994	38,782	2.3	
1995[1]	38,400	−1.0	1

Real income decline after six years = 6%.

[1] 1995 figure for RFI estimated from the real earnings data.

Source: Economic Report of the President, 1996; The Council of Economic Advisers, Washington, DC, p. 314.

Consumer prices also sank in the 1930s, so that real wages did not drop as much. In fact, real wages dropped only for three years and then began a sharp and steady ascent until 1937. Over the decade, they rose 17 percent. Another interesting feature is that in 1935, the sixth year after the start of the depression in 1929, the real wage had moved back to its old high of 34.3. Thus, after six years, the real wage drop was zero. During the 1990s, by contrast, family income had dropped by 6 percent after the sixth year. What is worse, families see no light at the end of the earnings tunnel.

The depression is already here in America, but it is quiet and festering, not as dramatic as the cataclysm of the 1930s. In some respects, however, it is worse. The agony in the 1930s was felt mostly by the unemployed millions, who were a fraction of

TABLE 10.3   Real weekly earnings in manufacturing during the 1930s (1947–1949 = 100): 1929–1939.

Year	Weekly Money Wages	CPI	Weekly Real Wages[1]	Percentage Decline	Years of Change
1929	$25.0	73.3	34.2		
1930	23.3	71.4	32.3	−5.6%	
1931	20.9	65.0	32.1	0	
1932	17.1	58.4	29.2	−9.0	3
1933	16.7	55.3	30.3	3.8	
1934	18.4	57.2	32.2	6.2	
1935[2]	20.1	58.7	34.3	6.5	
1936	21.8	59.3	36.7	6.9	
1937	24.1	61.4	39.2	6.8	
1938	22.3	60.3	37.0	−5.6	1
1939	23.9	59.4	40.2	8.6	

[1] Real wages obtained by dividing money wages by CPI and multiplying by 100.
[2] Real wage decline after six years = 0.
Source: Economic Report of the President, 1960, U.S. Government Printing Office, Washington, DC, pp. 184 and 200.

the population. Today's depression afflicts 80 percent of employed workers and at least 50 percent of families; it is spread out and not concentrated in a smaller group. The quiet depression of the 1990s has also been overshadowed by the booming stock market and the rising fortunes of the elite who are totally out of touch with reality. In sum, there is no unemployment depression—not yet anyway; but there is a family income depression, and it is worse than that of the 1930s.

The trend in median income after 1989 indicates that nearly 35 million families, or half of the total, have seen their real income fall in five of the six years from 1990 through 1995. By contrast, the Great Depression, at its worst, afflicted 25 percent of the workforce. In the 1990s, pain has been spread over a much larger group of people, and has remained under the surface, ignored by politicians, mocked by the stock exchange.

The median family in 1995 paid a Social Security tax of 7.65 percent and an average sales tax of 7 percent, or a total of 14.65 percent. After these taxes, the family income was only $32,774. In 1969, these tax rates added to 7.8 percent, which left $33,818 to a family. Excluding the income tax bite, which was essentially unchanged, the after-tax family income in 1995 was below that in 1969. In other words, 26 years of plodding improvement in family incomes had been wiped out by the quiet depression of the 1990s.

WEALTH DISPARITY AND DEPRESSIONS

Much of the flak that I caught from my critics in the 1980s was directed at my insistence that extreme disparities of wealth cause depressions.[13] Some people disliked the idea that inequality spawns economic disasters. They cited the equity–efficiency tradeoff endorsed by established economists. The tradeoff implies that although high taxes on the rich may shrink income equality, these taxes also hurt economic efficiency by discouraging the wealthy from working hard. Professor Samuelson puts it this way: "If we make income taxes more steeply progressive, decisions to invest in risky ventures and to work hard at one's profession will be profoundly affected."[14]

We have already seen that there is absolutely no historical connection between the level of investment and low taxes on the wealthy and on corporations. If anything, regressive taxes squeeze demand and, hence, lower investment. Similarly, why would high taxes levied on, say, a million dollars of annual income discourage anyone from hard work? He or she will still strive to earn the first million. If someone who made $5 million in 1995 refuses to work for a paltry million in 1996, there are many others who would be happy to take his or her place for that kind of money. A university president, after all, has tremendous expertise and responsibilities, but puts in 60 hours a week for just $300,000 or less.

Samuelson's idea is based on an exception. If a super-rich person would not work when a 70 percent marginal tax is imposed, that does not mean that one "does not work hard at one's profession," because 95 percent of the people are not affected by the top tax rate.

In the 1980s, when my critics objected to my idea that inequality creates depressions, they first denied there was any disparity. Then they accused me of cooking up the figures. Today, the disparity is so extreme that only diehard "experts" would refute it. Newspapers, magazines, and talk shows frequently focus on mounting executive pay and perks. I don't need to offer much evidence in this regard. Just compare the trends in the real wages of workers and of CEOs in Figure 10.3. Even excluding the huge sums that the executives receive from stock options and other perks, there has been an explosion in wage inequality since 1976.

I have taken great care in developing the CEO pay index. I updated it to 1995, using information from sources listed in Appendix Table A.11. The real wage index for both classes of employees starts at 1.0 and then quickly diverges, falling to 0.86 for workers and rising to 2.5 for executives by 1995. The contrast between the sharply different fortunes for the two groups is clear: The trend line for the CEOs climbs and the

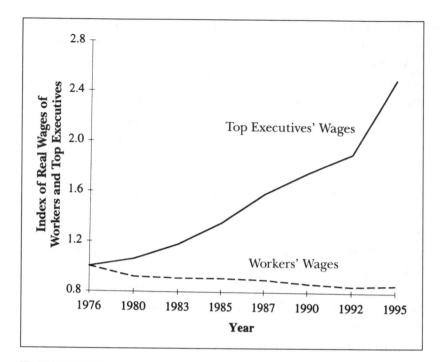

FIGURE 10.3 Index of real wages of workers and top executives: 1976–1995 (selected years). Since 1976 inequality between the real wages of workers and executives has soared. Workers' wage index fell 14 percent by 1995, while that of executives jumped 150 percent. (*Source:* Appendix Table A.11.)

workers' line sinks, while the distance between the two widens over time.

Why does extreme inequality create depressions? To answer this question, it is necessary to distinguish between income and wealth. *Income* is primarily the earning from your work in the current period; *wealth* is accumulated savings from past earnings or investments, or an inheritance from a relative. *Income inequality,* created by the tax structure or by soaring trade, has generated recessions and anemic growth. But the convulsion of a depression stems primarily from *wealth disparity,* because, as stated earlier, total wealth is normally four to five times the level of GDP.

In 1995, per-capita GDP was the highest since U.S. independence in 1776. So there should be few economic troubles in America today, right? Wrong. The country faces some of the worst economic dilemmas of its history. There can be only one cause: so much of our GDP and national wealth are enjoyed by an extremely small minority—just 1 percent of American families.

Currently, economists think that the U.S. government caused the Great Depression of the 1930s through its faulty monetary, trade, and tax policies. This is like blaming a doctor for his patient's sickness. The economy of the 1920s was already severely ill because of the extreme wealth disparity that led to a fragile banking system and a stock market euphoria out of sync with reality. It collapsed like a house of cards as soon as business declined a little in 1929. The government made matters worse by ignoring the true cause of the depression: wealth disparity. It raised taxes on everyone, including the poor and the middle class, in the midst of a severe downturn in 1931.

A depression is a response of free markets to great imbalances caused by extreme concentration of wealth. Extreme inequality creates poverty, which in turn generates high debt, as the poor and the middle class try to maintain their living standard through borrowing. When wealth concentration grows worse, the financial system becomes fragile, as bank failures rise because banks are now lending to people who are high credit risks.

Another effect of inequality is a sharp rise in speculation. Only the rich can afford to gamble money on risky investments. Therefore, all stock and real estate bubbles have been initiated by extreme wealth disparities. (Not surprisingly, these disparities generated another bubble in the 1980s.) Lured by quick and hefty profits made by the rich, the public joins the mania at a late stage. But every bubble bursts in the end, culminating in a depression.

The real estate bubble burst in 1989 and started a recession in 1990. The official miscues of NAFTA and the benign neglect of the virus of downsizing turned the 1990 recession into the quiet depression.

The benign neglect is reminiscent of the 1930s, when one bank after another failed and the Fed stood idly by. In the 1990s, one corporation after another cut high-paying jobs, but successive administrations adopted the policy of hear no evil, see no evil, stop no evil. During the 1930s, the classical economic ideology stood in the way of timely action by the government, even as millions lost their life-time savings in bank failures. In the 1990s, the ideology of laissez-faire and free trade hindered any official action as hundreds of prosperous companies decimated lifetime jobs for millions of Americans.

History suggests that inflation and depressions in the United States have followed regular patterns. Going as far back as the 1750s and omitting the aftermath of the Civil War, every third decade was the peak decade of inflation. For instance, inflation peaked in the 1970s, 1940s, 1910s in this century, and then in the 1860s, 1830s, 1800s, 1770s, and 1740s in the preceding centuries.[15]

However, depressions do not reveal such a clear-cut pattern. According to the historical record, there has been at least one recession every decade, but only four major depressions. There was one in the 1780s, one in the 1840s, another in the 1870s, and finally one in the 1930s. Of these, the depressions of the 1840s and the 1930s were the worst in history. In other words, a depression occurring at the interval of three decades was not as bad as the previous disaster; but a depression at the sixth-decade interval showed a cumulative effect and was worse than the previous worst.

Business activity thus seems to move in terms of three- or six-decade cycles. That is why the 1980s in America and Europe reminded us so much of the 1920s.[16] The 1920s were marked by low money growth, low inflation, and deregulation. The 1980s, relative to the immediately preceding decade, had the same characteristics. The same holds true with the merger activity among businesses. Both the 1980s and the 1920s reveal a sharp rise in industrial marriages and concentration.

By the same token, banks earned mediocre incomes during the 1920s. They did the same in the 1980s—in fact, a full-fledged crisis enveloped the failing savings and loan associations. Then, as now, the farm sector was highly depressed because of the loss of foreign markets and the low prices received by American farmers. Then, as in the 1980s, the coal industry was in the doldrums; so were textiles, shoes, shipping, and the railroads. Energy prices declined throughout the 1920s. They did the same in the 1980s.

Similarly, the economic events in the 1970s are reminiscent of many in the 1910s. Both decades experienced high money growth, high regulation, and high inflation. In both, the farm and energy sectors were very prosperous. Thus, a close look at history reveals, quite remarkably, the presence of a six-decade cycle of business activity. The three-decade cycle also exists, but the six-decade cycle is more pronounced.

Now, using Figure 10.4 and Table 10.4, let's examine the long-term pattern of wealth concentration in the United

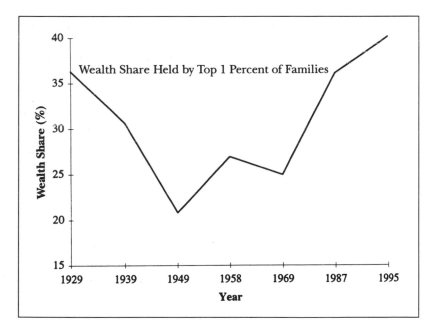

FIGURE 10.4   Concentration of wealth in America: 1929–1995 (selected years). U.S. concentration of wealth was the highest in 1995, higher than even in 1929, when the Great Depression began. (*Source:* Table 10.4.)

TABLE 10.4   Concentration of wealth in America: Share of wealth held by one percent of U.S. adults or families: 1810–1995 (selected years).

Year	Share of Wealth Held by the Richest Americans
1810	21.0%
1860	24.0
1870	27.0
1929	36.3
1939	30.6
1949	20.8
1958	26.9
1969	24.9
1983	34.3
1987	36.0
1995	40.0+

Source: Ravi Batra, *The Great Depression of 1990,* 1987, New York, Simon & Schuster, p. 118, and Steven Sass, "Passing the Buck," Regional Review, Boston Federal Reserve Bank, Summer 1995, p. 16.

States. I have taken this table from *The Great Depression of 1990* and updated it to 1995. Here we see that the wealth disparity was extraordinary around most catastrophes. In 1870, the richest 1 percent of the population held 27 percent of the country's wealth, thereby generating the great depression of the 1870s. The share of the richest soared to 36.3 percent in 1929, spawning the worst depression in history.

By 1987, when the stock market suffered a devastating crash, the disparity was back to the 1929 level, and the quiet depression started in 1990.

ANOTHER BURSTING OF THE BUBBLE

During the quiet depression of the 1990s, the stock market has been galloping like a bull. Indeed, according to many scholars, this is the most bullish market in U.S. history. The market of the 1920s at least had a long economic boom to back it. In the 1990s, the main stimulus to stock escalation has come from an interest rate plunge tied to the worst economic growth rate since the 1930s. The reason behind the stock boom is, of course, the 40 percent-plus figure for wealth disparity in 1995. In fact, 1995 was marked by one of the fastest jumps in share prices in U.S. stock market history. As *New York Times* reporter Floyd Norris puts it:[17]

> The run of the stock market since 1988, as it recovered from the 1987 crash and then moved on to new heights, has no parallels in market history. The Dow has hit record highs in every year since 1989, a run of eight consecutive years including this one . . . the longest previous stretch was six years, a string that ended with the 1929 crash.

All stock market bubbles have burst in the past, including the recent one on Wall Street in 1987 and another in Japan in 1990. The present bubble could also burst. There has not been any serious market correction between January 1991, when the current bullish trend began, and April 1996. This has never happened before, not even in the 1920s. In major bull markets in the past, there were negative interruptions of 10 percent or more. But, in the 1990s upswing, every correction has fallen short of that level.

Another stock market crash will be as devastating as its predecessors. People's savings in banks may be protected by government insurance this time, but who is going to protect their funds parked in stock mutual funds? Millions of people—the young, the middle-aged, the elderly—have poured billions into a casino called the stock exchange. Floyd Norris again: "Stocks and mutual funds have replaced real estate and bank deposits as the largest segments of net worth in American households. Not since the late 1960s have Americans been so heavily dependent on the stock market."[18]

The crash perhaps will not occur in just one day. It is more likely to imitate the Japanese variety in 1990, when share prices tumbled week after week by a few percentage points. Whatever its style, it will cause untold suffering in America. The quiet income and growth depression of the 1990s will then turn into a big bang.

When is the next crash likely to occur? The answer may come from the three-decade cycle of inflation. Using this cycle, I predicted that inflation and interest rates would tumble in the 1990s, and they have. Share prices have risen in response, because, in an anemic economy, there are no other financial assets to attract money. The same cycle of inflation now points to a mild uptick in the rate of inflation, coming most likely by the end of 1997. If inflation picks up, the interest rates are sure to rise, and the interest-driven stock market is likely to crash.

It is possible that things are different this time, as the proponents of bull markets always contend. But I have yet to discover a speculative bubble that did not burst. I hope the current share price mania is slowly contained without an explosion. A stock market crash today, unlike the one in 1987, will quickly turn the quiet income depression into a loud unemployment depression.

Since depressions are caused by extreme wealth concentration, the only way to contain the current quiet depression is to control the exploding incomes of the wealthy through significantly more progressive taxes and high tariffs. But such changes are unlikely to occur in the present political environment.

CHAPTER 11

The Destructive Tax System in Other Countries

A s indicated by its persistent trade deficit, the United States does not export enough products to the world. But it certainly exports its ideas in abundance, espe cially the bad ones. The virus of the regressive tax structure that evolved in America after the 1960s gradually infected other G-7 countries as well. Slowly but surely, the tax burden overseas switched from the rich to lower-income groups, as Social Security contributions soared and corporate taxes tumbled. Simultaneously, taxes on foreign goods gave way to those on local products to stimulate international commerce.

The results overseas have been the same as in the United States—slow growth and growing public suffering. However, the suffering in the G-7 nations of Canada, Europe, and Japan has been felt not in plunging wages but in mounting unemployment. Today, the economists and politicians in Europe parrot the same line as their U.S. counterparts: Taxes for wealthy individuals should be lowered to stimulate the economy. Much like the United States, the rest of the G-7 group has shifted from tax-and-spend to borrow-and-spend policies, with the same consequences.

The G-7 countries—more properly, their poor and middle class—are saddled with huge debt to their rich citizens. In some cases, the interest burden is crippling the people; in others, the tax toll is so high that nearly half of the GDP goes into taxes. The rich collect the interest while others pay the taxes.

The same forces that have destroyed the American dream are now demolishing people's dreams in Canada, the United Kingdom, France, Italy, Germany, and Japan. Voodoo economics has spread its vast tentacles to many nations.

Because of free trade, the giant corporations of most rich countries have been exporting factories and jobs to low-wage areas. As a result, manufacturing employment has dropped in G-7 nations, although not as steeply as in the United States. Unlike America, the other advanced economies do not have large and persistent trade deficits. Free trade, therefore, has not been as destructive for them as the damage has occurred for a shorter period.

The index of manufacturing jobs in Germany in 1980 was 103, but it sank to 86 in 1994.[1] In the United Kingdom, the fall was from 117 to 78 over the same period;[2] in Canada, the index tumbled from 108 in 1980 to 90 in 1994.[3] The story is the same in all the G-7 countries. Workers who were laid off from manufactured goods industries in America reluctantly accepted lower wages and went to work in services. Consequently, unemployment has remained low in the United States.

In other G-7 nations, however, this adjustment process broke down. They had earlier developed what is usually called a welfare state; generous benefits are provided to the unemployed, along with aid for healthcare and education. This generosity seems to have hindered the migration of workers from industries to services, raising the unemployment rate. Real wages did not fall—at most, they stagnated—but the jobless rate began a slow but steady climb.

Wages and unemployment are two sides of the same coin. Both are linked to economic growth and the degree of manufacturing; and when the latter declines, something has to give. In America, where free trade did the worst damage, the result was the real wage blight. In Europe and Canada, the result was the scourge of unemployment. Japan doesn't suffer from either affliction, but then Japan does not follow free trade either, and it dutifully protects its industries from foreign competition.

Low-wage competition from abroad is only one color pervading this bleak picture; there are others as well with familiar hues. Take, for instance, the matter of downsizing and inequality that are now infecting other G-7 nations. Table 11.1 shows that most advanced economies, including Australia, now have horrendous inequality. Japan's income disparity is somewhat reasonable; among all G-7 nations, it has the highest share of income for the poorest fifth of its population, and the lowest share for the richest fifth. Not surprisingly, its unemployment rate is the lowest, and its real wages have yet to fall.

Australia has the worst income inequality, and it is suffering from falling real wages along with high unemployment. It is in even worse shape than the United States.[4]

Downsizing now afflicts all the nations listed in Table 11.1. In Germany, Mercedes Benz, Volkswagen, and Deutsche Bank, among many other well-known corporate names, have announced major layoffs.

In 1995, Deutsche Bank earned almost $2 billion in profits but fired 10,000 employees. In total, about half a million workers became victims of downsizing in Germany that year. By

---

TABLE 11.1   Income share of the poorest 20 percent and the richest 20 percent of population in G-7 countries and Australia: 1988 or 1989.

G-7 Countries	Lowest 20 Percent	Highest 20 Percent
Canada	5.7%	40%
France	5.6	42
Germany	7.0	40
Italy	6.8	41
Japan	8.7	38
United Kingdom	4.6	44
United States	4.6	44
Australia	4.4	42

Source: World Development Report, World Bank, Washington, DC, 1995, p. 221.

comparison, Italy suffered job losses of only 200,000. Everywhere in Europe and Canada now, the story is the same. CEOs and directors announce fat raises for themselves at the expense of the workers. Between 1984 and 1992, executive compensation in Italy, France, and England tripled; in Germany, it more than doubled. At the same time, the unemployment rates broke new post-WWII records. Except for Japan, the economic landscape reveals the same pattern in all G-7 countries and Australia: soaring trade, climbing inequality, hefty CEO salaries, regressive taxation, and proletarian plight.[5]

Capitalism in Japan reveals a surprisingly humane face. Like the United States, the nation has suffered a quiet depression, but there have been few layoffs. People are kept on the company payroll even if there is not enough work for them. They may not receive a year-end bonus, but at least they have the peace of mind of having a job and are not a burden on the government. The unemployment rate in Japan is still a minuscule 3.4 percent after five years of zero or paltry GDP growth.

This is a snapshot of the G-7 nations and Australia today. But there are also differences among the countries, and I will now explore them one by one.

CANADA

If low taxes on wealthy individuals, corporations, and foreign trade stimulate savings, investment, and economic growth, let's see how this idea has worked in Canada. The country is almost totally dependent on trade with its giant neighbor. It had a free trade agreement with America in 1989, and joined NAFTA in 1994.

Canadian trends in household savings, investment, and GDP growth have differed sharply from those in America. Like the United States, Canada used to have a progressive tax structure in the 1960s, with low Social Security (SS) contributions and also somewhat lower taxation of corporations. However, Canadian tariffs were higher, and income inequality was lower than in its southern neighbor. All this generated a better economic performance: Canada excelled in terms of the rate of saving, investment, and GDP growth. Throughout the period between 1961 and 1995, Canada's economic performance was superior to America's in all respects except the rate of unemployment. After 1984, the unemployment rate began to soar in

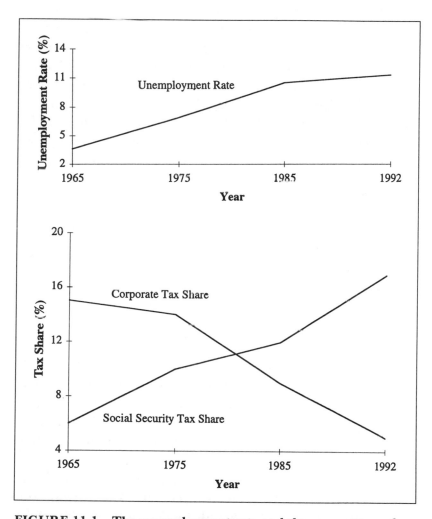

FIGURE 11.1 **The unemployment rate and the corporate and social security tax shares in Canada: 1965–1992.** As the Social Security tax rose and corporate taxes fell, the unemployment rate soared in Canada. Regressive taxation causes misery in society in the form of high joblessness. (*Source:* Appendix Table A.15.)

Canada, reaching a lofty 11.3 percent in 1992. The quiet depression of the 1990s has been louder north of the border because of high joblessness. The unemployment rate in February 1996 was still 9.6 percent.

The reason is obvious. The bandwagon of Reaganomics moved quickly northward in the 1980s. Canada cut tax rates for corporations and raised taxes on the poor in the form of SS contributions. Consequently, its rates of saving, investment, and GDP growth fell while unemployment rose, through much of the 1980s and the 1990s (see Figure 11.1 and Appendix Tables A.14 and A.15). The free trade agreement with America and Mexico did not, or could not, help Canada. Today, the country is stuck with a feeble currency, huge debt, high joblessness, and, above all, hopelessness. It needs to go back to its progressive tax system and place high tariffs on non-American goods.

Manufacturing job losses in America have spread to Canada. The two neighbors with similar economies and wages need to revive their industrial base through high tariffs on goods imported into North America. Tariffs should be low among neighbors with a similar salary structure. I will return to this point in the next chapter.

GERMANY

Germany is regarded as the powerhouse of Europe, the locomotive economy. But the German growth performance since 1960 has not been as spectacular as is generally believed. In fact, over the long run, it is no better than the French and Italian record.

The strength of Germany is its currency, buttressed by strict controls over inflation. The Deutsche mark is one of the strongest currencies in the world. In 1970, one mark bought 28 cents. In 1995, it bought 69. Germany also has the largest economy in Europe and the third largest in the world. This, along with the robust mark, has regained for the country the pride and prestige that were lost in a shattering defeat in the Second World War.

Germany rebuilt its economy in the old-fashioned way—through a high level of savings, investment, and quality control. Historically, it had a solid reputation for careful workmanship and precision, and that tradition of high-quality manufacturing came in handy after the end of the war. Unlike Japan and 19th-century America, postwar Germany maintained low customs on foreign products, especially those coming from its neighbors. But the neighborhood was inefficient relative to Germany's free markets. Products from socialist Britain, Italy, and France were no match for the intensely competitive goods of Germany. The communist Soviet Union and its satellites fared even worse.

Soon, within Europe, Germany regained its leadership in manufacturing, and consistently ran trade surpluses. As a consequence, the mark became Europe's dominant currency.

The German economy performed well in every respect until 1980, when Asian competition began to take its toll. Its growth rate was respectable and unemployment paltry, in spite of high Social Security taxes. Germany and other countries in Europe are quite often described, in a derogatory way, as welfare states that take care of the poor, the unemployed, the handicapped, and the retirees, among others. The inference is that the rich are financing a huge pyramid of social welfare that will eventually undermine the economy. This is completely misleading. The corporate tax burden in Germany has been extremely low—always below 10 percent, and only 4 percent since 1992. (See Appendix Tables A.16 and A.17.)

The welfare state is mostly financed by the middle class. In 1995, Deutsche Bank earned a huge profit even after making large Social Security contributions to the Treasury. However, it paid very little in corporate taxes, and its executive salaries climbed much faster than those of the workers.

A unique feature of the German economy is that the benefits of its productivity growth, unlike in the United States, accrue primarily to the workers. Real wage growth has been exceptional in Germany since the war. Today, the country has the highest real earnings and the lowest working hours in the world. Endowed with robust manufacturing, the nation is still highly competitive and enjoys a persistent trade surplus.

Yet all is not well with the German economy today. As elsewhere, the specter of downsizing hangs over its head like the sword of Democles. High wages are not safe anywhere in a global economy, as long as capital is free to migrate to low-wage nations and then send its products back to home countries.

Until 1980, Germany had little to fear from foreign competition, and its predominantly manufacturing-based economy generated millions of high-paying jobs, pouring billions into state spending. But then competition from Japan and the Asian tigers—South Korea, Singapore, Hong Kong, and Taiwan—caught up with it. At the same time, Social Security taxes went up further. Both forces discouraged the growth of industrial employment. Manufacturing jobs could no longer keep pace with the growing labor force.

The index of industrial employment was 103 in 1980, fell to 92.5 in 1984, and slowly inched to 100 by 1990. Then came the breakup of the Soviet Union and a vast pool of low-paid workers in Poland, Czechoslovakia, and Hungary, among other countries. Discouraged by high wages and payroll taxes at home, German companies began to open plants in former communist lands, exporting jobs with them. By 1994, the index of industrial employment had plummeted to 86—a 16 percent drop in just 4 years.[6] In the same year, German companies invested over 26 billion marks in other countries.[7]

When high-wage manufacturing jobs move abroad, one of two things must happen: workers must be laid off at home, or real wages must fall. In Germany, because of strong unions, wages continued to rise. So workers were laid off or new ones were not hired. The unemployment rate began to climb. By February 1996, it had jumped to 11.1 percent, the highest rate recorded since the war.

Germany faces tough choices today. Including the 2 million people on government programs, as many as 6 million

Germans, out of a labor force of 38 million, may be jobless. Mary Walsh, a staff writer for the *Los Angeles Times,* writes:[8]

> Only a minority of the official jobless are believed to be the victims of a temporary, cyclical downswing; most appear to have no long-term place in the workforce at all. The costs of this situation

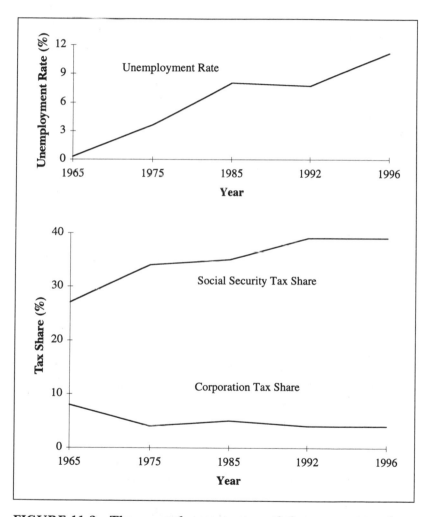

FIGURE 11.2 The unemployment rate and the corporate and social security tax shares in Germany: 1965–1996. Rising Social Security taxes and extremely low corporate taxes among others caused a huge jump in the unemployment rate in Germany. Regressive taxation hurts the economy. (*Source:* Appendix Table A.17.)

are daunting, not only in terms of human unhappiness, but also for the government, which must provide unemployment compensation, welfare and make-work programs for these burgeoning millions.

Clearly, Germany has also been suffering from a quiet depression in the 1990s. An unemployment rate of over 11 percent, compared to just 3.2 percent in 1980, is staggering and cannot be ignored. And the problem will only get worse in the near future. Nathaniel Nash, a journalist at the *New York Times,* underscores the gloomy prospect:[9]

> Corporate Germany has been producing a drumbeat of layoffs, downsizings, bankruptcies and the flight of jobs abroad. Individually, none of these has been of the magnitude of AT&T's plan to slash 40,000 jobs, but taken together they are producing the grimmest employment prospects in Europe's largest economy since the end of World War II.

Figure 11.2 shows how, in a globalized German economy, rising Social Security taxes and falling corporate levies have generated a lofty rate of unemployment.

THE UNITED KINGDOM

While Germany built a welfare state in the midst of a market economy, its neighbor across the English Channel tried to do the same via socialism. Soon after World War II, the United Kingdom launched a program of nationalization of key industries in public utilities, mining, and transportation. The belief was that workers would get a better deal in state-owned monopolies, and real wages and the living standard would grow faster.

Contrary to popular belief, progressive taxation is not identical with socialism. Socialism means a preponderance of companies owned or regulated by the state, whereas a progressive tax structure is one that spares the poor from taxation. In fact, some socialist states in Europe, including the United Kingdom, have had some of the most regressive taxes.

Britain had inherited a tradition of free trade designed to keep its colonies specializing in the production of farm goods and raw materials. Unlike Germany and the United States, both of which were protectionist in the 19th century, Britain had kept its tariffs low. According to Ohio University Professor Alfred Eckes, this was the main cause of Britain's economic decline.[10]

Initially, however, Britain was insulated from foreign competition. Its control over its colonies provided it cheap raw materials and also offered privileged access to their markets. In spite of these advantages, however, Britain lagged behind its protectionist competitors. In the absence of competition at home and foreign competition in the colonies, British industry could never develop the reputation and quality of the German companies.

As I have explained before and will do again in the next chapter, protectionism works best in an atmosphere of high domestic competition, which has to be preserved by the state through antitrust laws. Otherwise, protectionism hurts the economy. Britain, unlike the United States in the 19th century, adopted monopolistic free trade in its colonies. Its domestic monopolies cornered the markets of subject nations, and free trade could not undo the harm done by the absence of competition at home.

The lack of such tradition from the past, along with a socialistic bent, hindered the U.K. economy after the war. (For the results, see Appendix Tables A.18 and A.19.) In saving, investment, unemployment, and GDP growth, Britain trailed its neighbors, which routinely enjoyed growth rates of 5 percent or above in the early 1960s. But the U.K. was limited to a 3 percent level of expansion.

Like its neighbors, Britain did not tax its corporations hard; their tax share tended to be mostly below 10 percent. British Social Security taxes were also not as oppressive as those on the Continent. The main source of tax revenue was personal income, which, until 1980, yielded a tax share of 30 percent or higher.

Britain had what may be called a dual tax structure. On the one side, it had a steeply progressive income tax; on the other, it had regressive consumption taxes. Nevertheless, its tax structure was more progressive than that of Germany. Normally, this approach yields growth advantage to a country, as it did to the United States until 1970. But the British advantage in this respect was overwhelmed by its disadvantage in terms of the lack of domestic competition. Steep foreign competition from Germany only added to the problems. Britain's economic growth of 3 percent lagged behind its neighbors', as did wage growth and hence savings and investment.

Britain's constant balance-of-payments deficits led to repeated devaluations in the 1960s and the 1970s. The country tried to face these ills through subsidies to state-owned companies and mergers among sick private enterprises. This was a faulty prescription because domestic rivalry among firms, not their combination, is what yields efficiency, productivity, and growth.

The pound was depreciated time and again, but the British trade deficit would always make a comeback after a temporary disappearance. The country was a net importer of manufactures, and no medicine could heal the illness of deficient trade.

British unemployment began to climb after 1980, when manufacturing employment started its decline. The highest postwar rate of unemployment, 11 percent, occurred in 1985–1986, the time I had predicted Europe would experience a serious recession. By 1990, unemployment had shrunk, only to soar again in 1992 and reach a high of 10.3 percent in 1993 in the current cycle. The quiet depression of the 1990s has indeed been a global phenomenon.

In 1992, Britain severed the pound from its link with the Deutsche mark. The pound depreciated again and brought the unemployment rate down to 7.9 percent by the first quarter of 1996. But whether this will be any more than a temporary stimulus of devaluation, only time will tell. With British manufacturing in a long-term decline, the past record of such moves does not inspire confidence. The United Kingdom needs more than just devaluation to set its ailing house in order. Its income and wealth disparities are among the worst in the world. They, along with shallow business competition at home, are the evils that have impeded British economic performance. In this respect, the fat bonuses for directors since 1990 are a step in the wrong direction.

FRANCE

France has one of Europe's most generous welfare states, which is financed primarily by perhaps the most regressive tax structure in G-7 countries. Its corporate tax share has never exceeded 6 percent, and the Social Security tax share has not been below 34 percent since 1965, the first year for which such figures are available. France does not collect much from personal income tax. Instead, it has high consumption taxes. As in Germany, the French welfare state is financed by the middle class, not by wealthy corporations and individuals. (See Appendix Tables A.20 and A.21.)

The state benefits are as lavish as in Germany. Government workers may earn early retirement, with generous pensions, after 20 years of work. Workers put in some 1,755 hours of labor per year on average, compared to 1,896 in the United States. However, real wages are low compared to those in America.[11]

Recently, France has joined the brutal sport of downsizing. It's not hard to see why: On average, a French worker gets five weeks' paid vacation, 80 percent of salary when unemployed, free healthcare—and the list goes on. It is very difficult to fire an employee because of myriad government regulations. For this reason, and because of the high Social Security taxes needed to finance the welfare state, companies are reluctant to hire new workers. In March 1996, Alcatel Alsthom, Europe's largest maker of telecommunications equipment, announced a loss of $5.2 billion and simultaneously laid off 12,500 workers. The company plans to trim its employment further by another 30,000.[12] This may be easier said than done. France tried to cut subsidies of state-owned companies in late 1995, but the government met heavy resistance. Workers went on a month-long strike and nearly brought business to a halt.

It was not always like this. In spite of a regressive tax structure, France enjoyed remarkable growth in the 1960s. In fact, its performance was superior even to that of Germany. France is well endowed with fertile land and natural resources, and in the past it utilized them primarily for local industrialization and not for exports. The country had higher customs duties than its neighbors, and, in fact, impeded Japanese efforts to penetrate Europe's auto market.

But the secret of high French growth was a huge rate of saving—as high as 20 percent until 1975—and a correspondingly high rate of investment. Since the income tax collection was low, the high levels of payroll taxes did not discourage saving. But, after 1970, the Social Security tax began to rise, and the natural thriftiness of the French soon vanished. The saving rate displays a negative trend after 1980.

As savings declined, so did the rate of investment and GDP growth. With a fall in the price of oil, growth recovered somewhat between 1986 and 1990, only to be struck down again after 1991. As with most other advanced economies, France's annual growth of 1.2 percent during the 1990s has been the worst since the 1930s.

Unemployment began to rise after 1980, reached a high of 10.2 percent in 1985, and then slowly declined following 1986. After 1990, it resumed its upward crawl and reached a postwar high of 11.8 percent of the labor force in February 1996 (see Figure 11.3). One reason should be obvious by now: the crippling Social Security tax share, which rose above 41 percent in 1992 and thereafter. The other reason has also been discussed in the context of the G-7 countries: deindustrialization resulting from global competition. The French industrial employment index fell from 103 in 1981 to 89 in 1995.[13]

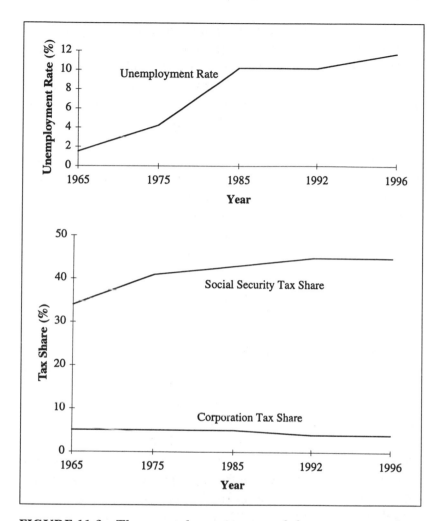

FIGURE 11.3　The unemployment rate and the corporate and social security tax shares in France: 1965–1996. Rising Social Security taxes and extremely low corporate taxes caused a huge jump in the unemployment rate in France. Regressive taxation hurts the economy. (*Source:* Appendix Table A.21.)

ITALY

Italy has the dubious distinction of having the highest rate of unemployment as well as the loftiest government debt as a percentage of GDP among the G-7. The nation typifies the peril facing a welfare state in a global economy.

Italy started out with the same great promise as its neighbors after World War II (see Appendix Tables A.22 and A.23). It imposed high levies for Social Security and collected paltry taxes from corporations and, initially, from individuals as well. Because of its extraordinary rates of saving and investment, the country displayed a better growth record than Germany or France. Just as it did elsewhere, the global recession of 1981 and 1982, however, crippled Italian growth, and Italy's rate of unemployment, always higher than in other G-7 nations, has never recovered from that blow.

To combat unemployment, payroll taxes were trimmed after 1975 and transferred partly to corporations but mostly to personal income, and the tax system remained as regressive as ever, choking the growth of demand in the process. After 1980, the growth rate remained anemic. In the 1990s, Italy, like its neighbors, has suffered the worst growth performance since the 1930s. Consequently, its unemployment rate jumped to a postwar high of 12.6 percent in February 1996. This happened even though the Social Security tax share was brought down to 31 percent, the lowest since 1965. Italy is also a victim of the twin forces of globalization and an ultraregressive tax system.

With declining payroll taxes, the Italian welfare state was financed by excessive government borrowing. As a result, the country had huge budget deficits in spite of one of the heaviest overall rates of taxation. At 125 percent, Italy's gross public debt as a percentage of GDP is the highest among advanced economies. In fact, its interest burden now far exceeds the government's new borrowing. This is the famous debt trap, and Italy is caught deep within it. A debtor who borrows money to pay off interest on past loans is said to be in the stranglehold of a debt trap. Not surprisingly, the country faces the worst dilemma among G-7 nations.

The virus of downsizing, which first migrated from the United States into Germany, is now spreading to Italy. Fiat has fired thousands in the 1990s. On top of that, the nation has been mired in corruption and political scandals. Its former strongman and prime minister, Giulio Andreotti, among other political leaders, has been on trial for bribery and conspiracy to murder. Only strong leadership and bold economic reforms can cure Italy's high unemployment.

JAPAN

Japan, the land of the rising sun as well as the rising living standard for 40 straight years between 1950 and 1990, is now in the same trouble as its G-7 cohorts. It is hard to believe that a country that routinely grew more than twice as fast as others after World War II is today in the same boat as its major trading partners. Japanese products built by the likes of Sony, Mitsubishi, Toyota, and Canon are still coveted around the world, but these companies have earned meager profits at home.

The causes for Japan's economic debacle are completely different from those of other advanced nations, however. Others were damaged by deindustrialization, soaring inequality, and an ultraregressive tax structure. Japan, in contrast, was hurt primarily by its trade surplus and the mindset responsible for it. This may come as a surprise to those who believe that a positive balance in the foreign account is always desirable. Yet, a large surplus is a symptom of a growing gap between productivity and wages.

The phenomenon—let us call it the wage gap—is somewhat similar to what has happened in the United States, where real wages have lagged behind a slow rise in productivity since 1972. In Japan, real wages never fell as they did in the United States. But Japanese productivity growth, since the early 1970s, was so far above the real wage growth that the wage gap climbed steadily over time.

Rising labor productivity generates rising supply. Increasing wages generate increasing consumer demand. If productivity grows much faster than wages, however, supply outpaces demand. Government spending may rise to plug or even reverse the direction of this gap, as happened in the United

States. In Japan, however, the wage gap was too strong to be overcome by rising government and investment spending. As a result, supply grew faster than demand. The excess of production over consumption had to go somewhere. It went abroad and became the country's trade surplus.

As long as foreign demand for Japanese products showed a healthy growth, Japan's GDP growth was strong despite anemic demand at home. But after 1989, the rest of the world went into a recession. That is when Japan's growing trade surplus—a demand gap—became the real problem. The gap had been building since the early 1970s, so it could not disappear easily.

Another source of trouble was the speculative mania that developed in the 1980s in land and stock prices. The Nikkei index on the Tokyo Stock Exchange jumped from about 7,100 in 1980 to near 39,000 on the last trading day of 1989—a rise of 450 percent in 10 years! Similarly, the land price index soared 200 percent between 1985 and 1990.

The global recession, along with a freak rise in the price of oil in the extreme winter of 1990, triggered a stock market crash. The land speculation bubble also burst in 1991, generating an unprecedented crisis for many banks that had loaned millions against land as collateral. The stock exchange plummeted to near 14,000 in June 1992, about 55 percent below its all-time peak, whereas land prices have yet to hit bottom. At the end of March 1996, the Nikkei index hovered around 21,000. The investor community has still not fully recovered from the crash. The banks are saddled with huge debts totaling half a trillion dollars.

Foreign demand continues to be anemic, because other G-7 nations are in a quiet depression. Japan cannot grow on the strength of its own demand, as its economy is geared to foreign needs. Consequently, a country that regularly grew at an average rate of over 6 percent for 40 years has annually grown by just 1.2 percent in the 1990s. (See Appendix Tables A.24 and A.25.)

The secret of the Japanese economic miracle in the past was rapid industrialization based on extraordinary rates of savings, investment, and protectionism. The miraculous growth sprang from low foreign competition and intense company rivalry at home. Small companies such as Sony, Toyota, and Nissan, battle-tested at home, easily bested their foreign rivals on their home turf. Later, however, excessive emphasis on surplus trade at the expense of domestic markets became a hindrance. Japanese growth suffered a precipitous decline from which it has yet to recover.

Japan's tax system was highly progressive until the 1970s and is still more progressive than the systems of other advanced nations. Its corporate tax share is higher, and the Social Security tax share lower than in most G-7 nations. But a feeble demand base at home has trapped the economy in a chokehold. Japan has rarely suffered from high unemployment. Nevertheless, its unemployment rate, at 3.4 percent in February 1996, was the highest since 1950. Millions of people are underemployed. Taking them into account, the rate of joblessness is above 10 percent. However, the Japanese corporate face is benevolent, unlike in America, where prosperous companies are comfortable destroying the lives of skilled and hardworking people.

Japan does not need further industrialization. Indeed, the country needs an expanding demand base at home to fully utilize the existing manufacturing base, as we shall see in the next chapter. The lesson from Japan is that exorbitant trade surplus can also generate economic ills. In other words, balanced trade, where exports roughly match imports, is the best policy.

AUSTRALIA

Let's now venture outside the G-7 arena and examine the saving, investment, and growth performance of another advanced country—Australia. Australia is a mirror-image of the United States. Both developed through high tariffs and then began to sink after the tariffs were cut. Today, both countries are plagued by high inequality in income and wealth. Both are mired in domestic and foreign debt. Both are dependent on services and have seen their real wages fall. Australia, however, has another headache. In addition to tumbling real wages, especially in services, it has suffered from high unemployment throughout the 1980s and the 1990s.

In the United States, about 15 percent of the workforce is engaged in manufacturing. In Australia, the rate is 16 percent, but it was much higher in the 1960s. At that time, annual economic growth averaged 5 percent and exceeded the performance in the United States.

Australia's tax structure was progressive in the 1960s as the contribution of Social Security taxes was relatively small at 25 percent of tax revenues. Corporate taxes, at 15 percent of the receipts, yielded a respectable level of revenue. All this generated a healthy rate of saving at 15 percent and investment at 25 percent. (See Appendix Tables A.26 and A.27.) In the 1970s, however, the country was flooded with manufactured goods from Japan and the rest of Asia. Manufacturing employment began to fall. In 1974, Australia trimmed its tariffs and transferred the tax burden to payroll taxes. The results were disastrous, in spite of the high level of inflation prevailing in the world at the time.

Australia was a major exporter of farm goods and raw materials, both of which registered impressive gains in prices because of global inflation. Despite a hefty rise in export prices, Australia suffered a drop in annual growth to 4 percent in the early 1970s. The drop was even more severe after the tariff cuts in 1974. Clearly, the culprits responsible for stagnation were deindustrialization and a fall in the progressivity in the tax system. And both arose from tariff reductions.

Tariffs continued to decline in the 1980s, and the Social Security tax share kept rising. Corporate tax yield also dwindled. The rate of saving fell, but GDP growth improved because of increasing foreign investment from the United States and Japan. Ford, General Motors, and IBM, among others, have invested heavily in Australia. However, the burden of the payroll taxes exacerbated the rate of unemployment, which displayed an upward trend in the 1980s.

After 1985, unemployment began a slow fall, but then came the quiet depression of 1990. By 1992, the unemployment rate had soared to the post-WWII high of 10.7 percent and was still at 8.6 percent in February 1996.

Australia is a major importer of manufactured goods. As a result, it has suffered from persistent trade deficits, which have not been corrected by periodic devaluation of its currency. Manufacturing real wages in 1995 were about where they were in 1985, but service wages had dwindled by over 10 percent. With payroll taxes at their highest levels in its history, the level of poverty was also near the peak.[14]

The story of Australian economic ills is much the same as in most G-7 countries: deindustrialization caused by the removal of many tariffs, a regressive tax structure, and extraordinary income and wealth disparities. As elsewhere, Australia's CEOs are flourishing while its workers are hurting. Not surprisingly, its household saving rate of 4 percent is as pathetic as in the United States. Figure 11.4 shows that the rising share of payroll taxes has all but destroyed the once high rate of saving in the 1960s.

SPAIN

The Spanish unemployment rate in February 1996 was 22.8 percent, comparable to U.S. unemployment rates in the Great Depression. Has it always been this high? No. The rate was as low as 2.4 percent in 1970, better than in most other countries in the world. It stayed low until 1975 and then soared.

We have seen repeatedly that whenever a country has developed economic troubles in the form of high unemployment, falling real wages, low growth, or trade deficits, two culprits are generally responsible: regressive tax system and/or tariff cuts leading to soaring trade. Spain offers no exception to this general principle.

From 1965 to 1975 everything was rosy in Spain. Investment and growth were excellent and unemployment was meager. Then tariffs were cut in the 1970s, and their tax burden was

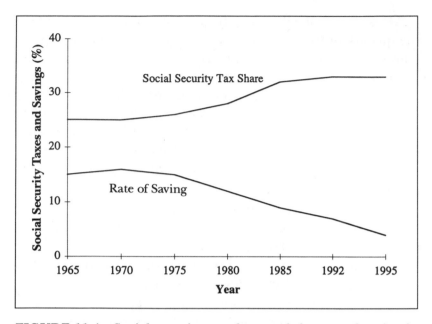

FIGURE 11.4   Social security tax share and the rate of saving in Australia: 1965–1995. Soaring Social Security taxes have crushed the rate of saving in Australia. (*Source:* Appendix Tables A.26 and A.27.)

passed on to the payroll taxes. At about the same time oil prices jumped. All these combined to cripple growth and boost the jobless rate. The unemployment rate reached 11.5 percent in 1980, as Social Security bore almost half of the total tax burden. Tariffs continued to fall and so did their tax share. Payroll taxes also fell after 1980 but could not overcome the harm done by dwindling tariffs. As manufactured imports and trade soared, growth fell even more between 1981 and 1985, whereas the unemployment rate rocketed to 21.5 percent. The global oil price plunge in 1986 boosted the growth rate, as in the G-7 countries, and joblessness declined somewhat. Then came the quiet depression of 1990, and jobs were lost again. In 1994, the rate of unemployment rose to 24.2 percent. Spain has been in a severe depression ever since 1990. (See Appendix Tables A.28 and A.29.)

Figure 11.5 displays the effect of Spanish trade on GDP growth. From 1965 to 1985, Spain's trade as a percentage of GDP rose steadily, and its growth also tumbled steadily. In 1965, trade was only 19 percent of GDP, but economic growth was a vigorous 8 percent. In 1985, the trade ratio jumped to 44 percent, but the rate of growth sank to 1.4 percent. Then trade fell by 1990 and growth jumped again, only to plummet once again with rising trade.

Trade usually hurts the nation that imports manufactures, and Spain reveals this effect dramatically. Figure 11.6 portrays the effects of tariff cuts on the rate of unemployment. As the customs share of taxes declined, the jobless rate generally went up.

Prior to 1973, Spanish trade was sometime in deficit, sometime in surplus. But after the tariff cuts in the early 1970s,

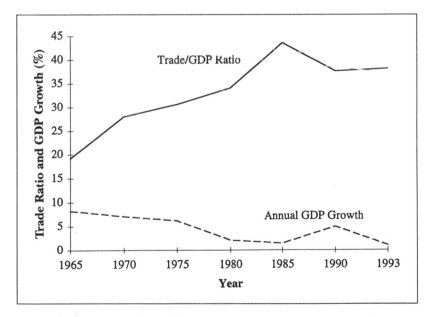

FIGURE 11.5   Trade and growth in Spain: 1965–1993. Whenever the contribution of trade to GDP rose in Spain, its economic growth fell, and conversely. (*Source: International Financial Statistics Yearbook,* 1985, 1992, and 1994, International Monetary Fund, Washington, DC.)

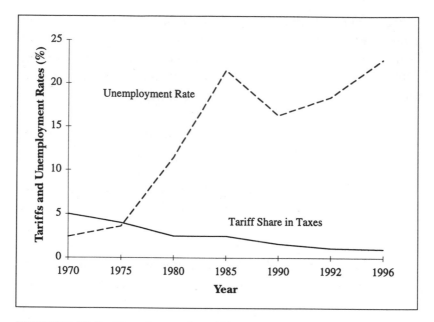

FIGURE 11.6   Tax share of tariffs and unemployment in Spain: 1970–1996. As the tariff rate began to fall starting with the early 1970s, the rate of unemployment began a relentless rise. (*Source:* Appendix Table A.29.)

trade was mostly in deficit. In fact, Spain has suffered deficient trade ever since 1978. This is one reason why unemployment has skyrocketed in spite of falling payroll taxes and oil prices. Jobs were created in 1995 but mostly in low-wage services. The Spanish depression reveals no signs of easing anytime soon.

A brief study of most advanced economies—G-7, Spain, and Australia—reveals that the quiet depression of the 1990s has been a global phenomenon. All these nations are suffering from minimal growth, tumbling real incomes, or gigantic rates of unemployment, in spite of heavy government spending and monetary expansion designed to produce low interest rates.

What is worse, there is no glimmer of light in a dark tunnel. Traditional remedies of deficit financing and government borrowing from the rich have already been tried by all nations, but have failed to contain the tentacles of gloom among the poor and the middle class. New diagnosis and medicines are needed. My prognosis is that the illness lies in a garbled tax system that smites the lower income groups and nurtures the wealthy. It invites copious imports from low-wage countries; chokes manufacturing, wages, and demand at home; and encourages the emigration of capital and factories to the Third World, which then becomes a victim of pollution and pell-mell industrialization that fattens the billionaire owners of multinational companies without providing for the basic necessities of local populations. In short, the global system today is oppressive, tyrannical, and inefficient. What can be done about it? To this I turn next.

CHAPTER 12

A Plan for American and Global Prosperity

Why are thousands of skilled and talented people being laid off by giant and frequently thriving corporations not just in the United States but also in Europe? Why are the masses in the Third World destitute, even though millions of them are now working for multinational companies?

The troubles that the global economies face can be summed up in four self-perpetuating vicious circles described and illustrated below.

VICIOUS CIRCLE I

Ultraregressive taxation today afflicts the poor and the middle class in almost all advanced economies. For a variety of reasons, payroll taxes have been frequently raised in all G-7 nations since the early 1960s. The burden of these levies is harshest on the indigent, who pay the largest percentage of their income in taxes.

Initially, the rise in payroll taxes was small, but, in the absence of strong opposition from their powerless victims, the taxes climbed further. (See Figure 12.1.)

The first effect of regressive taxation is to depress both savings and consumption. This in turn reduces investment. Low consumption and investment then produce low GDP, which in

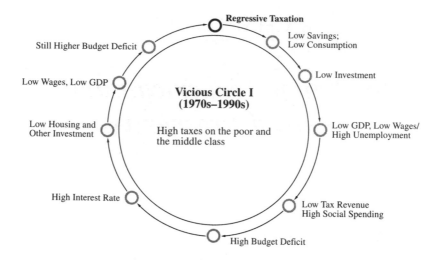

FIGURE 12.1   The vicious circle of regressive taxation in advanced economies: 1970s–1990s. These taxes include high payroll and consumption taxes. The vicious circle displays the cause and effect relationship in a clockwise motion, with each arrow starting with a cause and pointing to the effects. Thus, regressive taxation, the initial cause, leads to low savings and consumption, which generate low investment, and so on.

turn generates low tax revenue in spite of the initial rise in payroll tax rates. They also trigger lower wages and/or higher unemployment, both of which tend to raise state social spending. From all this comes a high budget deficit, which tends to boost the rates of interest, which in turn crimp investment in housing and factories. The results are low GDP, low wages, low tax receipts, and still higher budget deficits. Finally, the soaring deficit calls for further tax increases, which again fall on the defenseless sections of society—the poor. The circle is complete. One round of regressive taxation leads to another round, and on and on it goes until the public begins to revolt.

Look at the combined payroll tax rates on employers and employees in G-7 nations in 1993 (Figure 12.2). The highest

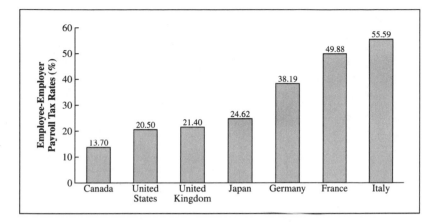

FIGURE 12.2 Employee–employer payroll tax rates in G-7 countries: 1993. Except for Canada, most G-7 countries have exorbitant payroll tax rates on employment, with Italy collecting more than half of a person's salary from the employee and employer. Such a tax system is ultra regressive, because its burden is the heaviest on the poor and small businesses. (*Source: Statistical Abstract of the United States,* 1995, U.S. Department of Commerce, Washington, DC, p. 861.)

tax rates are in France and Italy, and, not surprisingly, they also have the highest rates of unemployment among the G-7 economies. Canada's levies are the lowest in this respect, and the United States comes next.

The consumption tax is another type of regressive tax (Figure 12.3). The United Kingdom is the worst offender here, whereas Japan collects the lowest revenue from such duties.

Combining the two taxes, we find that Italy and France have the most regressive system among advanced economies. Italy's payroll tax rates are the highest, but enforcement is rather lax, so the French tax share of Social Security contributions is higher than Italy's.

The United States seems to be better placed in this regard, but the country collects 47 percent of its federal revenue from regressive taxes, of which 30 percent came from payroll contributions in 1992. In 1996, the regressive tax figure jumped to 54 percent.

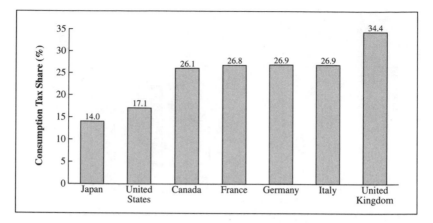

FIGURE 12.3   Consumption tax share in G-7 countries: 1992. Except for Japan, most G-7 countries have extremely high taxes on consumption, with the United Kingdom collecting the highest percentage of such levies. This makes the tax structure ultra regressive. (*Source: Statistical Abstract of the United States,* 1995, U.S. Department of Commerce, Washington, DC, p. 860.)

VICIOUS CIRCLE II

Another type of regressive taxation is tax cuts for wealthy individuals and corporations. When taxes were cut dramatically for corporations and the affluent, the results were supposed to be larger savings and investment in factories. This did not happen, however, because investment spending is normally linked to demand growth, which began to fall because of rising inequality and payroll taxes. Instead, funds sat idle in bank vaults and moved into the stock market or highly leveraged speculation—commodities, options, and futures. Corporations purchased their own stock instead of investing in new plant and equipment, or bought other companies in a wave of mergers and leveraged buyouts.

Vicious circle II was also sparked by regressive taxation via large tax cuts for the rich. The effects of these cuts had consequences mostly in financial markets. Indirectly, they perturbed the rest of the economy as well by wasting capital that could have gone into productive, job-creating activities. Vicious circle II (Figure 12.4) begins from a regressive tax structure and then moves toward idle funds among the rich to high stock prices and speculation, to megamergers and stock repurchase. Megamergers in turn led to downsizing, which in turn generated lower wages but huge corporate profits. High profits transformed rising stock markets into a speculative bubble, as share prices, unlike in the past, started to soar in low-growth economies. From the bubble came the stock market mania that has once again sucked millions of small business-people, savers, and retirees into mutual funds. Mutual funds generally lower risk, but, in a crashing stock market, they also collapse as in 1987.

Meanwhile, investment in factories suffered and GDP growth tumbled. With lower GDP growth came further demand from conservative economists and politicians for another round of tax cuts on top incomes, capital gains, and corporations.

This completed the vicious circle. So, one round of pro-wealthy tax cuts created a chain reaction that led to another

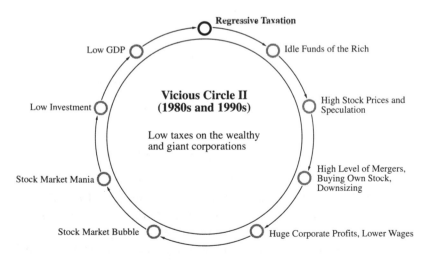

FIGURE 12.4 The vicious circle of regressive taxation in advanced economies: 1980s and 1990s.

round of pro-wealthy tax cuts. The process is self-perpetuating. The chain started in 1981, moved into high gear in 1986, was interrupted by minor changes by Presidents Bush and Clinton, but is now generating fresh demands in the form of a flat income tax no larger than 20 percent on all levels of income. Two rounds of this vicious circle have been completed, and the third could begin if Dick Armey, Newt Gingrich, and other GOP stalwarts have their way.

Except for Japan, no country in 1992 and thereafter collected more than 10 percent of its tax receipts from corporations. (Figure 12.5). The U.S. corporate revenue share was just 7.2 percent in 1992, compared to over 25 percent in the 1950s and the 1960s. Some experts suggest that corporations should not be taxed at all, because they pass their levies on to their customers, so that consumers end up bearing the burden.[1] If this were the case, companies would have no objection to these taxes. The fact that they fiercely oppose corporate duties suggests that they fear the burden of corporate taxes would fall on them.

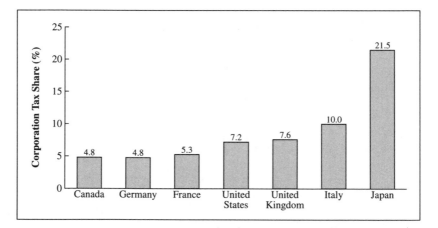

FIGURE 12.5   Corporate tax share in G-7 countries: 1992. Except for Japan, corporate taxes as a percentage of total tax revenues are extremely low in G-7 countries. This makes the revenue system extremely regressive, as rich corporations pay hardly any taxes. (*Source: Statistical Abstract of the United States,* 1995, U.S. Department of Commerce, Washington, DC, p. 860.)

VICIOUS CIRCLE III

Then there is the spiraling effect of falling tariffs since the 1960s. Lower tariffs invited manufacturing imports from low-wage countries and encouraged the migration of factories from rich to poor nations, where goods are produced but not sold. In fact, products are mostly shipped back to advanced economies, especially the United States, Canada, and Australia. This led to a rising trade deficit with protectionist nations, and lower real wages or higher unemployment at home.

If tariffs were beneficial to advanced economies in the past, how do we explain the pernicious effects of tariffs to which free traders constantly point? Tariffs hurt when businesses lack rivalry at home, but are an unmixed blessing when active enforcement of the antitrust laws generates strong domestic competition. I will explain this in detail later in the chapter.

Deindustrialization and growing trade deficits resulting from vanishing tariffs led to lower GDP growth and the expansion of services (Figure 12.6). As trade deficits continued, some advanced economies felt the need for export promotion

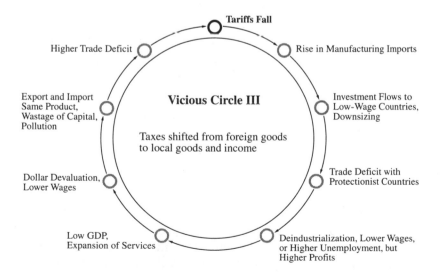

FIGURE 12.6   The vicious circle of transferring taxes from foreign goods to local goods and incomes.

through currency depreciation and through lower wages in exporting industries. The result was intraindustry trade, which means the export and import of nearly the same product. Countries began to export and import manufactured goods to each other. Today, America exports cars and also imports them. We ship out computers, appliances, furniture, office machines, and tractors, and we also import these goods from abroad.

According to many estimates, nearly 80 percent of U.S. trade is now in similar products.[2] All this trade involves two-way shipping across the seas as well as in the skies. A lot of capital is then tied up in the transportation industry, and the skies and seas become highly polluted. If the goods were mostly produced at home, this waste would vanish. If factories of either domestic or foreign corporations were located near population centers or mines, production would rise or be unchanged but pollution would tumble. I will return to this matter shortly.

Currency depreciations do not eliminate the trade deficits of countries that import manufactured goods. They make things worse, in spite of downsizing. The importers of manufactured products believed that their foreign trade shortfall resulted from the protectionist policies of surplus-producing nations. They invited these nations for further trade negotiations, which led eventually to another round of tariff cuts in the so-called GATT (General Agreement on Tariffs and Trade) treaties. This completed the vicious circle sparked by initial tariff cuts and set off the same negative economic trends in advanced economies again.

This vicious circle continues unabated. Most of the rich countries are suffering from the lowest growth rates since the 1930s, huge unemployment, or plummeting real wages.

VICIOUS CIRCLE IV

Finally, there is a spiral of debt, corruption, interest burden, and growing suffering among the masses of those developing economies that came into contact with multinational banks.

We've discussed what happened in the 1970s, when the global banking giants, awash with petro-dollars, went on a lending spree to poverty-stricken nations. Many people, bankers and government officials alike, made a lot of money in the process—bankers, from their fees and interest charges; state officers, by siphoning funds away into their Swiss bank accounts.

Corruption and monopolies already ran rampant in the developing world under the umbrella of what may be called monopolistic protectionism, which prevails when a nation grants tariff protection to regional monopolies at home. Bolstered by loans from the multinational banks, the monopolists bought up smaller companies in several industries, while funneling millions of dollars into foreign accounts. Thus, the first effects of the bank loans were to increase graft, strengthen the monopolies, and generate many wasteful projects (Figure 12.7).

Rising foreign debt and the resulting high level of interest to be paid in foreign exchange created a reverse flow of capital from the underdeveloped to the developed economies, and

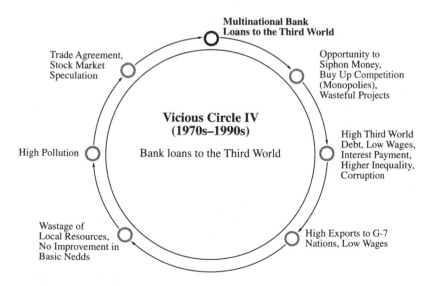

FIGURE 12.7   The vicious circle of foreign debt in the third world: 1970s–1990s.

could not but lower wages and exacerbate income and wealth disparities in the Third World.

Servicing the giant foreign debt at escalating interest rates in the late 1970s and early 1980s called for increased Third World exports to G-7 nations, where most of the lenders were located. Export promotion also required further wage restraint in Third World nations for an already poor mass of workers.

With local resources mobilized toward an export drive, the basic needs of the teeming Third World populations suffered. Instead of using precious resources to expand local supplies of clean water, electricity, housing, and healthcare—basic needs not adequately met in poor nations—goods such as textiles, shoes, carpets, and televisions were produced to be shipped thousands of miles away to Europe and the United States. However, even vast quantities of exports were insufficient to pay the ever-escalating interest burden. Mexico and Brazil, among others, were on the verge of default in the early 1980s. Their debts were rescheduled, but the total continued to climb.

In retrospect, bank loans to the Third World were a calamity. The living standard of the masses in Thailand, the Philippines, Venezuela, Brazil, Argentina, and Mexico sank as never before.

Export promotion at all cost to service the debt also meant pell-mell industrialization without regard for the environment. The Third World moved from one crisis to another in the 1980s, always under pressure to meet the next loan installment. Finally, bankers gathered around the world and began to form free trade agreements involving the debtor nations. In 1989, the Asia Pacific Economic Cooperation (APEC) was formed. It comprised a common market of 12 countries, which later expanded to 18. The regional block is led by Japan, whose banks had lent billions of dollars to the Pacific Rim countries. The other trade agreement, of course, was NAFTA, involving again a debtor–creditor combination. Here Mexico was and is the debtor, and U.S. and Canadian banks were the creditors. There has also been talk of expanding NAFTA to a Free Trade Area of the Americas (FTAA). This way, in theory, all the debtor countries of Latin America will have free access to the lucrative American market. They will earn dollars from their exports and pay off their loans to multinational banks.

The trade agreements encouraged multinational banks to buy local banks and lend even more money to Third World companies and governments. The vicious circle was thus complete. It started with bank loans to poor nations, created a chain of misery in the process, and then ended with even more loans following the formation of regional trading blocks.

Many developing countries can now boast of membership in a trading block, but their foreign debt is as high as ever. They still pay huge sums every year to service their debt. Their corrupt officials have siphoned millions, leaving the impoverished masses to foot the bill.

A watchdog group called Transparency International, based in Berlin, published a corruption index in 1995, ranking 41 nations in Asia, Europe, and the Americas on a scale of 1 to 10. The index was derived from a survey of those who had long work experience in these countries. Ranking was based on a reverse score: the higher the score, the lower the level of graft and sleaze.

Among the 41 nations, 10 were identified as the most corrupt, with a score close to 3 or lower. Of those 10, 9 are among the most indebted countries in the world. There is, in other words, a strong connection between corruption and external debt, which has soared for all the listed countries from 1980 to 1993 (Table 12.1). Excluding short-term private borrowing, Mexico had an external debt of $118 billion in 1993, up from $57.4 billion in 1980. Counting short-term loans, the Mexican foreign debt was $160 billion or nearly 45 percent of GDP in 1995, for which it had to cough up $20 billion in interest and service charges alone.[3] One-third of Mexico's export earnings goes just into debt servicing. Argentina is the only country that is somewhere in the middle on the scale of corrupt nations, but has a huge foreign debt, paying 46 percent of export earnings into debt charges in 1993. The cleanest country was New Zealand, with a score of 9.55. The United States had a tally of 7.79 and was ranked fifteenth among the least corrupt countries.[4]

TABLE 12.1   Corruption and foreign debt.

Country	Corruption Index[1]	External Debt (Billions)[2] 1980	External Debt (Billions)[2] 1993
Indonesia	1.94	$20.9	$ 89.5
China	2.16	4.5	83.8
Pakistan	2.25	9.9	26.1
Venezuela	2.66	29.3	37.5
Brazil	2.70	71.0	132.8
Philippines	2.77	17.4	35.2
India	2.78	20.6	91.8
Thailand	2.79	8.3	45.8
Mexico	3.18	57.4	118.0
Argentina	5.24	27.2	74.5

[1] A low score means high corruption.
[2] Excludes private short-term debt.
Source: Barbara Crossette, "A Global Gauge of Greased Palms," *New York Times,* August 20, 1995, p. E3. *World Development Report,* World Bank, Washington, DC, 1995, pp. 200 and 201.

Among the most corrupt, Brazil owed $133 billion in 1993. Indonesia owed $90 billion, China $84 billion, and India $92 billion. In Indonesia, external debt was nearly 60 percent of GDP; in Venezuela, it was 63 percent.[5] The downtrodden masses of these nations are caught in a debt trap; they keep paying interest year after year without seeing any relief from their obligations. Thus, there is a clear connection between debt and graft, and conversely.

Indonesia, the leader among corrupt countries, piled up a huge debt between 1980 and 1993. In the words of Edward Gargan, a reporter for the the *New York Times:*[6]

Some things never seem to change in Indonesia, where nepotism, favoritism and corruption have long been ubiquitous. Small and medium-sized businesses pay licensing fees off the books. Judges are paid to settle cases. Sweetheart deals are struck between foreign investors and local interests.

Again, we see a close connection between foreign investment and graft, which in turn leads to regional monopolies. As Gargan explains, friends of the ruling elites "control vast business empires, including monopolies and exclusive concessions . . . ."[7]

What has all this brought to Indonesia? "Thousands of low-paying, low-tech factories, producing clothing, shoes, electronics and toys for export," writes Gargan.[8] In other words, local resources are used to fatten the multinationals' profits, but not to satisfy the urgent needs of the destitute masses.

Indonesia is not unique. This is the story of much of Asia. Nothing can be done in these countries without greasing somebody's palm. In the process, poverty continues and populations mushroom. The best way to control the population is to improve the general standard of living, as has been the case in the First World of Europe and North America.

In terms of foreign aid, Europe and America are finally beginning to realize, says Howard French, another *New York Times* reporter, "that big cash outlays to central governments may only pave the way to corruption . . . that three decades of foreign developmental assistance in the Third World has failed to lift the poorest of the poor in Asia and Africa much beyond where they have always been."[9]

French goes on to cite Professor Peter Boone of the London School of Economics, and reports that "development assistance had fattened political elites . . . , but had done little to improve living standards in poor countries."[10]

True, growth in these nations is somewhat higher with foreign assistance, but its fruits are enjoyed by the local elites. This in areas where even drinkable water and shelter are not available to millions of people.

Of the 10 countries listed in the table, 7 are already members of some trade agreement, and the others have been invited to become members in the near future. Indonesia, China, the Philippines, and Thailand belong to APEC; Mexico is a part of NAFTA, whereas Brazil and Argentina are members of Mercosur, a trading bloc in South America. President Clinton, of course, seeks to involve all the Latin American debtors in a grand free trade area stretching from "Alaska to Argentina."[11]

SOME ECONOMIC PRINCIPLES

What can be done to escape these vicious circles? Before designing a master plan for global prosperity, we should explore some economic principles that cannot be violated with impunity. Chief among them are the forces of human nature and markets that in turn revolve around supply and demand.

Supply and demand are like the two wings of a bird that needs them both to fly. An economy must pay heed to both forces to function smoothly and enjoy healthy growth. If one of them is feeble, the other becomes weak as well. Suppose there is excessive demand for goods and services but not enough supply. Then production, and hence the living standard, will be limited to the level of supply. This is the main problem in the Third World.

On the other hand, suppose there is plenty of supply but not enough demand. Then total output will be limited to the level of demand, for businesses cannot produce more than they can sell. This is the main trouble in advanced economies today. Thus, for healthy output growth, demand and supply should be in proper balance. A bird cannot fly on one wing alone.

For wages to rise with productivity, the demand for local labor should rise faster than its supply. In the days of automation, this is possible only if new products are discovered and produced at home, so that the victims of downsizing can find lucrative jobs in emerging industries. This is how the United States enjoyed rising real wages for 19 straight decades after independence.

Consumption-driven trade deficits slash the local demand for labor. The deficit itself reflects a demand–supply imbalance; that is, national demand exceeds national production, so that the difference is met by excessive imports. In this case, the national demand for labor falls in proportion to the deficit. As a consequence, real wages must be lower. The demand–supply balance at home calls for balanced trade—neither deficit nor surplus.

DOMESTIC VERSUS FOREIGN COMPETITION

Competition is necessary among firms to induce them to produce high-quality goods at affordable prices. As an extreme example, let us assume that only one company produces all the cars in a nation. This is the case of a pure monopoly, where only one firm has control over the entire industry. When an auto giant has no competition, it is clear that first the producer will charge a very high price—in fact, the highest that customers can pay. Second, the product will be of poor quality and offer little choice. Auto workers will be rude to their captive customers. In fact, the workers themselves will be underpaid because the producer will not have to compete for their services with other companies. In short, with a pure monopoly, there are low-quality but over-priced goods, along with underpaid workers and irritated customers.

Such was the case in the Soviet Union and, until recently, with some industries in Britain, where public utilities were pure monopolies. The phone service in India, one of the worst in the world, is a monopoly.

The opposite of monopoly is intense competition. When an industry has a large number of companies, there is extreme competition among them. In this case, businesses compete with each other for workers and customers. Therefore, wages are high, production quality is superb, prices are reasonable, and customers are satisfied. *High competition, therefore, produces a prosperous, low-inequality economy.*

The main source of inequality in the world are the lofty profits that arise in industries with paltry competition. In general, the smaller the number of firms, the lower the competition within the industry and the higher the prices and profits. Inequality is also then exorbitant.

Governments should encourage high competition in most industries. This may be done through antitrust laws, through temporary subsidies to generate new firms, or both. Mergers should never be permitted among giant firms, especially where a corporation seeks to acquire another through borrowed funds. Even in a shrinking industry, giant firms should not be allowed to merge. They will choke competition and eventually harm consumers and workers. Some faltering companies seek a merging partner in order to survive. This should be permitted if intense competition still remains. Otherwise, the government should help a wobbly firm temporarily with low-interest loans, to be paid back after the borrower becomes profitable. This is how Chrysler survived in the 1980s and emerged as a strong corporation in the 1990s.

Although there are few pure monopolies in the world today, there are many regional monopolies. A corporation is a regional monopoly if it controls at least a third of the market. Pure monopolies are, of course, the worst for an economy, but regional monopolies (some call them oligopolies) can also cause havoc. General Motors has been a regional monopoly for a long time. That is why, even now, the U.S. auto industry has trouble competing with the auto companies of Japan and Germany. The U.S. auto industry is not as productive as others, even though foreign companies like Nissan, Toyota, Honda, BMW, and Mercedes Benz are producing cars in the United States. The government policy should be such that no company has a strong influence over the market price. Otherwise, the government should help set up new firms or break up the regional monopolies into two or more companies, as was done with AT&T in 1982.

Competition is by far the most critical force in raising a country's prosperity and in eradicating poverty. The origin of competition, however, can be domestic or foreign, and the two have disparate effects on industries. In both cases, companies have to respond to the challenge of rivals to survive, but the nature of this challenge is more important than the incentives it creates.

Within limits, foreign rivalry is a positive factor. But it can also be destructive, especially if it comes from producers in low-wage countries. *The best form of foreign competition springs from foreign rivals located on your own soil.* When foreign corporations produce goods in your country, they not only bring capital and new technology with them, they also generate new jobs and boost the demand for workers. This in turn tends to raise wages.

The best form of foreign competition thus comes from foreign investment. However, competition coming from foreign trade can demolish a country's economy if it causes a shrinkage of manufacturing. If imports lead to deindustrialization, then foreign competition is destructive and harmful to the country.

America has lost its economic edge over the world because its manufacturing has shriveled. Mounting competition from abroad has destroyed many manufacturing jobs, whereas rising exports of service goods have created millions of service jobs. But the net effect has been extremely negative because high-wage jobs have been replaced by low-wage "McJobs."

When manufacturing moves out of one country and into another, a hollowing-out of industry occurs. This is now happening in Western Europe and Japan as well. Many companies are moving production overseas to Eastern Europe and Asia. If this trend continues, other G-7 nations will go down the same way the United States has. In fact, they are already in trouble.

However, domestic competition poses no dangers. Import competition can decimate a local industry, but domestic competition normally has no such effect. Take the case of the television industry, which is now extinct in the United States. When inexpensive imports flooded the U.S. market, some TV manufacturers went bankrupt. Workers who were laid off could not find similar jobs with another TV manufacturer because all domestic firms were sinking. These workers could find work only in service industries at meager salaries.

But suppose domestic competition among American TV manufacturers had increased because another firm had decided to make TVs in America. Some existing firms would have lost ground, as occurs with any increased competition, but the fired workers would have found jobs with the new firm. The industry would have flourished. When cheap imports come in, jobs are created abroad, not in the home economy. However, domestic competition generates good jobs and quality production at home.

What encourages domestic rivalry is competitive protectionism, which the United States followed until the 1930s. When a large number of companies, secure behind tariff walls, struggle against each other to attract customers at home, then the state policy may be called competitive protectionism. In this case, the nation enjoys all the advantages of intense competition without the potential devastation of import competition. This was the secret of American success in the past and of Japan's rise since World War II.

America abandoned its winning formula and switched to what may be called monopolistic free trade, where mergers at home create regional monopolies, which are then exposed to foreign rivals. This is a recipe for self-destruction. Mergers decimate a company's efficiency and competitiveness, as happened to auto and electronics industries in the 1960s. There were only four auto producers in America in the 1960s—GM, Ford, Chrysler, and American Motors. In Japan, there were nine in a much smaller market—Toyota, Nissan, Honda, Subaru, Mitsubishi, Isuzu, and Suzuki, among others. As Harvard Business Professor Michael Porter explains in *The Competitive Advantage of Nations:* "The domestic market, not foreign markets, led industry development in the vast majority of Japanese industries. Only later did exports become significant."[12]

According to Porter, domestic rivalry is perhaps the best spark for industrial efficiency. In his words:[13]

Nations with leading world positions often have a number of strong local rivals, even in small countries such as Switzerland and Sweden. . . .

These examples belie the notion that world leadership grows out of one or two firms who reap economies of scale in the home market. . . .

Rivalry among a group of domestic competitors is different from and often takes forms far more beneficial to the nation than rivalry with foreign firms.

History shows that every nation that adopted competitive protectionism thrived. Such winners include all G-7 nations in the 19th century, modern Japan, South Korea, Malaysia, Taiwan, and, yes, Mexico. From 1940 to 1970, Mexico shielded its domestic industries from foreign competition, but within the country, there was a large number of competing companies. This policy generated what some have called the Mexican miracle, where real GDP growth routinely exceeded 7 percent per year. Between 1955 and 1970, the real wage grew at an annual rate of 5.5 percent, compared to negative wage growth since then.[14]

Trouble began when Mexico borrowed heavily from American banks and its state officers used a part of the funds to buy small companies and create regional monopolies. Competitive protectionism then turned into monopolistic protectionism, which is, of course, the worst type of commercial policy, worse even than monopolistic free trade. When free traders condemn tariffs, they in fact point to the monopolistic protectionism of India, Mexico, Brazil, and Argentina, among others. This type of protectionism is, of course, self-destructive, but that is not what I recommend.

Competitive protectionism is a combination of high tariffs and robust antitrust or antimonopoly measures. This policy has a proven record of great success for every country that tried it.

Monopolistic free trade, by contrast, has a record of failure. Its patrons, Britain, America, Canada, and Australia, have all suffered from falling real wages or rising unemployment since the early 1970s. In fact, all G-7 nations now have monopolistic free trade, and this is one reason for their mounting troubles.

MAXIMUM PRODUCTION WITH MINIMUM POLLUTION

Economic policy should generate maximum output with minimum pollution. Competitive protectionism does that; free trade, monopolistic or competitive, does not. In today's world of soaring intraindustry trade, trade liberalization simply adds to global pollution without increasing production. Hundreds of ships crisscross the oceans every year, transporting raw materials from America and Canada to Japan and then bringing them back to North America in the form of finished goods. If Japan wants to participate in American markets, it makes more sense, for global efficiency and environmental health, that Japan utilize U.S. raw materials to produce goods on U.S. soil. This will avoid the destruction of the seas in which oil is frequently dumped and spilled by cargo ships and tankers.

Japanese output of cars, TVs, and electronics sold in America will still be the same, but the environment will be in better shape. American consumers will still enjoy goods from Japan, but the global atmosphere will be cleaner. Free foreign investment, but not free foreign trade, will ensure this happy outcome.

If goods were produced near population centers, a lot of global transportation would become unnecessary. We could curtail the demand for oil and free up capital to produce other goods with greater usefulness. Oil prices will fall, and the production of basic necessities will rise.

Today, Boeing produces nuts in one country, wings in another, frame in yet another, and then transports these parts for assembly in Seattle. This does not enhance Boeing's output; it only lowers wages for American workers and creates a lot of pollution. Government policy should be such that transportation needs are minimized so that the same amount of global production can occur with less pollution and less use of oil. Competitive protectionism, along with free foreign investment will ensure that.[15] I will return to this point shortly.

PRINCIPLES OF TAXATION

Now let's turn to some basic principles of taxation.

The tax structure should be simple and easy to administer. Complexity is one of the chief flaws of the tax system in the United States, where even the experts find the tax laws difficult to comprehend. Thousands of rules and regulations govern a wide variety of levies and circumstances. The system must be simplified.

One Republican idea of simplification is a flat tax that would eliminate the progressive bands of tax rates. One rate would apply to all levels of income. But progressiveness is not the cause of the system's complexity, which derives mostly from the myriad definitions of income, depreciation, whether or not you live abroad for a while, your age, self-employment, personal exemptions, dependents, divorce, widowhood, refunds, credits, and so on and so forth. A flat tax would not simplify the system at all. Everyone would still have to estimate taxable income, and that is where the system becomes intractable.

The tax system should be fair to everyone. Those who can afford it should pay taxes in proportion to the benefits they receive from the government. The main function of the state is to protect our lives, liberty, and property. Life and liberty are equally dear to everyone, but we differ in the amount of our income and wealth. In other words, wealthy individuals and corporations receive far more from the government in the form of income and wealth protection; hence, they should pay a higher percentage of their earnings. That is why a progressive tax system is generally considered fair and equitable.

The tax system should be efficient so that it maximizes real wages and economic growth. Workers' real earnings should rise with their productivity, which depends on savings and capital formation. America's savings, economic growth, and real wages were the highest in times of a sharply progressive tax system. The same was true with all G-7 countries, as well as Australia and Spain. Clearly, the fairness and growth aspects of taxation are in harmony with each other.

The tax system should minimize pollution to preserve the environment. To achieve a certain amount of revenue, taxes that reduce the stench in the air are preferable to those that have no such effect. For instance, a gasoline tax that discourages the use of oil is preferable to, say, an excise tax on tires.

AN ECONOMIC PLAN FOR THE UNITED STATES

Almost all our economic ills arise from a distorted tax system, which, on the one hand, is a heavy burden on the poor, the middle class, and the self-employed, and, on the other, spares foreign manufacturers altogether from any import duties. In order to revive our economy, we need to spark our manufacturing and raise domestic demand. The following changes are recommended:

1. Corporate taxes should be raised from a 10 percent tax share to the 25 percent level that prevailed in the 1950s and 1960s, when America had the best growth record after World War II.

2. To simplify the tax structure and to remove its various loopholes, the corporate income tax should be replaced by a revenue tax. Today, corporate incomes are taxed at rates varying from 35 percent to 38 percent, but there are so many loopholes that most companies pay a much smaller fraction to the Treasury. In 1950, corporations paid 49 percent of their profits to the federal government; in 1995, they paid only 26 percent, almost half of the earlier figure.

A revenue tax, levied in a progressive manner, would remove all the loopholes, tax disputes, and complexities. A 5 percent to 10 percent tax on the revenue would raise enough funds to raise the corporate tax share to the level prevailing in the 1950s. The largest companies should pay 10 percent of their sales, whereas small companies with sales of $500 million or less may pay a 5 percent tax. The revenue tax will then be like the cost of doing business. Companies such as retailers that have large expenses for inventories may be taxed on their net revenue, or gross sales minus cost of inventories.

In 1994, corporate revenue equaled $3,258 billion. An average revenue tax of 8 percent would have generated federal receipts of $260 billion, instead of the $140 billion that the companies actually paid.[16] Since corporations earned $526 billion that year, a tax liability of $260 billion would have amounted to 49.4 percent, about what they paid in 1950.

3. The top-income-bracket tax rates should be raised to the levels of the 1960s, the decade with the best postwar growth performance. Today, a couple with a taxable income above $256,500 pays the maximum rate of 39.6 percent. This should be left unchanged, because it is close to the 1960s rate applicable to equivalent income today.

A couple with an annual income exceeding $400,000, however, should pay a marginal rate of 50 percent, and another couple with income above $1 million should pay the 70 percent rate. This will bring us to the same progressive tax structure that we had in the 1960s.

4. In 1960, Social Security contributed only 16 percent to federal receipts; in 1995, its burden was an intolerable 36 percent. This tax, the most regressive levy in America, needs to be cut by more than half. It should be cut to 3.5 percent for an individual and to 7 percent for the self-employed. In 1995, this tax cut would have shaved $272 billion off the federal revenue. But this can be easily made up from other proposed changes, as we shall soon see.

5. To achieve the growth rate of the 1960s, the level of imports and trade has to be lowered to the level prevailing in that decade. The trade/GDP ratio, at 23 percent today, was around 10 percent in the mid-1960s, about the same as in the 1920s. An average tariff rate of 40 percent, which prevailed at the time on most manufactured goods, should be ideal today. Labor-intensive products such as textiles and shoes should have lower tariffs than others such as machine tools, automobiles, computers, and electronics, so that the average rate is 40

percent. The same type of customs structure prevailed in the 1920s. Raw materials and oil should be spared from the tariff. We are not likely to attract foreign investment in labor-intensive sectors in spite of the tariff; a high tariff in these areas will not be as productive as in capital-intensive industries.

The tariff will cut our manufactured imports in half, from $550 billion in 1995 to $225 billion. An average tariff of 40 percent will then raise $90 billion. This will be the minimum collection from customs duties, because most likely a 40 percent tariff today would work like a 20 percent rate in the past. In view of dramatic reductions in transportation costs, trade barriers no longer restrain imports as much as they did in the past.

6. The income tax on self-employment earnings should also be changed to a revenue tax, to simplify the system. A graduated tax rate of 5 percent over revenue exceeding $50,000 will be equivalent to today's income tax liability. For instance, a small businessowner with a gross revenue of $200,000 would pay 5 percent of $150,000, or $7,500, as income tax.

This system should apply to all the self-employed except doctors, lawyers, and consultants, who should use the current system and pay the income tax rates proposed above. This group of workers has fewer costs and its revenue approximates its net income.

7. The hourly minimum wage should be raised from $4.25 in April 1996 to $6.00, which, in terms of current prices, prevailed in the 1960s. With wages lagging productivity, this is one of the best cures for inadequate demand and high inequality.

8. A panel of experts should be appointed to simplify the individual income tax system *without* sacrificing its progressive nature because, without tax progression, savings, consumer demand, investment spending, and growth all plummet.

POSSIBLE OBJECTIONS TO THE TAX PLAN

The tax plan suggested above represents a major overhaul of the system and is likely to invite harsh criticism from many quarters. Let me anticipate and tackle them one by one.

1. Conservative economists and politicians will attack the progressive traits of the above plan. They will accuse me of being a socialist and an enemy of free enterprise, bent on destroying savings, work incentives, and capital formation. These objections can be easily brushed aside. If we want the growth rates of the 1960s, we have to adopt the tax policies of the 1960s. It is as simple as that.

In the late 1960s, the top-income-bracket tax rate was 70 percent, the corporate tax share was 25 percent, and, in spite of all the loopholes, the effective income tax rate on lofty incomes was above 60 percent. In the 1950s, on the other hand, the top effective tax rate was over 70 percent, and that is one reason why the United States had an annual growth rate of 4 percent compared to the lowly 1.7 percent in the 1990s.

2. Some may suggest that my tax plan will jeopardize the Social Security system by eliminating the trust fund. First, the fund is empty now. It has little cash, just billions of dollars of IOUs from the federal government, which is itself in hock by $5 trillion. Second, my plan is revenue neutral. The revenue loss from the cut in the Social Security tax would be $272 billion. But the plan would raise an extra $120 billion from corporations.

It would also raise an extra $80 billion from wealthy individuals, whose tax rates would rise substantially. In 1992, affluent couples with incomes above $500,000 paid an average tax rate of 26 percent, and an actual tax equaling $72.3 billion.[17] If my proposals were in effect that year, their average tax rate would have been 50 percent and their tax bill an extra $67 billion. Since their incomes went up at least 20 percent by 1995, their tax liability in 1995 would be an additional $80 billion.

With $90 billion coming from new tariffs, the revenue loss of $272 billion from cuts in payroll taxes would be easily made up from revenue gains from corporations, wealthy individuals, and duties on foreign goods. Hence, Social Security and other social programs would not be jeopardized by my tax proposals. In fact, my plan would offer a tax cut totalling $182 billion to at least 95 percent of Americans without adding to the budget deficit.

3. Another objection will come from free traders. As we impose tariffs, so will other countries, and our exports will tumble proportionately with our imports. There could be a trade war.

A trade war cannot hurt a nation with a trade deficit like ours. Let us take the extreme case in which we import nothing but oil in exchange for our farm goods. In 1995, our trade deficit in nonfarm goods and services was about $140 billion; exports equaled about $600 billion and imports $740 billion. If a trade war escalates to a point where our nonfarm exports and imports fall to zero, then our companies will lose all their foreign business worth $600 billion, but they will gain all our domestic business, currently going abroad, worth $740 billion. Therefore, in the worst-case scenario of zero nonfarm trade, our companies will have a net gain of $140 billion, which equals our nonfarm, non-oil trade deficit.

The national output will then rise by the same amount. Since every $54,000 of GDP creates one good job, the worst-case scenario will generate 2.6 million net American jobs. In the best case, where we may actually have a small trade surplus as in the 1920s, the job gain would be larger. America should not fear a trade war.

Who would we sell our exports to? To ourselves, as we did all through our history until the late 1960s, with lower rates of unemployment than today. Global tariffs will have minimal business disruption today, because 70–80 percent of our trade is in similar products. We export cars and also import them; we export tractors and also buy them from abroad. Brand names are different, but the products bought and sold are the same.

4. What about goods that we don't produce in America anymore—TVs, VCRs, radios, consumer electronics? The U.S. market is still the most lucrative in the world. The moment we announce our intention to impose high tariffs, U.S. and foreign companies will rush to move their factories back onto American soil to avoid customs duties. The threat of tariffs and the devaluation of the dollar have already attracted many foreign companies to the United States. Sony, BMW, Toyota, Mercedes Benz, and Honda, among many others, have opened plants in America, and tariffs would hasten the process. Recall

that, in the 19th century, our tariff-driven economy attracted far more foreign investment than today.

With factories relocated back home, tariffs would not restrain competition for our own firms, which would still have to face the challenge of home-based foreign companies.

If, for some reason, foreign companies fail to move some of their plants to the United States, then we would have to invoke our antitrust laws and break up the regional monopolies to create competition at home. Companies have been split in America before with great success. AT&T, Standard Oil, U.S. Shoe, among others, have been broken up in the past to preserve domestic competition.[18] The same should be done if tariffs threaten to choke business rivalry at home. But most likely we will not have to use this weapon.

5. Could tariffs hurt our consumers and raise inflation? No. Throughout American history, consumer prices fell in high-tariff decades. American tariffs raised domestic supply much more than demand, so that prices had to fall. The relentless rise in prices is a disease of the post-WWII U.S. economy, in which trade has soared. In the past, prices rose mostly during wars, and then fell in the aftermath. Furthermore, in my tax plan, any price rise from the tariff would be more than offset by a huge cut in the payroll and self-employment tax rates that affect everyone. The consumer cannot possibly suffer. In fact, the consumer, being the worker as well, would benefit a great deal from a jump in real wages resulting from the elimination of the trade deficit and from the Social Security tax cuts.

VAST BENEFITS OF THE TAX PLAN

I have already noted some benefits of the tax plan. But there are others.

1. The tariff would redirect American demand away from foreign goods and toward home goods. As imports fall, domestic manufacturing will hum again. The trade deficit will be

immediately eliminated, and at least 2.6 million new manufacturing jobs will be created. A sharp pickup in labor demand will first raise real wages in manufacturing, and those workers who have been migrating to services since 1980 will go back to their old jobs. This will create labor shortages in services, raising their wages as well.

2. As foreign and U.S. multinationals rush their plants to America, manufacturing jobs will expand further. New American inventions will be translated into production inside America, thereby absorbing all those who may be downsized today and in the future. With high tariffs, it will no longer be profitable for companies to bring vast quantities of foreign goods to America, because now they will have to pay a sizable tax on them. And whatever comes in will generate revenue, so that other taxes could be reduced.

In the auto industry, foreign production in existing U.S.-based plants will pick up immediately, and the trade deficit in this product will soon disappear.

3. As real wages rise, poverty and inequality will fall. Once the American manufacturing potential is unleashed, there will be a revival of optimism, and some of the social ills will recede.

4. Payroll and self-employment tax cuts will boost domestic demand and spur investment in spite of higher taxes on corporations. Remember that no one would risk money on an investment project without the assurance of a ready market. Rising demand and investment will raise GDP growth.

5. As the high-productivity manufacturing sector expands at the expense of the low-productivity service sector, productivity growth will climb, further spurring GDP growth.

6. We know from the persistent trade deficits that U.S. domestic demand outpaces domestic production. As imports and then exports tumble, exporters will sell their products to Americans earning rising wages. Exporters will no longer need to cut wages to sell their products to low-wage countries. Therefore, in spite of falling exports, real wages will rise in export industries as well.

7. Social Security tax cuts will boost the rate of saving. Savings will enable people to afford down payments for homes, spurring the demand for housing. The rate of home ownership, which has been falling since the early 1980s, will expand, and so will the industries connected to it—appliances, furniture, decorations, carpets.

8. Higher GDP growth will generate high tax revenue growth. Our budget deficit will vanish. The so-called entitlement crisis of today will become a memory of the bad old days. We do need to eliminate waste and fraud from the social safety net that the state offers to the needy, but there is no reason to alter the system. This is because the growth of government spending has been meager since 1980. The paltry tax growth due to low GDP growth is primarily responsible for the persistent federal deficit.

9. As trade plummets globally, the need for oil will fall. Oil prices will sink, and much of the world will see faster GDP growth. Sea and sky pollution will also then abate without any cut in global production.

All the country has to do is to try the proven formula of the 1960s—progressive income taxation along with low trade.

A PLAN FOR OTHER ADVANCED ECONOMIES

The medicine for the European Union and Canada is the same as that for the American illness. All the common market countries should raise tax collection from their corporations and wealthy individuals, while giving tax breaks to the poor and the self-employed. This is the only way to spur domestic demand and enable small businesses to create jobs. They should also create more flexibility in the hiring and firing of workers. If a business cannot lay off workers when economic conditions demand, it will be reluctant to hire them during an upturn.

The 15 members of the European Union (EU) will have to act in concert, so that the same tax policies prevail everywhere. In addition, they should consider shifting taxes from local goods to foreign goods. Britain, for instance, has a 17 percent value-added tax (VAT) on local goods but very low taxes on imports. It would be better to cut this tax in half and impose, say, a 20 percent tariff on imports from EU countries. This notion, of course, contradicts the current concept of a trade union. However, our objective should not be trade but a high living standard with minimum pollution. If the VAT is partly replaced by tariffs, then the same or a better lifestyle can be attained in a healthier environment. The idea is to encourage the location of factories near demand centers, and cut the wastage of capital and pollution in transportation of goods across Europe. Being a trade-deficit nation, Britain has more demand than domestic production, so it will attract more foreign investment. Spain would also profit from the tariff.

Here again, the EU members should act in concert and approve a uniform 20 percent tariff on each other's exports while trimming other consumption taxes. Since they are exporting and importing more or less the same products, there will be only minor business disruptions, especially when consumption taxes are cut at the same time.

The EU should also impose an average 40 percent tariff on imports from the United States and other countries. The revenue should be used to trim Social Security taxes, because these are among the levies most responsible for mounting unemployment. The tariffs would arrest the growing deindustrialization of the European Union and keep factories from relocating to low-wage areas. Similarly, Canada and America should impose a 20 percent tariff on each other's products, but a 40 percent tariff on the products of other countries.

True, my plan calls for sweeping changes in the current system, but the price of inaction, as in the 1930s, is Nazism, which is already raising its ugly head in Europe. Columnist Mark Hunter, writing on April 21, 1996, is duly alarmed by the disturbing trend:[19]

A page of history has turned: For the first time since World War II a wave of aggressively nationalist, extreme right parties have swept into municipal, regional, national and European parliament offices from the English Channel to the edge of the former Soviet empire . . . . In election after election, this hard right—which calls the traditional right soft—is proving its power to survive and grow, pushing its roots deeper and deeper.

We must take timely action, before the current quiet depression generates another catastrophe like the rise of fascism.

Japan

The remedies suggested above would be only modestly effective in Japan, which still has a progressive tax system and is not suffering from deindustrialization. Its real problem is a feeble demand base at home, for which its exorbitantly expensive housing is mostly to blame.

Affordable housing is the main source of demand in a developed economy. This is because a home buyer also needs to buy many other products. Japan should launch an all-out assault on its troubled housing industry, especially through a housing tax credit. I have recently tackled this subject in another book, *Japan: The Return to Prosperity*, where I offer detailed solutions.[20]

A PLAN FOR THE THIRD WORLD

Much of the Third World today has dual economies, in which rural and urban areas manifest dramatically different lifestyles. The urban sector is extremely small relative to the village economy. Nevertheless, with exploding populations, the smallish city sector has millions of people.

City dwellers tend to be literate factory workers who are generally richer than villagers living in huts, filth, and gripping poverty. Even within cities, there is incredible inequality, with mansions surrounded by slums, skyscrapers and five-star hotels coexisting with squalor. Multimillionaires and billionaires live among homeless masses surviving on a subsistence diet and minimal income.

Technologically, the rural sector uses obsolete techniques inherited from the Middle Ages, while the urban regions boast some of the most advanced, modern, capital-hungry methods of production. In China, Indonesia, and India, a small section of rocket scientists may work alongside a teeming mass of farmers using bullocks and ploughs.[21]

Economic development in the bulk of the Third World has been extremely one-sided and bypassed the vast majority of people. Some countries, such as Thailand and Indonesia, have recently grown at a fast pace, but mostly with the help of foreign investment, which brings little improvement in living conditions for the locals.

The rural areas, hosting as much as 80 percent of the population, need clean water, sewage facilities, brick houses, literacy, electricity, and healthcare. Instead, foreign plants produce cars, Coca-Cola, carpets, Nike shoes, and computer parts, mostly for export to the First World of Europe and North America.

The model of development that some of the fastest growing developing countries have followed is this: Invite multinational companies from G-7 countries to use their low-paid workers and produce goods for export to the United States. Indonesia, Malaysia, China, and the Philippines have enjoyed high GDP growth rates in the 1990s. But they also have mountains of foreign debt, for which they have to make huge interest payments every year. Their growth relies crucially on trade surpluses with the United States.

In Table 12.2, look at the U.S. trade balance with the highly indebted countries, all of which have grown faster than the United States in the 1990s. Except for Argentina, the United States has a negative balance, or trade deficit, with every nation. A development model in which multinationals are invited to dump low-wage production primarily into the United States cannot succeed for long. How long can American workers be expected to sacrifice real wages before they revolt against the whole system?

The vicious circle that piles foreign debt on the Third World in spite of impressive growth and export earnings is

TABLE 12.2   U.S. trade balance with highly indebted developing countries: 1994/1995.

Country	Trade Balance (millions)
Indonesia	$ −3,712
China	−29,494
Pakistan	−293
Venezuela	−4,337
Brazil	−590
Philippines	−1,830
India	−3,005
Thailand	−5,446
Mexico	−15,400
Argentina	2,741
Malaysia	−7,012

Source: *Statistical Abstract of the United States,* 1995, U.S. Department of Commerce, Washington, DC, pp. 819–822.

fundamentally unstable, not just for the developing countries, but also for America. In order for the bankers to recover their loans, America must have deficient trade with the low-income countries, leading to further U.S. deindustrialization. If America tried to correct its trade imbalance through tariffs, the Third World economies would be devastated. (But this can easily be offset with debt forgiveness, as we shall see.) Since the 1970s, America's loss has been the gain of other countries, but this cannot continue. In fact, this system hurts the poor and the middle class in both regions. The masses in low-income nations are as poor as ever, while real wages tumble in the United States. The only beneficiaries are the rich in America and in the developing economies—the bankers and executives of the multinationals.

The Third World masses also suffer from pervasive corruption and regional monopolies that pay pennies per hour in wages while pocketing millions in profits. Is there a comprehensive economic plan that would raise the real wages of the

American worker while relieving the Third World masses of poverty and official decadence?

I believe there is. The First World should forgive the foreign debt of the Third World in exchange for the purge of corrupt officials and the breakup of the monopolies into smaller companies. We should invite the Third World governments to file bankruptcy petitions in the World Court. The bankers should collect what is normal in Chapter 11 filings, something like 10 cents on the dollar, and let the system start anew.

The Third World has already paid more money in interest charges than the original amount of the loans. The banks have also made billions in fees. The system victimizes not just the Third World masses but also the American workers. Therefore, debt forgiveness will be a win–win proposition around the globe.

Corrupt officials in developing countries must be purged. They should at least be removed from their posts and, if possible, prosecuted for graft. At the same time, regional monopolies should be split into many smaller units and begin competing with each other. The next step is to grant them tariff protection. This way, the developing world will be able to follow the proven developmental model of competitive protectionism, and the competing firms will turn their attention to local needs. The precious resources of local capital and the environment will then be used to alleviate the suffering of the masses.

The First World will also benefit from this plan, because it will not have to endure persistent trade deficits that lead to deindustrialization. Manufacturing will be preserved in all parts of the planet, and balanced development will occur everywhere.

When monopolies are broken up from Mexico to Argentina, from India to Thailand, corruption, decadence, and inequality will fade away and living conditions will improve for the vast majority of people. The rich will also benefit in the end, because they will no longer be surrounded by an ocean of hostile humanity.

Debt forgiveness is not as radical as it sounds. It has been done a few times before. In the 1930s, desperate Latin American countries repudiated their external obligations, and were forgiven by lending banks and governments within a decade. In fact, they were given a fresh start with new loans after the war.

In the 1980s, with the Third World in the throes of another debt trap, many economists suggested debt forgiveness as a way out of the crisis. That was when the world's largest banks in America, Europe, and Japan were heavily involved in Third World loans.

In 1989, Treasury Secretary Nicholas Brady supported a debt reduction plan, including partial forgiveness. Multinational banks were reluctant to go along, but the secondary market price of the debt was already down to 30 cents of its face value. Finally, the banks cooperated, and Mexico and Brazil were able to reduce their obligations by about 10 percent.

The Brady plan made a modest start, but it also set a precedent. Today, multinational banks have much less exposure to developing country loans, of which about a third are with international agencies such as the World Bank and the International Monetary Fund. As Professor Krugman points out, "The total value of all loans to troubled debtors is less than 1 percent of the wealth of the creditor nations; the debt service on those loans less than 1 quarter of 1 percent of the national incomes of the creditors."[22]

In early 1996, the World Bank forgave about $2 billion of external obligations of sub-Saharan Africa, the poorest region in the world. *New York Times* columnist Peter Passell remarks: "Debt forgiveness alone would not open the door to growth in heavily indebted poor countries with wretched domestic economic policies. But it is a start—and apparently the current inclination of official leaders."[23]

In fact, it is a promising start; but the "wretched domestic economic policies," along with official corruption, have to be purged at the same time. Here also there are signs of fresh thinking among the nations involved in foreign aid as well as private investment in developing countries. In April 1996, the richest nations took a giant step to fight corruption in international business deals. They agreed that bribes to foreign officials would no longer be tax deductible. David Aaron, a U.S. representative at the Paris-based Organization for Economic Cooperation and Development, says, "This is a sea change, a very important step in breaking the international chain of corruption. It takes governments out of the business of subsidizing corruption by giving tax breaks for bribery."[24]

This indeed is an important first step, but it also confirms the existence of an axis between foreign investment and corrupt administrations in developing countries. Morally as well as legally, those who offer bribes are just as culpable in crime as the recipients. One may reasonably ask at this point: Why should the destitute masses of the Third World be responsible for sanctioning the decadent practices of private foreign lenders and their own elites? This is exactly what they would be doing by honoring obligations in which they had no say. Similarly, the governments of rich nations are morally bound to withdraw legal protection from those who have aided and abetted graft in foreign countries.

No G-7 government openly tolerates kickbacks inside its own borders. Why then should that crime be tolerated overseas? Fortunately, the United States is taking a lead to outlaw bribes in future aid and loan dealings. The Organization of American States (OAS) adopted the "Inter-American Convention Against Corruption" in March 1996.[25] But the antibribery campaign should be extended to past episodes of greased palms as well. This means that all or a substantial part of the Third World debt should be forgiven, especially when it would also benefit the First World economies.

In exchange, of course, the Third World must follow the path of competitive protectionism, purge corrupt officials, and break up its monopolies. Otherwise, the fresh start provided by debt forgiveness would be all for naught, and the masses will remain destitute. If some banks get into trouble, the donor governments may divert a part of foreign aid to rescue them.

Debt forgiveness may be phased out over five years to mini-mize the annual impact on large banks. Governments should also alter regulations, permitting banks to write off the Third World debt without a charge against their capital and earn-ings. Once the public realizes that debt forgiveness is ethical, as well as a win–win proposition for all involved countries, it will become politically feasible, especially when large multi-national banks no longer have the same loan exposure as before.

EPILOGUE

"It was 50 years ago when," according to Jeff Faux, the Presi-dent of the Economic Policy Institute, "a headline in the *Wall Street Journal* proclaimed, 'GOP Plan: Cut Taxes, Balance Bud-get, Remove Control from Business.'"[26] So much has changed in America since the end of the Second World War. No longer is the country a global economic leader. Manufacturing shriv-els by the day, while services flourish. The industrial employ-ment share has been cut in half; the persistent trade surplus of that time has turned into a persistent deficit. Trade has soared, the federal government is saddled with a debt of $5 trillion; ultraregressive taxation has replaced the ultrapro-gressive system of the past. The country has gone through many convulsions since the mid-1940s, yet the Republicans have not budged one bit. They still chant the same mantra of cutting income taxes to balance the budget.

Soon after the war, the Democrats at least offered an alter-native view of society, one that was committed to prosperity for all through fair and progressive taxation. Today the De-mocrats have become Republican clones. Both parties are slightly different sides of the same coin. They have joined hands to transfer taxes from foreign goods to local goods and incomes, and then transfer them again from affluent individ-uals and corporations to the poor, the middle class, and the self-employed. The results are now clear for everyone to see.

I have offered an alternative and comprehensive plan in this chapter. It is designed to bring prosperity to the world while minimizing pollution. It works through market forces that require a balance between demand and supply in every economy. It derives from a proven idea that domestic competition is preferable to foreign competition, an idea that, in the past, transformed all agrarian nations into thriving industrial societies. If the status quo persists, then American real wages and family incomes will continue to fall, manufacturing will keep shedding workers, and we will remain in the clutches of the quiet depression that has plagued the world since 1990.

Today America is confused. There are so many competing theories that all seem to make some sense. But the best ideas are those that derive from common sense and are backed by facts. History, not ideology, should decide what measures should be adopted to shake off the stranglehold of obsolete dogmas and revive the elusive American Dream. I have devised my global economic plan with great care, and I am sure you will see nothing but common sense in it.

Notes

Chapter 1

1. John Maynard Keynes, *The General Theory of Employment, Interest, and Money* (London: Macmillan, 1936), p. 383.
2. Ravi Batra, *The Myth of Free Trade* (New York: Macmillan, 1993), pp. 190–192.
3. Andres Oppenheimer, *Bordering on Chaos* (Boston: Little, Brown, 1996). Quoted by Richard Reeves, "Mexico: Nation's Decline Is a Time Bomb for Clinton Campaign," *Dallas Morning News*, April 9, 1996, p. 15A.
4. Ravi Batra, *The Great Depression of 1990*, first edition (Dallas: Venus Books, 1985); second edition published by Simon and Schuster, New York, 1987.
5. Quoted by Susan Feeney, *Dallas Morning News*, April 14, 1996, p. J1 ("Sunday Reader" section).
6. Jill Smolowe, "The Stalled Revolution," *Time*, May 6, 1996, p. 63.
7. Elias Tuma, *European Economic History: Tenth Century to the Present* (New York: Harper & Row, 1971), pp. 359–360. *Also see* Angus Maddison, *Economic Growth in the West* (New York: Twentieth Century Fund, 1952), p. 220.
8. Donald Barlett and James Steele, *America: What Went Wrong* (Kansas City, MO: Andrews and McMeel, 1992). The authors write: "Congress has written the government rule book so that Social Security taxes consume an ever larger share of the weekly paychecks of low and middle-income Americans, while the affluent are exempted from similar increases" (p. 46). *Also see* William Greider, *Who Will Tell the People: The Betrayal of American Democracy* (New York: Simon and Schuster, 1992), Ch. 3.

Chapter 2

1. Richard L. Berke, "Candidates Clash Over Trade Issues Heading Into Vote," *New York Times*, February 20, 1996, p. A1; James Bennet, "Buchanan, Exalted, Pushes Economic Insecurity Theme," *New York Times*, February 22, 1996, p. A1. What prompted Dole's remarks was

the unexpected but temporary surge of another presidential candidate in the primary, Pat Buchanan.

2. Ravi Batra, *The Myth of Free Trade: A Plan for America's Economic Revival* (New York: Charles Scribner's Sons, 1993), Ch. 2. *Also see* Barry Bluestone and Bennett Harrison, *The Deindustrialization of America: Plant Closings, Community Abandonment, and the Dismantling of Industry* (New York: Basic Books, 1992); Paul D. Staudohar and H. E. Brown, *Deindustrialization and Plant Closure* (Lexington, KY: D.C. Heath & Co., 1987); Katherine S. Newman, *Falling from Grace* (New York: The Free Press, 1988); Gary Burtless, *A Future of Lousy Jobs* (Washington, DC: The Brookings Institution, 1990); Wallace Peterson, "The Silent Depression," *Challenge,* July–August 1991, pp. 29–34.

3. Lester Thurow, *The Future of Capitalism: How Today's Economic Forces Shape Tomorrow's World* (New York: William Morrow, 1996), p. 23. *Also see* Donald Barlett and James Steele, *America: What Went Wrong* (Kansas City, MO: Andrews and McMeel, 1992), and Ravi Batra, "The Fallacy of Free Trade II" *Review of International Economics,* vol. 2, February 1994, p. 88. Barlett and Steele write: "The share of the workforce enrolled in a pension plan guaranteed by the Pension Benefit Guarantee Corporation has fallen steadily from 39.4 percent in 1975 to 29.9 percent in 1988." Similarly, the fraction of Americans enjoying hospital benefits rose from 1960 to 1975 and declined thereafter. See *Statistical Abstract of the United States,* 1988, U.S. Department of Commerce, Washington, DC, p. 92.

4. *Statistical Abstract of the United States,* 1995, U.S. Department of Commerce, Washington, DC, p. 383. Even the Clinton Administration recognizes the long-term problem. Joseph Stiglitz, Chairman of the Council of Economic Advisers, concedes that "the anxieties are real. Perhaps that is because of a 20-year period in which real wages have declined." Quoted in David Sanger, "Workplace Fears Disputed in Politically Delicate Study," *New York Times,* April 24, 1996, p. C3.

5. Jerry Jasinowski's views were reported in "Downsizing Fears Not Supported," *Dallas Morning News,* April 19, 1996, p. 11D.

6. *Statistical Abstract,* 1995, op.cit., p. 379. How do we explain the popular perception of American Prosperity under President Reagan? Most people believe that the economy did extremely well when Ronald Reagan was president. His record certainly looks brilliant when compared to what the nation had endured during the term of his predecessor, Jimmy Carter. During the Carter years, the country was demoralized not only from the twin evils of high unemployment and high inflation, but also from the president's constant indecision and foreign policy failures in Iran.

   Before Reagan could put the nation back on the road to prosperity, he had to undo the mess that Carter had created since 1977. During Reagan's eight years, inflation, interest rates, and unemployment fell steadily, and the economy grew at a rapid rate, especially after 1983.

   This is the bright side of Reaganomics. But there is a sordid side as well, one that bequeaths a massive headache to future generations, which are already buried under the weight and culture of deficits that soared after 1980. Moreover, the vast majority of Americans either saw vicarious gains or actually suffered a loss in inflation-adjusted earnings.

7. Allan Sloan, "The Hit Men," *Newsweek,* February 26, 1996, p. 45.

8. Louis Uchitelle and N. R. Kleinfeld, "On the Battlefields of Business, Millions of Casualties," *New York Times,* March 3, 1996, p. A1.

9. Lyle Spencer Jr., *Reengineering Human Resources* (New York: John Wiley, 1993), Ch. 10.

10. G. C. Fite and J. E. Reese, *An Economic History of the United States* (Boston: Houghton Mifflin, 1973), p. 355.

11. Ibid.

12. George J. Church, "Are We Better Off?" *Time,* January 29, 1996, p. 37.

13. Newt Gingrich and Dick Armey, *Contract with America* (New York: Random House, 1994), p. 4.

14. Newt Gingrich, *To Renew America* (New York: HarperCollins, 1995).

15. Paul R. Krugman and Maurice Obstfeld, *International Economics: Theory and Policy,* third edition (New York: HarperCollins, 1994).

16. Quoted in Al Franken, *Rush Limbaugh Is a Big Fat Idiot* (New York: Delacorte Press, 1996), p. 177.

17. Rush Limbaugh, *The Way Things Ought To Be* (New York: Pocket Books, 1993), p. 41.

18. Ibid., p. 41.

19. Karen Tumulty, "Why Subsidies Survive," *Time,* March 25, 1996, p. 46.

20. *Statistical Abstract of the United States,* 1995, U.S. Department of Commerce, Washington, DC, pp. 416 and 424.

21. George Will, "Why Are We Unhappy When We've Never Had It So Good?" *Dallas Morning News,* January 27, 1996, p. 27A.

22. Bob Herbert, "Politics of Meanness," *New York Times,* February 9, 1996, p. A15.

Chapter 3

1. There are many books on the Reagan presidency—its failures as well as its achievements. Notable among these are: John H. Makin and Norman J. Ornstein, *Debt and Taxes* (New York: Random House, 1994); David Stockman, *The Triumph of Politics: How the Reagan Revolution Ended* (New York: Harper & Row, 1986); William Niskanen, *Reaganomics: An Insider's Account* (New York: Oxford University Press, 1985); Paul Craig Roberts, *The Supply-Side Revolution: An Insider's Account of Policymaking in Washington* (Cambridge: Harvard University Press, 1984); Michael Boskin, *Reagan and the Economy* (San Francisco: ICS Press, 1987).

2. *Economic Report of the President,* 1996, The Council of Economic Advisers, Washington, DC, p. 367.

3. John K. Galbraith, *The World Economy Since the Wars: A Personal View* (Boston: Houghton Mifflin, 1994), p. 227.

4. Philip Howard, *The Death of Common Sense: How Law Is Suffocating America* (New York: Warner Books), 1994.

5. The theory of rational expectations is now a standard menu item in most textbooks. Prominent among them are Rudiger Dornbusch and Stanley Fischer, *Macroeconomics* (New York: McGraw-Hill, 1994); Robert B. Carson, *What Economists Know: An Economic Policy Primer for the 1990s and Beyond* (New York: St. Martin's Press, 1990); Roy Ruffin and Paul Gregory, *Principles of Economics* (New York: HarperCollins, 1993); Richard Lipsey and Paul Courant, *Economics* (New York: HarperCollins, 1996).

6. Robert E. Lucas, Jr., *Models of Business Cycles* (Oxford: Basil Blackwell, 1987); *Studies in Business-Cycle Theory* (Cambridge, MA: MIT Press, 1981), Ch. 3.

7. Proponents of this view believed in what is known as the Phillips Curve, named after London School of Economics Professor A. W. Phillips, "The Relation between Unemployment and the Rate of Change of Money Wages in the United Kingdom, 1861–1957," *Economica,* November 1958. The Phillips Curve suggests that there is a trade-off between inflation and unemployment, so that inflation becomes a price for low unemployment. The theory has critics, of whom Milton Friedman and Robert Lucas are the most prominent. Cf. Dornbusch and Fischer, op. cit., p. 480.

8. P. A. Samuelson, "The Gains from International Trade," *Canadian Journal of Economics and Political Science,* 1939, pp. 195–205; reprinted in H. S. Ellis and L. A. Metzler, *Readings in the Theory of International Trade* (Philadelphia: Balkiston, 1949). *Also see* Samuelson, "The Gain from International Trade Once Again," *Economic Journal,* 1962, pp. 820–829.

    Others who believe in unilateral tariff reduction are Milton and Rose Friedman, *Free to Choose: A Personal Statement* (New York: Harcourt Brace Jovanovich, 1990); W. M. Corden, "The Normative Theory of International Trade," in R. W. Jones and P. B. Kenen (editors), *Handbook of International Economics,* Vol. I (New York: North Holland, 1984), Ch. 2. This article contains an extensive bibliography on the gains from trade.

9. Paul Samuelson, "International Trade and the Equalization of Factor Prices," *Economic Journal,* 1948, pp. 165–184, and "International Factor Price Equalization Once Again," *Economic Journal,* 1949, pp. 181–197. Other prominent participants in this controversy are Jagdish Bhagwati, "The Pure Theory of International Trade: A Survey," *Economic Journal,* 1964, pp. 1–78; Murray Kemp, *The Pure Theory of International Trade and Investment* (Englewood Cliffs, NJ: Prentice-Hall, 1969). Also see Ravi Batra, *Studies in the Pure Theory of International Trade* (London: Macmillan, 1973), Ch. 3.

10. Milton and Rose Friedman, op. cit., p. 44; Paul Krugman, *The Age of Diminished Expectations* (Cambridge, MA: MIT Press, 1994).

11. This was the rationale for replacing the tariff with the income tax, via an amendment to the Constitution in 1913. See William Gill, *Trade*

Wars Against America (New York: Praeger, 1990); and Makin and Ornstein, op. cit., Ch. 5.

12. Robert Hall and Alvin Rabushka, *The Flat Tax* (Stanford, CA: Hoover Institution Press), 1995; Dick Armey, "Flat Tax Would End the Confusion," *Dallas Morning News,* April 15, 1995, p. 11A; Henry Aaron and Joseph Pechman, *How Taxes Affect Economic Behavior* (Washington, DC: Brookings Institution, 1981).

13. Martin Feldstein, *Taxes and Capital Formation* (Chicago: University of Chicago Press, 1987); Roger Gordon and Joel Slemrod, "Do We Collect Any Revenue from Taxing Capital Income?" in Lawrence Summers (editor), *Tax Policy and the Economy* (Cambridge, MA: MIT Press, 1988).

14. Hall and Rabushka, op. cit.

15. Paul Samuelson, *Economics* (New York: McGraw Hill, 1976), Ch. 40; David Hyman, *Economics* (Homewood, IL: Irwin, 1991), Ch. 23; Edwin Mansfield and Nariman Behravesh, *Economics* (New York: Norton), Ch. 24.

16. Samuelson, *Economics,* op. cit., pp. 421–429.

17. John Galbraith, *Economics in Perspective: A Critical History* (Boston: Houghton Mifflin, 1987). This book offers a lucid history of many economic ideas.

18. Galbraith, *Economics in Perspective,* op. cit., Chs. 8–10. Dornbusch and Fischer, op. cit.; Carson, op. cit.; Ruffin and Gregory, op. cit.; Lipsey and Courant, op. cit.; Ravi Batra, *The Great Depression of 1990* (New York: Simon and Schuster, 1987), Ch. 6.

19. Ravi Batra, *Surviving the Great Depression of 1990* (New York: Simon and Schuster, 1988), Ch. 17.

20. Charles Kindleberger, *Manias, Panics and Crashes* (New York: Basic Books, 1978); Leonard Ayres, *Turning Points in Business Cycles* (New York: Macmillan, 1939).

21. Galbraith, *Economics in Perspective,* op. cit., Chs. 17 and 18. Professor Galbraith describes how prominent economists were incensed with Keynes for blending practicality with economic theory. *Also see* Robert Lekachman, *The Age of Keynes* (New York: Random House, 1966).

22. Carson, op. cit., Ch. 5.

23. Ravi Batra, *Regular Economic Cycles: Money, Inflation, Regulation and Depressions* (New York: St. Martin's Press, 1990), Ch. 3.

24. In *Models of Business Cycles,* op. cit., Professor Lucas argues that the "decision to model unemployment as voluntary was, and still is, subjected to ignorant political criticism," p. 66. On the next page he continues in the same vein and lumps unemployment together with leisure: "Whether modeling unemployment in a competitive way . . . (and hence lumping unemployment together with 'leisure' and all other non-work activities) is a serious strategic error in trying to account for business cycles. I see no reason to believe that it is." Actually, Lucas borrowed the concept of voluntary unemployment from another Nobel laureate, George Stigler, "The Economics of Information," *Journal of Political Economy,* June 1961, pp. 213–235.

25. N. Gregory Mankiw, "Real Business Cycles: A New Keynesian Perspective," *Journal of Economic Perspectives*, 1989, p. 85.

26. Samuel Morley, *Macroeconomics* (New York: Dryden), p. 167. On p. 138, Morley writes: "It may seem surprising to the reader that unemployment exists in equilibrium. . . . That the reader should keep in mind that the unemployment we are speaking of here is voluntary."

27. Milton Friedman also subscribes to this view. See his "Inflation and Unemployment," in Martin Baily and Arthur Okun (editors), *The Battle Against Unemployment and Inflation* (New York: Norton, 1982), p. 49.

28. "U. S. Economist Wins Nobel Prize," *Reuters News Media*, October 10, 1995.

29. Peter Passell, "A Nobel Award for a University of Chicago Economist, Yet Again," *New York Times*, October 11, 1995, p. C1.

30. "The Downsizing of America," *New York Times*, March 3 to March 10, 1996. The quote is from the March 4 issue, p. A9.

31. Albert Rees, "On Equilibrium in Labor Markets," *Journal of Political Economy*, 1970, p. 308.

32. Quoted in Passell, op. cit.

Chapter 4

1. Jack Kemp, "Lower Taxes, Higher Revenues," *New York Times*, February 11, 1996, p. 15; Dick Armey, "Flat Tax Would End the Confusion," *Dallas Morning News*, April 15, 1996, p. 11A; Nancy Gibbs, "Steve Forbes Has Wrinkled the G.O.P. Race by Spending a Fortune to Push His Flat Tax," *Time*, January 29, 1996, pp. 22–27.

2. Armey, ibid.; Kemp, ibid.; Milton and Rose Friedman, *Free to Choose: A Personal Statement* (New York: Harcourt Brace Jovanovich, 1990), p. 306.

3. *Statistical Abstract of the United States*, 1981, U.S. Department of Commerce, Washington, DC, p. 260.

4. *Statistical Abstract of the United States*, 1995, U.S. Department of Commerce, Washington, DC, p. 379.

5. Thorstein Veblen, *The Theory of the Leisure Class* (New York: Modern Library, 1934). *Also see* John Galbraith, *Economics in Perspective: A Critical History* (Boston: Houghton Mifflin, 1987), pp. 171–176.

6. Donald Barlett and James Steele, *America: What Went Wrong* (Kansas City, MO: Andrews and McMeel, 1992), p. 48. According to the authors: "In 1970, individuals and families with incomes between $500,000 and $1 million paid, on average, $304,408 in combined income and Social Security taxes. By 1989, individuals and families in that income group paid $168,714—or $135,694 less than nineteen years earlier. That amounted to a tax cut of 45 percent."

7. Robert Hall and Alvin Rabuska, *The Flat Tax* (Stanford, CA: Hoover Institution Press, 1995); Newt Gingrich, *To Renew America* (New York: HarperCollins, 1995); Jude Wanniski, "The Mundell-Laffer Hypothesis—A New View of the World Economy," *Public Interest*, No. 39, Spring 1975; John Makin and Norman Ornstein, *Debt and Taxes* (New York: Random House, 1994), Ch. 2.

8. Ravi Batra, *The Great Depression of 1990,* second edition (New York: Simon and Schuster, 1987), Ch. 6. John K. Galbraith, *The World Economy Since the Wars: A Personal View* (Boston: Houghton Mifflin, 1994), Chs. 6 and 7.

9. Rudiger Dornbusch and Stanley Fischer, *Macroeconomics* (New York: McGraw-Hill, 1994), p. 47; Richard Lipsey and Paul Courant, *Economics* (New York: HarperCollins, 1996), p. 444.

10. Hall and Rabuska, op. cit., p. 46. Few people have any choice between work and leisure. Ask the 40,000 employees of AT&T who faced layoffs in January 1996, or the 17,000 workers of GTE Corporation who were laid off in January 1994. These people had no choice except to accept the leisure that was forced on them.

11. William Greider, *Who Will Tell the People: The Betrayal of American Democracy* (New York: Simon and Schuster, 1992), p. 91.

12. Samuel Morley, *Macroeconomics* (New York: Dryden), p. 500.

13. At the time of this writing (April 1996), the Republican leaders continue to demand lower taxes on individual incomes and capital gains, while making no mention of the Social Security taxes, as if such taxes do not lower disposable incomes.

14. Gingrich, op. cit., p. 116.

15. Makin and Ornstein, op. cit., p. 192.

16. Kevin Phillips, *The Politics of Rich and Poor* (New York: Random House, 1996), p. 11.

17. Dick Armey and Newt Gingrich, *Contract with America* (New York: Random House, 1994).

Chapter 5

1. Paul Samuelson, *Economics* (New York: McGraw-Hill, 1976), pp. 164–166; Charles Bastable, *Public Finance* (New York: Macmillan, 1903); Alfred Buehler, *Public Finance* (New York: Macmillan, 1948); Hugh and Baron Dalton, *Principles of Public Finance* (London: Routledge & Sons, 1936); Otto Eckstein, *Public Finance* (Englewood Cliffs, NJ: Prentice-Hall, 1979); Ursula Hicks, *Public Finance* (New York: Pitman, 1947); Harvey Plank, *Public Finance* (Homewood, IL: Irwin, 1953); Earl Rolph, *Public Finance* (New York: Ronald Press, 1961); Carl Shoup, *Public Finance* (Chicago: Aldine Publishing Co., 1969); Richard Musgrave, *Public Finance in Theory and Practice* (New York: McGraw-Hill, 1976).

2. Rush Limbaugh, *The Way Things Ought To Be* (New York: Pocket Books, 1993), Ch. 7; Herbert Stein, *Presidential Economics* (Washington, DC: American Enterprise Institute, 1988); Robert Bartley, *The Seven Fat Years* (New York: The Free Press, 1992).

3. Ravi Batra, *Surviving the Great Depression of 1990* (New York: Simon and Schuster, 1988), Ch. 16.

4. Home ownership per person declined throughout the 1980s. See *Economic Report of the President,* 1996, The Council of Economic Advisers, Washington, DC, p. 339. Modern economies function smoothly through the mechanism of what is aptly called a circular flow in the

system. One side of this circle is *demand,* arising mostly from household spending; the other side is *supply,* stemming from the actions of producers. Households pay money to businesses in exchange for goods and services. Out of that money received, companies pay the same households income in the form of wages, rents, interest, and dividends. This enables the households to purchase goods again in the next round, and so on. This way, the wheel of the economy keeps moving. But if money sits idle in the bank accounts of the rich, or moves primarily into the stock market and does not go to the producers, a shortage of demand occurs in the economy.

5. David Birch, *Job Creation in America* (New York: The Free Press, 1987).

6. Donald Barlett and James Steele, *America: What Went Wrong* (Kansas City, MO: Andrew and McMeel, 1992). A chapter entitled "The Disappearing Pensions" explodes the conservative propaganda about rising pension benefits in America. According to *Statistical Abstract of the United States,* 1995, p. 437, only 39.2 percent of employees enjoyed pension benefits in 1993, and about half of employed workers lacked a group health plan.

Chapter 6

1. Alfred Eckes, *Opening America's Markets: U.S. Foreign Trade Policy Since 1776* (Chapel Hill: North Carolina Press); Robert Hall and Alvin Rabushka, *The Flat Tax* (Stanford, CA: Hoover Institution Press, 1995); John H. Makin and Norman J. Ornstein, *Debt and Taxes* (New York: Random House, 1994).

2. Eckes, op. cit., p. 49.

3. Ravi Batra, *Studies in the Pure Theory of International Trade* (London: Macmillan, 1973), Ch. 3; Jagdish Bhagwati, "The Pure Theory of International Trade," *Economic Journal,* 1964, pp. 1–78. For Ricardo's numerical example, see Dominick Salvatore, *International Economics* (New York: Macmillan, 1993), pp. 37–40.

4. Quoted in Sidney Ratner, *American Taxation* (New York: Norton, 1942), p. 173.

5. James Davidson, William Gienapp, Christine Heyrman, Mark Lytle, and Michael Stoff, *Nation of Nations* (New York: McGraw-Hill, 1990), p. 781.

6. Ibid., pp. 850–851.

7. William Gill, *Trade Wars Against America* (New York: Praeger, 1990), p. 48. Also see Frank Taussig, *The Tariff History of the United States* (New York: Putnam, 1923).

8. Davidson et al., op. cit., p. 855. *Also see* Davis Dewey, *Financial History of the United States* (New York: Longman, 1931).

9. Davidson et al., op. cit., p. 906.

10. Even though the tariff bill of 1930 is famous as "Smoot-Hawley Tariff," the actual title is Hawley-Smoot Tariff Act. Eckes, op. cit., Ch. 4.

11. Paul Krugman, *The Age of Diminished Expectations* (Cambridge, MA: MIT Press, 1994), p. 125.

12. Keynes and his followers also blamed the Hoover-Roosevelt tax rise for transforming a recession into a depression in the United States. Ravi Batra, *The Great Depression of 1990* (New York: Simon and Schuster, 1987), Chs. 6 and 7.

13. Davidson et al., op. cit., p. 1068.

14. This assumption is commonly made in the theory of tariffs. See, for instance, Murray Kemp, *The Pure Theory of International Trade and Investment* (Englewood Cliffs, NJ: Prentice-Hall, 1969), Ch. 4.

15. W. Max Corden, "The Normative Theory of International Trade," in R. W. Jones and Peter Kennen (editors), *Handbook of International Economics,* Vol. I (New York: North Holland), Ch. 2. A good survey of the literature on the gains from trade; offers a nontechnical analysis.

16. Paul Samuelson, "The Gains from International Trade," *Canadian Journal of Economics,* 1939, pp. 195–205; and "The Gains from International Trade Once Again," *Economic Journal,* 1962, pp. 820–829.

17. Richard Caves, *Trade and Economic Structure* (Cambridge, MA: Harvard University Press, 1967), p. 224.

18. Milton and Rose Friedman, *Free to Choose: A Personal Statement* (New York: Harcourt Brace Jovanovich, 1990), p. 39.

19. Ibid., p. 50.

20. *Statistical Abstract of the United States,* 1995, U.S. Department of Commerce, Washington, DC, p. 462. *Also see* Chapter 8.

21. A. Dixit and V. Norman, Theory of International Trade (Cambridge: Cambridge University Press, 1980).

22. Wolfgang Stolper and Paul Samuelson, "Protection and Real Wages," *Review of Economic Studies,* 1941, pp. 58–73.

23. Murray Kemp, op. cit.

24. Sylvia Nasser, "Top 1% Had Greater Net Worth than Bottom 90% of U.S. Households," *New York Times,* April 21, 1992.

25. Paul Krugman and Maurice Obstfeld, *International Economics: Theory and Policy* (New York: HarperCollins, 1994), p. 55.

26. Ibid.

27. Milton and Rose Friedman, op. cit., p. 41.

28. Lincoln is quoted in Eckes, op. cit., p. 33.

29. See the two articles by Paul Samuelson, "International Trade and the Equalization of Factor Prices," *Economic Journal,* 1948, pp. 163–184; and "International Factor-Price Equalization Once Again," *Economic Journal,* 1949, pp. 181–197.

30. Michael Todaro, *Economic Development in the Third World* (New York: Longman, 1977), Ch. 12.

31. Ravi Batra, *The Myth of Free Trade* (New York: Macmillan, 1993), Ch. 6. *Also see* Chapter 9 in the present book.

32. *Historical Statistics of the United States: Colonial Times to 1970,* 1975, U.S. Department of Commerce, Washington, DC, Series D 683, D 726, and D 737. *Also see* Batra, *The Myth of Free Trade,* op. cit., p. 48.

33. *The Economic Report of the President,* 1996, The Council of Economic Advisers, Washington, DC, p. 332.

34. Batra, *The Myth of Free Trade,* Chs. 3, 4, and 5.

35. Bob Davis, "How Buchanan Came to Be a Protectionist," *Wall Street Journal,* February 22, 1996, p. A4.

36. Krugman, op. cit., p. 126.

Chapter 7

1. According to Professor Samuelson, "The tariff may even increase money wages; but it will tend to increase the cost of living by more than the increase in money wages, so that real wages will fall as labor becomes less productive." *Economics* (New York: McGraw-Hill, 1976), p. 694.

   This 1976 statement contradicts Samuelson's earlier contribution with Wolfgang Stolper in 1943, where he argued that the tariff raises the real or inflation-adjusted wage in a nation such as the United States, which imports labor-intensive products from the Third World. See W. Stolper and P. Samuelson, "Protection and Real Wages," *Review of Economic Studies,* 1943, pp. 58–73. *Also see* discussion in Chapter 6.

   When free trade lowers the real wages of 90 percent of the population and raises the real incomes of the other 10 percent (the owners of capital), how can trade be beneficial to the country as a whole? If it was a 50–50 problem or even a 60–40 problem, there could be ambiguity about the result. But when the vast majority loses, the overall result is a major loss for the country.

2. Stolper and Samuelson, ibid.

3. Most experts are under the impression that the Hawley-Smoot tariff, at 59 percent, was the highest in U.S. history. Actually, the highest average tariff rate, 62 percent, occurred in 1830.

4. *World Development Report,* 1995, The World Bank, Washington, DC, p. 167, note a.

5. Other possible reasons for constantly rising prices are excessive money creation, budget deficits, depreciation of the dollar, and new regulations.

6. Herbert Stein, *Presidential Economics* (Washington, DC: American Enterprise Institute, 1988), p. 116.

7. Ibid., p. 117.

8. Alfred Malabre, *Beyond Our Means* (New York: Random House, 1987), p. 117. According to Malabre, transfer payments cost $1.5 billion in 1930, and had risen to half a trillion dollars by 1986.

9. John H. Makin and Norman J. Ornstein, *Debt and Taxes* (New York: Random House, 1995), pp. 177–179.

10. Ibid. *Also see* Peter Peterson, *Facing Up: How to Rescue the Economy from Crushing Debt & Restore the American Dream* (New York: Simon and Schuster, 1993).

11. *The Economic Report of the President,* 1996, The Council of Economic Advisers, Washington, DC, p. 368.

Chapter 8

1. Quoted in Lester Thurow, *The Future of Capitalism: How Today's Economic Forces Shape Tomorrow's World* (New York: William Morrow, 1996), p. 70.

2. The bulk of international trade today consists of manufactures; trading partners end up exchanging the same or similar products. This phenomenon, known as intraindustry trade, now constitutes over 60 percent of world trade. See Paul Krugman and Maurice Obstfeld, *International Economics: Theory and Policy* (New York: HarperCollins, 1994).

3. Milton and Rose Friedman, *Free to Choose: A Personal Statement* (New York: Harcourt Brace Jovanovich, 1990), p. 45.

   Everyone who has a choice among specializations would choose a higher-paying job. But the free trade theory takes that choice away from a nation's people. Furthermore, in the Friedmans' world, a lawyer should do lawyering and a secretary, typing. But in today's real world, countries export and import the same products. In other words, the lawyer is typing as well as lawyering, and the secretary is crossing over into other functions. Today's international trade violates the Friedmans' law of global efficiency.

4. Diana Kunde, "Texas Sees Growth in Lower-Skilled Jobs," *Dallas Morning News,* July 11, 1992, p. 1F; *Outlook: 1990–2005,* U.S. Department of Labor, Bureau of Labor Statistics, May 1992, p. 50.

5. *Statistical Abstract of the United States,* 1995, U.S. Department of Commerce, Washington, DC, p. 131.

6. A branch of international economics initiated by Harvard University Professor Everett Hagen argues that free trade may hurt the nation in the presence of interindustry wage differentials. But this argument has been traditionally limited to the Third World, where salary differences are reported to be substantial. However, free traders fail to acknowledge that wage differentials are also large in the United States.

   For more on the gains from trade under wage differentials, see E. Hagen, "An Economic Justification of Protectionism," *Quarterly Journal of Economics,* 1958, pp. 496–514; Jagdish Bhagwati, "The Pure Theory of International Trade: A Survey," *Economic Journal,* 1964, pp. 1–78; Ravi Batra, *Studies in the Pure Theory of International Trade* (London: Macmillan, 1973), Ch. 9; W. Max Caden, "Normative Theory of International Trade," in R. Jones and P. Kennen, *Handbook of International Economics,* Vol. I (New York: North Holland, 1984), Ch. 2.

7. Stephen Cohen and John Zysman, *Manufacturing Matters* (New York: Basic Books, 1987), p. 3.

8. G. C. Fite and J. E. Reese, *An Economic History of the United States* (Boston: Houghton Mifflin, 1973), p. 222.

9. Ibid., p. 223.

10. Gerald Gunderson, *A New Economic History of America* (New York: McGraw-Hill, 1976), p. 174.

11. Quoted in Alfred Eckes, Jr., *Opening America's Markets* (Chapel Hill: University of North Carolina Press, 1995), p. 30. *Also see* Roy Basler

(editor), *Collected Works of Abraham Lincoln* (New Brunswick, NJ: Rutgers University Press, 1953–1955), pp. 407–416.

12. Eckes, ibid., Ch. 2.

13. Ravi Batra, *The Myth of Free Trade* (New York: Macmillan, 1993), Chs, 2–4.

14. Thurow, op. cit., Ch. 2.

15. *Wall Street Journal,* "High Tech Explains Widening Wage Gaps," April 22, 1996. *Also see* Jagdish Bhagwati and Vivek Dehejia, "Freer Trade and Wages of the Unskilled—Is Marx Striking Again?" in Bhagwati and Kosters (editors), *Trade and Wages,* American Enterprise Institute, Washington, DC (1994); John Bound and George Johnson, "Changes in the Structure of Wages During the 1980s: An Evaluation of Alternative Explanations," *American Economic Review,* June 1992, pp. 371–392; Robert Lawrence, "Trade, Multinationals and Labor," NBER Working Paper No. 4838, August 1994; Edward Leamer, "A Trade Economist's View of U.S. Wages and Globalization," Brookings Institution Conference, 1995; Frank Levy and Richard Murnane, "U.S. Earnings Level and Earnings Inequality: A Review of Recent Trends and Proposed Explanations," *Journal of Economic Literature,* 1992, pp. 1333–1381; Joseph Stiglitz, *Economics* (New York: HarperCollins, 1993).

16. John H. Makin and Norman J. Ornstein, *Debt and Taxes* (New York: Random House, 1994), pp. 140–141.

17. *The Economic Report of the President,* 1996, The Council of Economic Advisors, Washington, DC, p. 225.

18. Harry Richardson, *Regional Economics* (Urbana: University of Illinois Press, 1979).

19. Fite and Reese, op. cit.

20. Cohen and Zysman, op. cit., Ch. 17; David Clark, *Post-Industrial America* (New York: Methuen, 1985).

Chapter 9

1. Jim Landers, "NAFTA Rivals Debate Impact on Jobs," *Dallas Morning News,* February 26, 1996, pp. 1D and 4D.

Ask any college freshman about GDP. He or she will tell you what every textbook teaches: GDP includes consumption, investment, government spending and exports minus imports. Ask any politician or establishment economist; he or she will say that GDP comprises consumption, investment, government spending, and exports. Why such a blatant difference about the treatment of imports? The reason lies in the North American Free Trade Agreement (NAFTA) and its precursor, the persistent trade deficit of the United States. Politicians, eager to show that exports create jobs, ignore the job-destroying impact of imports. This implies that GDP excludes imports.

Even now, the NAFTA acolytes claim that the trade agreement has created extra jobs in the United States. For this to happen, output must rise from trade with Mexico. *The Economic Report of the President* defines GDP in the same way as every textbook does. President

Clinton and his advisers and other elites cannot change this defini-
tion without inviting ridicule, but they still insist that imports don't
hurt jobs. If imports are subtracted from national demand, then rising imports lower GDP and hence employment.

   Politicians like to have it both ways. Al Gore himself argued in
1993 that NAFTA would be good for America because of its potential
to raise the U.S. trade surplus with Mexico. His thinking was backed
by the entire establishment. If the surplus had indeed risen, they
would all be bragging now—and justifiably so. Instead, the surplus
has turned into a hefty deficit.

2. Thea Lee, "Fake Prophets: The Selling of NAFTA," *Economic Policy Institute Briefing Paper,* July 1995, pp. 1–20.

3. Susan George, *A Fate Worse Than Debt* (New York: Grove Press, 1988).

4. Andres Oppenheimer, *Bordering on Chaos* (Boston: Little, Brown,
   1996).

5. Ravi Batra, *The Myth of Free Trade* (New York: Macmillan, 1993), Ch. 6.

6. Christopher Whalen, "Going South," *The Nation,* January 23, 1995,
   p. 80.

7. Batra, op. cit.

8. An avalanche of articles has appeared in support of NAFTA. Some of
   them are as follows: Bill Bradley, "NAFTA Is About Opportunity,"
   USA Today, November 8, 1993; "What If NAFTA Loses? The Conse-
   quences for the World Could Be Dire," *Business Week,* November 22,
   1993, pp. 32–42; Rudiger Dornbusch, "If Mexico Prospers, So Will
   We," *Wall Street Journal,* April 11, 1991; and "Workers Will Lose the
   Most If NAFTA Dies," *Business Week,* November 8, 1993, p. 20;
   Lawrence S. Eagleburger, "NAFTA: Good for America," *Washington
   Post,* July 4, 1993; Phil Gramm, "Leaving Mexico at the Altar," *Washing-
   ton Post,* June 1, 1993; Henry Kissinger, "NAFTA: Clinton's Defining
   Task," *Washington Post,* July 20, 1993; Nora Lustig, Barry P. Bosworth,
   and Robert Z. Lawrence (editors), *North American Free Trade: Assessing
   the Impact* (Washington, DC: Brookings Institution, 1992); Ernest S.
   McCrary, "Mexico Arrives: A New Player in the Global Big Leagues,"
   Global Finance, Vol. 7, Issue 12, pp. 95–96, 1993; Merrill Lynch, *Latin
   American Economic Outlook,* Newsletter, September 16, 1994;
   Allen R. Myerson, "U.S.–Mexico Trade Advances Sharply under New
   Accord," *New York Times,* July 6, 1994; Don E. Newquist, "Perot Is
   Dead Wrong on NAFTA," *New York Times,* May 10, 1993; Robert
   Samuelson, "Scare Talk about NAFTA," *Washington Post,* September
   15, 1993; John P. Sweeney, "Don't Blame NAFTA for the Mexican Cri-
   sis," Backgrounder No. 239 (Washington, DC: Heritage Foundation,
   February 13, 1995); Philip Trezise, "Clinton v. Perot: On Free Trade,
   Clinton Has the Better Case," *Washington Post,* June 22, 1993; *Washing-
   ton Post,* "Free Trade with Mexico," March 3, 1991; *Washington Post,*
   "Progress on NAFTA," August 18, 1993.

      However, there were also a handful of opponents: AFL-CIO,
   NAFTAmath: The First Year (Washington, DC, 1995); Robert Blecker,
   "NAFTA, the Peso, and the Contradictions of the Mexican Economic
   Growth Strategy," paper presented at the Eastern Economics Associa-
   tion meetings (New York, March 17, 1995); Jeff Faux, *The Failed Case*

for NAFTA: The Ten Most Common Claims for the North American Free Trade Agreement and Why They Don't Make Sense, Briefing Paper Series (Washington, DC: Economic Policy Institute, 1993); Jeff Faux and Thea Lee, *The Effect of George Bush's NAFTA on American Workers: Ladder Up or Ladder Down?* Briefing Paper Series (Washington, DC: Economic Policy Institute, 1992); Carlos G. Heredia and Mary E. Purcell, *The Polarization of Mexican Society: A Grassroots View of World Bank Economic Adjustment Policies* (Washington, DC: The Development Group for Alternative Policies, 1994); Christopher Whalen, "Mexico's Government Creates Another Debt Crisis," *Wall Street Journal,* March 12, 1992.

9. Donald Barlett and James Steele, *America: What Went Wrong* (Kansas City, MO: Andrews and McMeel, 1992).

10. Lee, op. cit.

11. Batra, op. cit., p. 190.

12. Whalen, op. cit.

13. "The Rescue of Mexico," *U.S. News and World Report,* January 23, 1995, pp. 48–49; "The Mexican Crisis: Anatomy of a Rescue Mission," *Business Week,* February 13, 1995, pp. 32–34; "Mexico Is Still in a World of Hurt," *Business Week,* February 13, 1995, pp. 36–38; Clay Chandler, "Latin Ministers Ponder Peso's Fall," *Washington Post,* April 7, 1995; Michael Clements and Bill Montague, "Will Peso's Fall Prove Perot Right? *USA Today,* January 17, 1995; Bob Davis, "NAFTA Is Key to Mexico's Rescue of Peso; U.S. Exporters May Not See Tariff Help," *Wall Street Journal,* January 4, 1995; Anthony DePalma, "Mexico Outlines an Economic Plan of Extended Pain," *New York Times,* March 10, 1995; "A Fork in the IMF's Road," *The Economist,* January 28, 1995, p. 14; Mark Fineman, "Mexican Currency Plunges in Value," *Austin American-Statesman,* December 23, 1994; Ken Geppert, "NAFTA Booster Scrambles to Adapt to Unstable World of Free Trade," *Wall Street Journal/Southeast Journal,* January 25, 1995; Tim Golden, "More Mexican Anguish than Gratitude," *New York Times,* February 3, 1995; Jim Hoagland, "Treasury's Mexican Mysteries," *Washington Post,* March 23, 1995; Ronald I. McKinnon, "Flood of Dollars, Sunken Pesos," *New York Times,* January 20, 1995; Kelly McParland, "Mexican Peso Crisis Fuels U.S. Doubts about NAFTA," *Financial Post,* January 31, 1995; Allen R. Myerson, "Peso's Plunge May Cost Thousands of U.S. Jobs," *New York Times,* January 30, 1995; Floyd Norris, "How Foreigners Invest, and Lose Their Shirts," *New York Times,* January 29, 1995; Nancy Nusser, "Peso Drags Ecology Projects Down with It," *Washington Times,* May 14, 1995; Frederick Rose, "Mexican Crisis to Hurt U.S. Economy with Substantial Loss of Jobs, Exports," *Wall Street Journal,* February 24, 1995; David E. Sanger, "Accord's Dark Side," *New York Times,* January 4, 1995; David E. Sanger, "Dollar Dips as the Peso Falls Again," *New York Times,* March 10, 1995; Sara Silver, "Stocks and Pesos Up, But Mexicans Down as Economic Crisis Lingers," Associated Press, May 14, 1995; Lee Smith, "After Mexico, Who's Next?" *Fortune,* March 6, 1995; R. Jeffrey Smith and Clay Chandler, "Peso Crisis Caught U.S. by Surprise," *Washington Post,* February 13, 1995; Henry Tricks, "Peso, Mexican Stocks Plunge," *Calgary Herald,* December 28, 1994.

14. Quoted in Enrique Rangel, "Mexico's GDP Shows 6.9% Slide," *Dallas Morning News,* February 17, 1996, pp. 1F and 11F.
15. Ibid.
16. Enrique Rangel, "Foreign Banks to Counter Gloom at Mexico Convention," *Dallas Morning News,* March 14, 1996, pp. 1D and 10D.
17. Cited in Jennifer Files, "NAFTA Report Cites Drawbacks," *Dallas Morning News,* March 26, 1996, pp. 2D and 9D.
18. Lee, op. cit., p. 1. Is it possible for real wages to decline with decreasing unemployment? This certainly wasn't the case in tariff-driven 19th-century America, but the American labor market has drastically changed since the adoption of NAFTA. It didn't take long for the new trade treaty to bring American workers down to their knees.
19. Gary Clyde Hufbauer and Jeffrey Schott, *North American Free Trade: Issues and Recommendations* (Washington, DC: Institute for International Economics, 1992); and *NAFTA: An Assessment* (Washington, DC: Institute for International Economics, 1993).
20. Jeffrey Garten, "The Big Emerging Markets: Changing American Interests in the Global Economy," address to the Foreign Policy Association, New York, January 20, 1994, p. 18; quoted in Lee, op. cit., p. 10.
21. Lee, ibid., p. 2.
22. Ibid.
23. *Economic Report of the President,* 1996, op. cit., p. 241.
24. Ibid., p. 250.
25. There are two measures of the U.S. trade deficit. The first and more important measure, called the merchandise trade deficit, examines trade in goods only. The other, more comprehensive measure includes the trade in services and is called the current account deficit. For purposes of high-wage jobs, the merchandise trade deficit matters more, because it is an indicator of a country's prowess in manufacturing.

    The United States has had a trade shortfall no matter what measure is adopted, although the current account deficit is somewhat smaller.
26. Milton and Rose Friedman, *Free to Choose: A Personal Statement* (New York: Harcourt Brace Jovanovich, 1990).
27. Ibid., p. 41.

Chapter 10

1. Ravi Batra, *The Downfall of Capitalism and Communism* (London: Macmillan, 1978); second edition published by Venus Books, Dallas, 1990.
2. Lester Thurow, *The Future of Capitalism; How Today's Economic Forces Shape Tomorrow's World* (New York: William Morrow, 1996).
3. Ravi Batra, *The Great Depression of 1990,* first edition (Dallas: Venus Books, 1985); second edition published by Simon and Schuster, New York, 1987.

4. Friedman's forecasts are described in Paul Krugman, *The Age of Diminished Expectations* (Cambridge, MA: MIT Press, 1994), p. 107.

5. Peter Passell, "Big Firms Getting Rid of In-House Economists," *New York Times,* February 4, 1996, p. 15.

6. Jason DeParle, "Class Is No Longer a Four-Letter Word," *New York Times Magazine,* March 17, 1996, p. 41.

7. John K. Galbraith, *The World Economy Since the Wars: A Personal View* (Boston: Houghton Mifflin, 1994), p. 210.

8. David Levy, "1990s: A Contained Depression," *Challenge,* July–August 1991, pp. 35–42.

9. Peter Peterson, *Facing Up: How to Rescue the Economy from Crushing Debt & Restore the American Dream* (New York: Simon and Schuster, 1993), p. 60.

10. Lawrence Hunter, "The Never-Ending Recession," *Wall Street Journal,* September 14, 1991, p. A14.

11. Wallace Peterson, *The Silent Depression* (New York: Basic Books, 1994), p. 29.

12. As quoted in *New York Times,* April 16, 1996, Senator Kennedy said to the Senate, "The 'quiet depression' facing American workers is the central economic, social and political issue of 1996. When the economy is wrong, nothing else is right," p. A10.

13. Ravi Batra, *The Great Depression of 1990,* second edition (New York: Simon and Schuster, 1987) and *Surviving the Great Depression of 1990* (New York: Simon and Schuster, 1988).

14. Paul Samuelson, *Economics* (New York: McGraw-Hill, 1976), p. 800.

15. Batra, op. cit., *The Great Depression of 1990,* Ch. 4.

16. Ibid., Chs. 6 and 7.

17. Floyd Norris, "Flood of Cash to Mutual Funds Helped to Fuel '95 Bull Market," *New York Times,* January 20, 1996, p. 1.

18. Ibid.

Chapter 11

1. *International Financial Statistics Yearbook,* 1995, The International Monetary Fund, Washington, DC, p. 389.

2. *Statistical Abstract of the United States,* 1995, U.S. Department of Commerce, Washington, DC, p. 866.

3. Ibid.

4. By 1995, the United States had the worst inequality among all advanced economies including Australia. The lowest 20 percent consumed only 3.6 percent of national income; the top fifth enjoyed nearly half of the income pie. See Michael Cox, "It's Not a Wage Gap, But an Age Gap," *New York Times,* April 21, 1996, p. E15.

5. Lester Thurow, *The Future of Capitalism: How Today's Economic Forces Shape Tomorrow's World* (New York: William Morrow, 1996), Ch. 2. European economic conditions are also described in: "Europe and the Underclass," *The Economist,* July 30, 1994, p. 19; "Homeless in France,"

International Herald Tribune, December 20, 1994, p. 1; Martin Orth and Rudiger Edelmann, "Flexible Working Times: Only a Trendy Concept?" *Deutscheland,* No. 2, February 1994.

6. *International Financial Statistics Yearbook,* op. cit.

7. Thurow, op. cit.

8. Mary Walsh, "Germany's Reckoning," *Los Angeles Times,* February 25, 1996, p. D13. *Also see* German Information Center, *Unemployment in Germany,* March 1994.

9. Nathaniel Nash, "In Germany, Downsizing Means 10.3% Jobless," *New York Times,* March 7, 1996, p. C1.

10. Alfred Eckes, Jr., *Opening America's Markets* (Chapel Hill: University of North Carolina Press, 1995), Ch. 2.

11. Walsh, op. cit., p. D1.

12. *New York Times,* March 29, 1996, p. C5. *Also see* Marlise Simons, "In French Factory Town, Culprit Is Automation," *New York Times,* May 12, 1994, p. A3.

13. *Statistical Abstract of the United States,* op. cit.

14. Ravi Batra, *The Myth of Free Trade* (New York: Macmillan, 1993), Ch. 6.

Chapter 12

1. Robert Hall and Alvin Rabushka, *The Flat Tax* (Stanford, CA: Hoover Institution Press, 1995), Ch. 2.

2. Peter Lindert, *International Economics* (Homewood, IL: Irvin, 1990); Nigel Grimwade, *International Trade* (London: Routledge, 1989); Ravi Batra, *The Myth of Free Trade* (New York: Macmillan, 1993). In some sectors, intraindustry trade is higher than 90 percent. See Paul R. Krugman and Maurice Obstfeld, *International Economics: Theory and Policy,* third edition (New York: HarperCollins, 1994), Ch. 6.

3. Christopher Whalen, "Going South," *The Nation,* January 23, 1995, p. 80.

4. Barbara Crossette, "A Global Gauge of Greased Palms," *New York Times,* August 20, 1995, p. 3.

5. *The World Development Report,* 1995, The World Bank, Washington, DC, pp. 206–207.

6. Edward Gargan, "Family Ties That Bind Growth: Corrupt Leaders in Indonesia Threaten Its Future," *New York Times,* April 9, 1996, p. C1.

7. Ibid.

8. Ibid., p. C2.

9. Howard French, "Donors of Foreign Aid Have Second Thoughts," *New York Times,* April 7, 1996, p. 5.

10. Ibid.

11. Quoted by Diana Schemo, "Unity Cracking as American Nations Meet to Plan an Economic Zone," *New York Times,* March 24, 1996, p. 6.

12. Michael Porter, *The Competitive Advantage of Nations* (New York: The Free Press, 1990), p. 401.

13. Ibid., pp. 116 and 118.

14. Ravi Batra, *The Myth of Free Trade* (New York: Macmillan, 1993), Ch. 6.

15. Ibid., Chs. 9 and 12.

16. *The Economic Report of the President,* 1996, The Council of Economic Advisers, Washington, DC, pp. 369, 379, and 382.

17. *Statistical Abstract of the United States,* 1995, U.S. Department of Commerce, Washington, DC, p. 346.

18. Batra, op. cit., Ch. 9.

19. Mark Hunter, "Europe's Reborn Right," *New York Times Magazine,* April 21, 1996, p. 39.

20. Ravi Batra, *Japan: The Return to Prosperity* (Tokyo: Sogo Horei, 1996). (In Japanese only.)

21. Michael Todaro, *Economic Development in the Third World* (New York: Longman, 1977).

22. Paul Krugman, *The Age of Diminished Expectations* (Cambridge, MA: MIT Press, 1994), p. 188.

23. Peter Passell, "Private Capital Is King in the New Order of World Investment," *New York Times,* March 21, 1996.

24. Quoted by Marlise Simons, "U.S. Enlists Rich Countries in a Move to End Business Bribes to Foreign Officials," *New York Times,* April 12, 1996, p. A7.

25. Ibid.

26. Jeff Faux, "Overview: New Eyes on a New Country," in Todd Schafer and Jeff Faux (editors), *Reclaiming Prosperity* (New York: M. E. Sharpe, 1996), p. 7.

Appendix

UNITED STATES: A.1–A.13

CANADA: A.14 AND A.15

GERMANY: A.16 AND A.17

UNITED KINGDOM: A.18 AND A.19

FRANCE: A.20 AND A.21

ITALY: A.22 AND A.23

JAPAN: A.24 AND A.25

AUSTRALIA: A.26 AND A.27

SPAIN: A.28 AND A.29

A.1 Maximum social security tax in current and constant dollars (1982–1984 = 100): United States 1980–1993 (selected years).

Year	Social Security Tax	CPI	Real Social Security Tax[1]
1980	$1,588	82.4	$1,927
1985	2,792	107.6	2,595
1987	3,132	113.6	2,757
1988	3,380	118.3	2,857
1989	3,605	124.0	2,907
1990	3,924	130.7	3,002
1991	5,123	136.2	3,761
1992	5,329	140.3	3,798
1993	5,529	144.5	3,826

[1] SS tax divided by CPI and multiplied by 100.

Source: Statistical Abstract of the United States, 1995, U.S. Department of Commerce, p. 379; Economic Report of the President, 1996, The Council of Economic Advisers, Washington, DC, p. 343.

A.2 The social security tax rates, actual and effective percentages: United States 1980–1993 (selected years).

Year	Actual SS Tax Rate	Maximum Taxable Wage Base	Maximum Effective Tax Rate
1980	6.13%	$25,900	6.13%
1985	7.05	39,600	8.26
1987	7.15	43,800	8.77
1988	7.51	45,000	9.09
1989	7.51	48,000	9.25
1990	7.65	51,300	9.55
1991	7.65	53,400	11.97
1992	7.65	55,500	12.08
1993	7.65	57,600	12.17

Source: Statistical Abstract of the United States, 1995, U.S. Department of Commerce, Washington, DC, p. 379.

Note: In 1980, the real value of the taxable wage base was $31,432, which is obtained by dividing the actual taxable wage of $25,900 by the CPI of 82.4 and multiplying by 100. The actual SS tax rate of 6.13, when applied to this wage base, gives us the real value of the maximum SS levy in 1980 at $1,927. Dividing the fourth column of Table A.1 by the 1980 constant real wage base of $31,432 then furnishes the effective maximum SS tax rate on that constant 1980 base. This is displayed in the fourth column of Table A.2.

A.3   GNP and net exports during the worst years of the Great Depression: United States 1929–1933.

GNP = Domestic Demand + Net Exports

1. Fall in GNP between 1929 and 1933 = $48 billion.
2. Between 1929 and 1933, fall in Net Exports = $700 million = 1.5 percent of the fall in GNP.
3. Fall in Domestic Demand
    = $47.3 billion between 1929 and 1933;
    = 98.5 percent of the fall in GNP.

Hence, the 1932 Hoover-Roosevelt income tax rise from 25 percent to 65 percent crushed domestic demand and caused the Great Depression.

Source: Economic Report of the President, 1991, The Council of Economic Advisers, Washington, DC.

A.4   Weekly real wages in manufacturing (1982 dollars): United States 1909–1994 (selected years).

Year	Money Wages	CPI[1]	Inflation-Adjusted Wages[2]
1909	$ 9.74	9	$ 108
1920	26.02	20	130
1930	23.00	17	135
1940	24.96	14	178
1950	58.32	24	242
1960	89.72	30	299
1970	134.00	39	344
1972	166.50	44	378
1980	289.80	82	352
1990	442.00	131	337
1994	507.00	148	343

[1] CPI figures prior to 1950 are obtained by dividing them by 3 to account for inflation and to combine two data series.
[2] Money wages divided by CPI and multiplied by 100.

Source: Historical Statistics of the United States: Colonial Times to 1970, 1975, U.S. Department of Commerce, Washington, DC, pp. 169 and 210; *Economic Report of the President,* 1992 and 1996, The Council of Economic Advisers, Washington, DC, pp. 340 and 343; *Statistical Abstract of the United States,* 1995, U.S. Department of Commerce, Washington, DC, p. 431.

A.5 GDP percentages: U.S. exports, imports, trade and growth: United States 1950–1995.

Year	GDP			Average Growth Per Decade (1950s*–1990s)
	Exports	Imports	Trade	
1950	5.1%	4.3%	9.4%	4%
1955	5.2	4.4	9.6	
1960	5.5	4.3	9.8	4.4
1965	4.9	4.4	9.3	
1970	5.5	5.4	10.9	3.2
1975	8.4	7.5	15.9	
1980	10.0	10.6	20.6	2.8
1985	7.2	10.0	17.2	
1990	9.7	11.0	20.7	1.7
1995	11.2	12.5	23.7	

*Figures for 1950 and 1955 use GNP data.

Source: Economic Report of the President, 1992 and 1996, The Council of Economic Advisers, pp. 286 and 280.

A.6 Cumulative deficits in the United States under successive presidents (Truman to Clinton) since the Second World War.

President	Average Deficit as Percentage of GDP	Gross* Federal Debt (billions)
Truman (1947–1952)	−1.2%	$ 271
Eisenhower (1953–1960)	0.6	259
Kennedy (1961–1963)	0.9	291
Johnson (1964–1968)	1.1	316
Nixon-Ford (1969–1976)	2.1	366
Carter (1977–1980)	2.5	644
Reagan (1981–1988)	4.4	909
Bush (1989–1992)	4.1	2,601
Clinton (1993–1995)	3.2	4,002–4,921

*At the start of each administration.

Source: Economic Report of the President, 1996, The Council of Economic Advisers, Washington, DC, pp. 367 and 368.

A.7   Growth in real government spending: United States 1950–1995.

Year	Government Spending (billions)	CPI (1982 = 100)	Real Government Spending*	Average Growth in Government Spending
1950	$ 42.6	24.1	$177	
1960	92.2	29.6	311	5.8%
1970	195.6	38.8	504	4.9
1980	590.9	82.4	717	3.6
1990	1,252.7	130.7	958	2.9
1995	1,514.4	152.4	993	0.7

*Government spending divided by CPI and multiplied by 100. Average annual growth of real government spending is then obtained for each decade (final column), which is a compound growth rate per year.

Source: Economic Report of the President, 1996, The Council of Economic Advisers, Washington, DC, p. 369.

A.8   Growth in real tax receipts: United States 1950–1995.

Year	Tax Receipts (billions)	CPI (1982 = 100)	Real Tax Receipts*	Average Growth in Real Tax Receipts
1950	$ 39.4	24.1	$163	
1960	92.5	29.6	313	6.7%
1970	192.8	38.8	497	4.7
1980	517.1	82.4	627	2.4
1990	1,031.3	130.7	789	2.3
1995	1,350.6	152.4	862	0.8

*Tax receipts divided by CPI and multiplied by 100.

Source: Economic Report of the President, 1996, The Council of Economic Advisers, Washington, DC, 1996, p. 369.

Note: The federal revenue after inflation is presented in the fourth column of Table A.8, and average annual growth per decade appears in the fifth column of Table A.8. This is also a compound growth rate per year.

A.9   California's manufacturing employment share and per-capita income advantage over U.S. per-capita income: United States 1960–1994.

Year	Manufacturing Employment Share	Income Advantage Over U.S. Per-Capita Income
1960	27%	23%
1970	23	14
1980	20	14
1990	17	11
1994	15	3

Source: Statistical Abstract of the United States, 1995, U.S. Department of Commerce, Washington, DC, p. 461 and various issues.

A.10   U.S. economic growth, by decades: United States 1880–1995.

Decade	Average Annual GDP Growth
1880s	3.2%
1890s	4.5
1900s	4.8
1910s	2.4
1920s	3.6
1930s	0.8
1940s	4.8
1950s	4.0
1960s	4.4
1970s	3.2
1980s	2.8
1990s (1990–1995)	1.7

Source: Historical Statistics of the United States: Colonial Times to 1970, 1975, U.S. Department of Commerce, Washington, DC, pp. 224–227; *Economic Report of the President,* 1996, The Council of Economic Advisers, Washington, DC, p. 283.

A.11 Indexes of real wages of nonsupervisory workers and CEOs, in 1982 prices (1982 = 100): United States 1976–1995 (selected years).

Year	Workers	CEOs
1976	1.0	1.0
1980	0.92	1.06
1983	0.91	1.18
1985	0.91	1.35
1987	0.90	1.58
1990	0.87	1.75
1992	0.85	1.90
1995	0.86	2.5

Source: Scott Burns, "CEO Pay Not What It Used To Be—It's Better," *Dallas Morning News,* March 3, 1987, p. 1-D; Margaret Blair, "CEO Pay: Why Such a Contentious Issue?" *Brookings Review,* Winter 1994, p. 24; Louis Uchitelle, "1995 Was Good for Companies and Better for a Lot of CEOs," *New York Times,* March 29, 1996, p. 1.

A.12 Median family income during recessions, in 1994 prices: United States 1947–1959.

Year	RFI*	Percentage Change	Years of Decline
1947	$20,173		
1948	19,674	−2.5%	
1949	19,184	−2.5	2
1950	20,178	5.2	
1953	23,564		
1954	23,055	−2.2	1
1955	24,520	6.4	
1956	26,151		
1957	26,131	0	
1958	26,112	0	2
1959	27,592	5.7	

*RFI = Real Family Income. Figures were multiplied by 4.98 to convert them into 1994 prices, as suggested by the 1996 *Economic Report of the President.*

Source: Economic Report of the President, 1965, The Council of Economic Advisers, Washington, DC, p. 210.

A.13   Median family income during recessions, in 1994 prices: United States 1960–1982.

Year	RFI*	Percentage Change	Years of Decline
1960	$27,109		
1961	27,386	1.0%	0
1969	36,759		
1970	36,301	−1.2	
1971	36,279	0	2
1972	37,959	4.6	
1973	38,739		
1974	37,376	−3.5	
1975	36,414	−2.6	2
1976	37,319	2.5	
1979	39,227		
1980	37,857	−3.5	
1981	36,825	−2.7	
1982	36,326	−1.4	3
1983	36,714	1.1	

*RFI = Real Family Income. Figures were multiplied by 1.48 to convert them into 1994 prices.

Source: Economic Report of the President, 1984, The Council of Economic Advisers, Washington, DC, p. 252.

A.14   GDP percentages: Household savings, investment, and growth per five-year period: Canada 1961–1995.

Period	GDP Savings	GDP Investment	Average Growth
1961–1965	14%	22%	5.7%
1966–1970	14	22	4.8
1971–1975	12	22	5.0
1976–1980	13	23	3.1
1981–1985	15	20	2.7
1986–1990	10	20	3.0
1991–1995	9	18	2.4

A.15   Social security and corporate tax shares, and the unemployment rate: Canada 1965–1996.

Year	SS Tax Share	Corporate Tax Share	Unemployment Rate
1965	6%	15%	3.6%
1970	9	10	5.8
1975	10	14	6.9
1980	10	12	7.5
1985	14	8	10.5
1990	17	5	11.3
Feb. 1996	NA	NA	9.6

Source for Table A.14 and A.15: *OECD Economic Outlook,* 1986, 1991, and 1995; Revenue Statistics of OECD Member Countries, 1965–1993. Both are published in Paris, France. *The Economist,* March 16, 1996, p. 106. The same sources apply to all other tables following this one, i.e., to Tables A.16–A.29.

A.16   GDP percentages: Household savings, investment, and growth per five-year period: Germany 1961–1995.

Period	GDP Savings	GDP Investment	Average Growth
1961–1965	16%	24%	5%
1966–1970	16	24	4.2
1971–1975	15	23	2.2
1976–1980	13	21	3.5
1981–1985	12	21	1.2
1986–1990	13	20	3.4
1991–1995	12	19	2.3

A.17   Social security and corporate tax shares, and the unemployment rate: Germany 1965–1996.

Year	SS Tax Share	Corporate Tax Share	Unemployment Rate
1965	27%	8%	0.3%
1970	31	5	0.8
1975	34	4	3.6
1980	34	5	3.2
1985	37	6	8.0
1990	37	5	6.2
1992	39	4	7.7
Feb. 1996	39	4	11.1

A.18   GDP percentages: Household savings, investment, and growth per five-year period: U.K. 1961–1995.

Period	GDP Savings	GDP Investment	Average Growth
1961–1965	11%	18%	3.1%
1966–1970	10	19	2.5
1971–1975	11	20	2.1
1976–1980	11	19	1.6
1981–1985	11	17	2.0
1986–1990	7	18	3.4
1991–1995	19	16	1.3

A.19   Social security and corporate tax shares, and the unemployment rate: U.K. 1965–1996.

Year	SS Tax Share	Corporate Tax Share	Unemployment Rate
1965	15%	7%	2.2%
1970	14	8	3.0
1975	17	6	3.6
1980	17	8	5.3
1985	18	13	11.0
1990	17	11	5.9
1992	18	8	9.9
Feb. 1996	NA	NA	7.9

A.20   GDP percentages: Household savings, investment, and growth per five-year period: France 1961–1995.

Period	GDP Savings	Investment	Average Growth
1961–1965	21%	22%	5.8%
1966–1970	20	23	5.4
1971–1975	20	24	4.0
1976–1980	19	22	3.3
1981–1985	16	20	1.5
1986–1990	12	18	3.2
1991–1995	14	18	1.2

A.21 Social security and corporate tax shares, and the unemployment rate: France 1965–1996.

Year	SS Tax Share	Corporate Tax Share	Unemployment Rate
1965	34%	5%	1.5%
1970	37	6	2.5
1975	41	5	4.2
1980	43	5	6.3
1985	43	5	10.2
1990	44	5	8.9
1992	45	4	10.3
Feb. 1996	45	4	11.8

A.22 GDP percentages: Household savings, investment, and growth per five-year period: Italy 1961–1995.

Period	GDP		Average Growth
	Savings	Investment	
1961–1965	24%	22%	5.2%
1966–1970	25	20	6.2
1971–1975	26	21	2.4
1976–1980	24	20	3.8
1981–1985	21	19	1.4
1986–1990	18	20	2.7
1991–1995	16	18	1.2

A.23 Social security and corporate tax shares, and the unemployment rate: Italy 1965–1996.

Year	SS Tax Share	Corporate Tax Share	Unemployment Rate
1965	34%	7%	5.3%
1970	38	7	5.3
1975	46	6	5.8
1980	38	8	7.5
1985	35	9	10.1
1990	33	10	11.5
1992	31	12	10.7
Feb. 1996	NA	NA	12.6

A.24 GDP percentages: Household savings, investment, and growth per five-year period: Japan 1961–1995.

Period	GDP		Average Growth
	Savings	Investment	
1961–1965	22%	30%	10.0%
1966–1970	23	33	11.2
1971–1975	23	34	4.6
1976–1980	20	31	5.0
1981–1985	16	29	4.5
1986–1990	15	32	4.5
1991–1995	15	26	1.2

A.25   Social security and corporate tax shares, and the unemployment rate: Japan 1965–1996.

Year	SS Tax Share	Corporate Tax Share	Unemployment Rate
1965	19%	18%	1.2%
1970	24	18	1.1
1975	29	16	1.9
1980	29	22	2.0
1985	30	21	2.6
1990	29	22	2.1
1992	32	17	2.2
Feb. 1996	NA	NA	3.4

A.26   GDP percentages: Household savings, investment, and growth per five-year period: Australia 1962–1995.

Period	GDP Savings	Investment	Average Growth
1962–1965	15%	25%	NA
1966–1970	16	27	5.6%
1971–1975	15	26	4.0
1976–1980	12	25	2.7
1981–1985	9	25	3.1
1986–1990	7	25	4.2
1991–1995	4	22	2.8

A.27   Social security and corporate tax shares, and the unemployment rate: Australia 1965–1996.

Year	SS Tax Share	Corporate Tax Share	Unemployment Rate
1965	25%	16%	NA
1970	25	16	1.6%
1975	26	16	4.9
1980	28	12	6.0
1985	32	9	8.1
1990	33	14	7.0
1992	33	15	10.7
Feb. 1996	NA	NA	8.6

A.28   GDP percentages: Household savings, investment, and growth per five-year period: Spain 1965–1995.

Period	GDP		Average Growth
	Savings	Investment	
1965–1970	NA	23%	6.5%
1971–1975	NA	19	5.6
1976–1980	13%	22	2.0
1981–1985	12	19	1.4
1986–1990	10	23	4.5
1991–1995	11	19	1.0

**A.29   Social security and corporate tax shares, the
unemployment rate, and the tax share of tariffs: Spain
1965–1996.**

Year	SS Tax Share	Corporate Tax Share	Unemployment Rate	Tax Share of Tariffs
1965	28%	25%	NA	7.0%
1970	37	20	2.4%	5.0
1975	48	22	3.6	4.0
1980	49	26	11.5	2.5
1985	41	26	21.5	2.5
1990	35	31	16.3	1.6
1992	37	30	18.4	1.1
Feb. 1996	NA	NA	22.8	1.0

Index